DOGME
UNCUT

DOGME
UNCUT

Lars von Trier, Thomas Vinterberg, and the Gang That Took on Hollywood

Jack Stevenson

SANTA
MONICA
PRESS

Published by:
Santa Monica Press LLC
P.O. Box 1076
Santa Monica, CA 90406-1076
1-800-784-9553
www.santamonicapress.com
books@santamonicapress.com

Printed in the United States

Santa Monica Press books are available at special quantity discounts when purchased in bulk. Please call our Special Sales department at 1-800-784-9553.

ISBN 1-891661-35-3

Library of Congress Cataloging-in-Publication Data

Stevenson, Jack, 1955–
    Dogme uncut : Lars von Trier, Thomas Vinterberg, and the gang that took on Hollywood / by Jack Stevenson.
      p. cm.
    Includes bibliographical references and index.
    ISBN 1-891661-35-3
    1. Experimental films—History and criticism. 2. Dogme 95 (Group) I. Title.
    PN1995.9.E96 S73 2003
    791.43'3—dc21

                                  2003013845

Book and cover design by Lynda "Cool Dog" Jakovich

Contents

Much appreciation is owed to Hans Peter Rosenmeier and Morten Rosenmeier for key technical assistance, and to Mads Nielsen, Maren Pust, Knud Romer Jørgensen, and Charlotte Day for essential help in other areas.

"The hardened old men with hearts of stone must die!"

—Lars von Trier

Introduction

The "Godfather of Dogme," manuscript studies professor Mogens Rukov, has stated that no film "wave" ever lasts longer than eight years.

In that case, Dogme's number is up.

But if Dogme's impact as a revolutionary call-to-arms has faded, its ability to sell tickets and impress critics is anything but exhausted. *Italian for Beginners*, Dogme film #5—the first of the second-wave of Dogme—smashed box office records in Denmark and was a big hit in most foreign markets, becoming, for example, one of the most-seen Danish films ever in America.

Danish Dogme films #6 and #7, *Truly Human* and *Kira's Reason—A Love Story*, won most of the major Danish awards in 2001 and were praised by American critics upon their U.S. releases. And Susanne Bier's *Open Hearts* (#8), which premiered on September 6, 2002 to impassioned accolades in the Danish press, went on to set the record for opening weekend grosses for a Dogme film. In America the film met with wildly positive audience response at Sundance 2003 where *Variety* praised it as "poignant, thoughtful and utterly absorbing." And the two most recent Danish Dogme films, by up-and-coming women directors, Natasha Arthy and Annette K. Olesen, have subsequently also been deemed successes.

To the joy of its fans and the torment of its detractors, Dogme lives!

Much has already been said and written about the first three Dogme films, *The Celebration, The Idiots,* and *Mifune,* directed respectively by Thomas Vinterberg, Lars von Trier, and Søren Kragh-Jacobsen. They made the first splash. Their films constituted a kind of first wave that swept through the film world in a spray of hype and controversy. Seemingly every film journalist wrote a piece about Dogme and every film magazine ran a spread on it. Dogme was hot stuff in 1998 and 1999. It was an audacious challenge to the powers-that-be, a tantalizing riddle that just might be "the answer" . . . the flag under which the Davids of the film world could unite against the Hollywood Goliath.

At the start of 1999, young, fresh-faced Thomas Vinterberg himself visited the Cave of the Cyclops to have lunch with Steven Spielberg and challenge him to make a Dogme film. Heady stuff for the young filmmaker from little Denmark who came clutching what was just his second feature film. Dogme was his ticket to the inner-sanctums of the Hollywood Temple, the magic key to film festival acclaim and adulation around the world. Dogme gossip and Dogme rumors seemed to dominate every film-related cocktail party and every indie-film panel discussion. There was no escaping the reach of Dogme "talk"—even if there were only three movies up to this point.

But under the sizzling glare of so much media scrutiny, the novelty of Dogme began to evaporate. Dogme became typecast, or rather "hypecast." The film world didn't crumble and Hollywood kept making movies stuffed with expensive special effects, glossy production values, and weak stories. And while film nerds the world over continued to devote themselves to arcane speculation as to which of the rules in the Vow of Chastity so-and-so director had violated, the general film-going public tired of the obscurantism Dogme had wrought. The promise of Dogme had yet to be redeemed and many interesting questions were left hanging in the air. Some people were, in fact, alienated by all the hype and branded the whole thing a publicity stunt. The backlash had begun.

Finally indifference set in. By late 2000, Dogme seemed to have run out of gas.

In fact much was about to happen with the movement.

Italian for Beginners, as noted, kicked off a kind of second wave and Dogme found a new head of steam as more films were released. It now entered what was perhaps its most diverse and interesting phase, and certainly its most successful if judged by the impressive box-offices grosses. And of course that was a problem in its own right. Dogme had "almost turned into a genre formula, and that was never the intention," as the final press-release from the Dogme secretariat stated in June of 2002, on the occasion of its shut down and the cessation of the issuance of certificates.

One Danish critic described the closing of the Secretariat as "the burial of Dogme," but if that were true then it appears to have been a premature burial. As noted, two more Danish Dogme films have come out since the official counting stopped and more films, both Danish and international, are in the pipeline.

The Brothers had created something beyond their control. Maybe they even created a Frankenstein.

Thomas Vinterberg might know something about that. He ran so many victory laps after *The Celebration* that it took him almost five years to get his next movie, *It's All About Love*, onto screens. He gave so many interviews about Dogme that he eventually grew sick of it and tried to make this film as anti-Dogme as possible. "I spit in the face of Dogme with this movie," he stated in issue #22 of the Danish trade publication, *Film*, which was printed in English and distributed for free at the 2002 Cannes festival. Vinterberg's face was on the cover, pictured in profile—dashing, intense, determined—because everybody assumed it was a given that *It's All About Love* would be in-competition that year. Hadn't *The Celebration* been the talk of the 1998 festival, playing to a full house in their biggest theater and winning salvos of thunderous applause at the end? So much greater the shock, then, when the selection committee rejected it. They told him they found it too "American" and were disappointed he hadn't given them something more in the spirit of *The Celebration*.[1]

Upon the film's release in Denmark, the critics, despite bending over backwards to say something nice about the country's favorite film son, largely agreed. "The Celebration is Over" announced one headline, while another paper declared that "Vinterberg screwed up."[2] American critics at Sundance 2003, where the film's premiere took place, were similarly underwhelmed. "The most ardent admirers of the raw, truth-telling qualities of Dogme will no doubt be disappointed," opined *Variety*'s Todd McCarthey in a piece headed "Vinterberg Disappoints with Comeback." "Concept Takes Precedence over Narrative," chimed in *Screen*.

Horrors! Vinterberg had sold out the gospel of Dogme: "acting and story, acting and story" (repeat until Hollywood listens). Now what kind of muddled story was this? In launching his new film he laid so much stress upon the fact that it was the opposite of Dogme that it began to seem like that was *all* that it was. It was quite a bit more than just that of course, but Vinterberg seemed to have psyched himself out. He could not escape Dogme's embrace which he had earlier so encouraged.

Despite the closing of the Secretariat, Dogme in 2003 is anything but dead. It has in fact changed, broadened, developed . . . "grown up" as Toronto film festival officials put it in 2002 on occasion of the screening of *Open Hearts*. While the founders might well cringe at the prospect of their snotty love-child growing up and "maturing," it has in any case survived. It has survived the departure of the four founding Dogme brothers and it has moved out from under the shadow of Lars von Trier. It has survived the failure of individual films and it has survived the *success* of individual films, such as *The Celebration* and *Italian for Beginners* whose popularity threatened to overshadow what Dogme was all about—the will to challenge oneself and experiment. It has survived innumerable charges of hype and fraud, and it has survived what many consider to be the failure and illegitimacy of many of the foreign (non-Danish) Dogme films.

The first chapter is over and much about Dogme that was inscrutable can now be examined with the benefit of hindsight. The next chapter is writing itself as we speak, and the jury is still out in many respects.

Many say it has proven to be a more elastic and adaptable concept than was originally thought possible. At the same time suspicions are voiced, by among others, Mogens Rukov, that the "great experiment" ended with the first four films.[3] To some the subsequent films have proven that Dogme has indeed become the "uniform" that von Trier promised it would be—a mere cloak or covering so to speak, a dress code, a label . . . something easily donned or shed for purposes of convenience (or profit). Others assert that yes, Dogme is adaptable, but in the best sense, that it provides a framework that is loose enough to let each film breathe on its own. Dogme, they say, is still ripe for experimentation and can still lead to new discoveries.

In fact there is still much to discover even about Dogme's past, for in spite of all the intense scrutiny it has received over the years, it was originally constructed as a kind of Rubik's cube, and few have managed to get a grip on what von Trier himself described as the movement's "impossible and paradoxical rules."[4] Even insiders, such as von Trier pal, Jesper Jargil, have struggled with the central mystery of Dogme.

"Despite all that's been said and written about Dogme, I spent almost a year simply figuring out what the manifesto actually meant," Jargil commented in issue 22 of *Film* on occasion of the release of his documentary about the movement, *The Purified* (which also had its American premiere at Sundance 2003).

Despite Dogme's longevity, the mystery lingers. The debate goes on, more polarized than ever. This Dogme discussion, carried on among otherwise polite critics, professors, and film buffs, has actually turned into a shoving match. In fact today there is a scuffle taking place amongst cineastes, a brawl between partisans that is tinged with the scent of class warfare as charges of heresy, sell-out, and rank opportunism fly through the air. If Dogme has managed nothing else, it has made people passionate about film again and re-injected a bit of radical politics back into the mix, the likes of which hasn't been seen since the '50s or '60s.

Within these pages it is my objective to consider the movement from all perspectives, particularly from the "insider" perspective—the Danish perspective—since it is in Denmark that the movement is still being actively celebrated, dismissed, debated, loved, and hated. That is a central aim of this book, drawing as it does upon many sources of information and opinion thus far confined to the Danish language.

Dogme is a legitimate movement that should be taken seriously by film scholars, but it is also a story that contains a lot of the grist of raw human drama. There is hubris and humility, perseverance and perfidiousness, back-slapping and bandwagon jumping. . . .

It is the story of a great success that was never expected or predicted, a story that the film world is still attempting to understand. A story that is still unfolding.

Jack Stevenson
Allerød, Denmark

"The Dogme Manifesto" and "Vow of Chastity"
by Lars von Trier

Dogme 95 is a collective of film directors founded in Copenhagen in the Spring of 1995.

Dogme 95 has the expressed goal of countering "certain tendencies" in the cinema today.

Dogme 95 is a rescue action!

In 1960 enough was enough! The movie was dead and called for resurrection. The goal was correct but the means were not! The New Wave proved to be a ripple that washed ashore and turned to muck.

Slogans of individualism and freedom created works for a while, but no changes. The Wave was up for grabs, like the directors themselves. The Wave was never stronger than the men behind it. The anti-bourgeois cinema itself became bourgeois, because the foundations upon which its theories were based was the bourgeois perception of art. The auteur concept was bourgeois romanticism from the very start and thereby . . . false!

To Dogme 95 cinema is not individual!

Today a technological storm is raging, the result of which will be the ultimate democratization of the cinema. For the first time anyone can make movies. But the more accessible the media becomes, the more important the avant-garde. It is no accident that the phrase "avant-garde" has military connotations. Discipline is the answer . . . we must put our films into uniform, because the individual film will be decadent by definition!

Dogme 95 counters the individual film by the principle of presenting an indisputable set of rules known as THE VOW OF CHASTITY.

In 1960 enough was enough! The movie had been cosmeticized to death, they said: yet since then the use of cosmetics has exploded.

The 'supreme' task of the decadent filmmaker is to fool the audience. Is that what we are so proud of? Is that what the '100 years' have brought us? Illusions via which emotions can be communicated? . . . By the individual artist's free choice of trickery?

Predictability (dramaturgy) has become the golden calf around which we dance. Having the characters' inner lives justify the plot is too complicated, and not "high art." As never before, the superficial action and the superficial movie are receiving all the praise.

The result is barren. An illusion of pathos and an illusion of love.

To Dogme 95 the movie is not illusion!

Today a technological storm is raging of which the result is the elevation of cosmetics to God. By using new technology anyone at any time can wash the last grains of truth away in the deadly embrace of sensation. The illusions are everything the movie can hide behind.

Dogme 95 counters the film of illusion by the presentation of an indisputable set of rules known as THE VOW OF CHASTITY.

"I swear to submit to the following set of rules drawn up and confirmed by Dogme 95"

1. Shooting must be done on location. Props and sets must not be brought in (if a particular prop is necessary for the story, a location must be chosen where the prop is to be found).
2. The sound must never be produced apart from the images, or vise versa. (Music must not be used unless it occurs where the scene is being shot.)

3. The camera must be hand-held. Any movement or mobility attainable in the hand is permitted. (The film must not take place where the camera is standing; shooting must take place where the film takes place.) (Ed: What is rightly meant by this oddly translated last phrase is that the film must not take place in front of a *stationary* camera, and that shooting must take place where the film takes place, ruling out cranes, helicopter shots and other techniques used to convey distant point-of-views.)

4. The film must be in color. Special lighting is not acceptable. (If there is too little light for exposure the scene must be cut or a single lamp may be attached to the camera.)

5. Optical work and filters are forbidden.

6. The film must not contain superficial action. (Murders, weapons, etc., must not occur.)

7. Temporal and geographical alienation are forbidden. (That is to say that the film takes place here and now.)

8. Genre movies are not acceptable.

9. The film format must be Academy 35mm. (Ed: This rule was later clarified to mean the exhibition format, not the shooting format, and hence digital and video cameras were permitted and became almost *de rigeur*.)

10. The director must not be credited.

Furthermore, I swear as a director to refrain from personal taste! I am no longer an artist. I swear to refrain from creating a "work," as I regard the instant as more important than the whole. My supreme goal is to force the truth out of my characters and settings. I swear to do so by all means available and at the cost of any good taste and any aesthetic considerations.

Thus I make my VOW OF CHASTITY.

Copenhagen, Monday, 13 March 1995
On behalf of Dogme 95
Lars von Trier, Thomas Vinterberg

John Cassavetes, Jean-Luc Godard, and the Gang That Influenced Dogme

The American Underground

"The official cinema all over the world is running out of breath. It is morally corrupt, aesthetically obsolete, thematically superficial, temperamentally boring. Even the seemingly worthwhile films, those that lay claim to high moral and aesthetic standards and have been accepted as such by critics and the public alike, reveal the decay of the Product Film. The very slickness of their execution has become a perversion covering the falsity of their themes. . . ."[5]

This paragraph could easily have been penned by Lars von Trier and included in his 1995 Dogme manifesto. He meant precisely all this. Yet this passage was in fact part of another manifesto, one written 34 years earlier in the summer of 1961 by a group of angry young American filmmakers. They were part of what was then called the "New American Cinema," or, in the vernacular, the "Underground."

Von Trier was no doubt aware of this movement and familiar with some of its works, and a startling number of parallels exist between it and Dogme.

Von Trier's idol, John Cassavetes, was, with his first feature, the low-budget semi-improvised *Shadows* from 1960, a founding father of the New American Cinema. The film was one of the cornerstones of

A scene from Shadows *(1960), the very influential and semi-improvised film by John Cassavetes.*

John Cassavetes, left, gives direction on the set of Too Late Blues.

the movement, and was held out as evidence that something new was happening, something raw and real and spontaneous.

Cassavetes virtually pioneered the technique of the shaky hand-held camera in combination with improvised acting, a kind of style that would become a signature of Dogme. Yet there were other film-makers in the movement who took these technical approaches to even more radical extremes. Jack Smith, for example, with his film, *Flaming Creatures*, and Ken Jacobs with *Blonde Cobra* and *Little Stabs at Happiness.* These films were pure experiments in alchemy—fragile, rickety attempts to capture the spirit of the moment and the moody, unpredictable cavortings of various flamboyant personalities. They were beyond improvisation . . . audacious, primitive little films stripped down to the core, largely incomprehensible in a narrative sense. Naked films.

In 2002 von Trier was finally able to pay homage to Cassavetes by hiring one of his old actors, Ben Gazzara—"the great god," as von Trier described him—for his movie, *Dogville.* "I saw him first in the work of John Cassavetes," enthused von Trier at a press-conference mid-way through production. "It's great that he is on board!"

Also kith and kin to the New American Cinema and somewhat interchangeable with it was the "Direct Cinema" (also known as the "Living Cinema") movement which focused on the documentary film and included filmmakers such as Richard Leacock, Robert Drew, and D.A. Pennebaker (*Primary,* 1960 / *Mooney VS Fowle* AKA *Football,* 1961 / *Don't Look Back,* 1967, respectively), as well as the Maysles brothers (*Salesman,* 1969/ *Gimmie Shelter,* 1970) and Frederick Wiseman (*Titticut Follies,* 1967). They worked from a set of principals and put into practice a number of technical approaches that would find an echo in Dogme.

For example, Direct Cinema downplayed the role of the director and instead emphasized the importance of the cameraman whom they felt was the most important link to the subject matter (this approach was also favored by the French *cinema verite* movement which developed at about the same time, in the late '50s and early '60s). Dogme shares this view: Vow of Chastity #10 states that "The director must never be credited" and attacks, both implicit and direct, against the *auteur* concept are to be found in the manifesto ("The *auteur* concept was bourgeois romanticism from the start." and "I swear to refrain from creating a 'work,' as I regard the instant to be more important than the whole," etc.) Neither Direct Cinema nor Dogme had any use for this old-fashioned type of director in all his dictatorial glory. The subject matter was *more* important.

The cameraman in Dogme occupies a central position and has been given heretofore unusual amounts of freedom and authority. In *The Idiots*, von Trier functioned more as the cameraman than the director. In *The Celebration*, cameraman Anthony Dod Mantle, wielding a tiny Sony digital camera, was able to melt into the action and practically become one with the cast. In this way, Dogme took advantage of the latest technology which gave the cinematographer ultimate mobility and autonomy. The new digital equipment was key to this approach. The ability of the small, totally mobile camera to erase the last vestiges of formal separation between cast and crew is invariably mentioned as one of the highlights of the Dogme approach.

But all this was being done within the framework of existing technology back in the '60s with Direct Cinema. They favored the use of equipment that was as portable and lightweight as possible and preferred to work without cumbersome crews or lighting apparatus—available light was used whenever possible—in the cause of capturing spontaneous "real life" situations. Direct Cinema sought, as did Dogme, to divest itself of the hardware that characterized studio-style filmmaking which tended to inhibit the people being filmed.

As Ephraim Katz phrases it, "Direct cinema used the camera as a silent observer that allowed people to reveal themselves in unguarded moments while forgetting about the presence of the camera or the crew."[6]

This Direct Cinema approach of using the camera as a passive and invisible tool to record moments of un-posed "truth" is, however, something Dogme does not subscribe to. Dogme is, after all, not about making documentaries, despite the fact that some Dogme films invariably have the veneer of documentary about them. Von Trier's thoughts about documentary filmmaking have been expressed in the separate *"Dog*-umentary" manifesto (see appendix), and the one documentary filmmaker, Anne Wivel, who was included in the original Brotherhood, quit soon after because, according to Kristian Levring, she wanted to continue making documentary and wasn't interested in fiction.

Dogme, in the final analysis, is about commercial fiction filmmaking, not documentary, and the camera, at least in the hands of Lars von Trier was anything *but* invisible. He used it as a tool to search out the truth rather than to passively record it. In *The Idiots* he uses the camera as a means by which to invade the actor's personal sphere, to get right in their faces, to become one with them. In his next film, *Dancer in the Dark*, he used the camera in an ever more intrusive fashion.

As Jesper Jargil commented on von Trier's shooting method: "It means a lot to Lars to be the one who films, to look through the camera and at the same time talk with the actors." In this fashion he attempts to prod a specific reaction or performance from them. It's the same technique he reportedly used in *Dogville* and it is anything but "fly on the wall."

"He makes the most of long shooting sequences," Jargil continues. "He drove Björk almost insane with that in *Dancer in the Dark* because he tries to penetrate the protective layer of professionalism an actor or performer has and reach down to something deeper, something else. He tries to pull the carpet out from under the actors."[7]

Although others are often given credit for cinematography on his films, it is actually von Trier behind the camera most of the time. On top of that, in *The Idiots* you can actually *see* a camera crew once in a while. That was fine with von Trier who believed that eventually audiences would accept the visible presence of the crew. He had a desire to make the filmmaking process visible and felt that it would not bother audiences or infringe upon a film's credibility to see the crew in action once in a while. This technique of the "visible crew," as it might be called, was in evidence to an almost absurd degree in the first edition of *Project D-Day* where all four actors were each shadowed by their own cameraman, and during one scene when they are all together, you can clearly see them all being filmed—eight people in the scene instead of four. In this sense von Trier believed in transparency, not invisibility. And if he liked to challenge actors, he also liked to challenge the audience.

Of course other Dogme directors had a different take on this, but generally speaking Dogme reordered the way films were prepared for and the way they were shot. And in this regard Dogme and Direct

Cinema were in accord: they were both rebellions against the way Hollywood made movies, the way Hollywood staged everything, the way Hollywood fooled audiences with their endless procession of technical "tricks." The two Vows of Chastity that preclude post-production manipulation, #2 and #5, go right to the heart of this issue. Direct Cinema, on the other hand had no need for such rules since they suffered no such temptations. After all, Dogme had been created to give freedom to the makers of big commercial films, filmmakers who supposedly had already been tempted, compromised, and corrupted, while the filmmakers of Direct Cinema were already coming from a milieu of purity or at least humility (television, for example), and they were not attempting to come *back* to a state of purity. In that sense they were not rebelling so much as they were pioneering. They were trying to make good honest documentaries—not save cinema.

Various miscellaneous technical approaches that Dogme would also come to exploit had parallels in New American Cinema. As noted, in his recent films, von Trier has taken advantage of the capabilities offered by new digital cameras to shoot scenes in long takes of sometimes up to almost an hour. This gives him the flexibility to follow the momentum of a scene and take it in unexpected directions.

The "king of the long take" is of course '60s underground icon, Andy Warhol, who sometimes just set up his camera in front of the actors, or *things*, such as the Empire State Building, turned it on and left the room. (As will be noted, von Trier also made extensive use of the "unmanned camera" in *Epidemic*.)

The difference is, of course, that Warhol's camera was always fixed on a tripod. Warhol believed in the fixed camera as much as von Trier believes in the mobile camera. Von Trier for his part is exploiting the latest technology which gives him this mobility and this option to shoot long takes, while Warhol had some flunky do the grunt work of reloading the film every few minutes.

Obviously, any comparison between Dogme and historical movements must take into consideration the relative technologies that were available and affordable to filmmakers at the time. Sound-synch equipment in the '60s was very much Hollywood gear at that point—cumbersome and expensive to rent. Hence a majority of the "underground" films at the time had the sound laid on after the images were shot. Most filmmakers had no choice. This naturally had a great bearing on the style of their films and pushed them in a more impressionistic and non-narrative direction. It wasn't until the dawn of the '70s that light sound-synch cameras became available to underground filmmakers, and this in turn led to the making of films with a more documentary style. Rule #2 in the Vow of Chastity—"The sound must never be produced apart from the images, or visa versa"—would have simply denied low-budget filmmakers in the '60s the ability to pursue their art. In this way, technology (and affordability) always leaves a stamp on the cinema of the times, always deeply effects the aesthetic decisions that are made. For its part, Dogme is in a technological sense just as much a product of the '90s as, for example, Warhol's *Chelsea Girls* was a product of the '60s.

And take Vow of Chastity #4—"The film must be in color." Today, it's cheaper to shoot in color stock than black-and-white because so few film labs do black-and-white processing anymore, but back in the '60s it was far cheaper to shoot in black-and-white. Surely one would expect Dogme to be sympathetic to a poor impoverished filmmaker. Additionally, color stock must be processed in a lab, while an ultra-diligent filmmaker can process 16mm black-and-white film stock at home.[8] Why hand over your hard earned cash to some film lab? . . . another advantage of black-and-white with which one might expect Dogme to be in sympathy. In reality though, Dogme is not the least concerned with impoverished undergrounders. By 1995, von Trier had no trouble financing any kind of film he wanted to make, and as he himself said, Dogme was not an economic concept but an artistic one. To state the paradox that echoes through this book, Dogme was aimed at established commercial filmmakers, but its most enthusiastic converts were impoverished independents.

Dogme's disavowal of black-and-white was of course based upon an understandable desire to avoid overt stylistic excesses, to avoid a single dominating aesthetic motif that can be seen in films like *The Elephant Man* (1980), *Rumble Fish* (1983), and *The Last Picture Show* (1971), to name just three examples. However successful all these films were in their own right, by 1995 black-and-white was almost exclusively associated with a kind of petrified nostalgia that smacked of "obvious aesthetic" in capital letters.

Warhol and von Trier are the polar opposites in other ways as well. Warhol almost never edited his film while von Trier is a firm believer in editing. Editing, in fact—the easiest way to manipulate all the "truths" that von Trier assumedly holds dear—is, curiously enough, not touched upon at all in any of the Vows of Chastity. Dogme could have, for example, decreed a whole set of rules for editing, but it did not. And by shooting so much footage, hundreds of hours in some cases (so much, as von Trier noted in regard to *The Idiots*, that it was almost impossible to look through), freedom to edit became all the more essential to the construction of a Dogme film.

Nonetheless, however much the two filmmakers differed in almost every other respect, they used long takes for the same reason: to force genuine reactions and emotions out of actors who were trained to give "performances" and to get the real stuff from amateurs who, given the first opportunity, would try to "act." Warhol did this by literally forcing the actors to take over the film in the absence of direction, while von Trier, by contrast, actively seeks to provoke or to prod them and to strip away their protective coating of professionalism. He pulls the carpet away while Warhol left the carpet nailed to the floor, two opposed strategies that often produced something of the same result—real situations, real reactions, real emotion.

Another interesting aspect about the Dogme manifesto in relation to the American film tradition is the declaration that "I am no longer an artist." In America, filmmakers have generally never considered themselves artists to begin with. Businessmen, craftsmen, and/or entertainers, yes, but rarely *artists*. This would be particularly true of the big commercial filmmakers to whom Dogme was purportedly addressing itself. American filmmakers never had this European *auteur* baggage to

Andy Warhol in the '60s, on the set of Lonesome Cowboys.

shed in the first place, rendering their allegiance to the Dogme cause somewhat problematic from the outset. I am not an artist? No, of course I am not an artist, I don't wear a beret and paint expressionist landscapes. In America, the *auteur* concept was a point of debate among film critics, resulting in a famous feud between Andrew Sarris and Pauline Kael, but it was never an issue with filmmakers.

To repeat the words of Mogens Rukov, most waves don't last longer than seven or eight years, and by 1967 The New American Cinema was not new anymore either and was taking its share of criticism from those who accused it of being a sham and a publicity stunt. That same year, in his December 21st column in *The Village Voice,* indefatigable champion of New American Cinema, Jonas Mekas, sarcastically confessed in print to an anonymous doubter that yes, you called our bluff—the New American Cinema was always just a joke, a con, a put-on.

We decided to work out, to connect, a few very 'unusual'
kooky ideas and gimmicks—like hand-held cameras, out of

focus shots, shaky camera techniques, improvised acting, single frames, jump cutting . . . things like that . . . and it worked, Hollywood picked up our bait . . . Today in Hollywood they are running in the studios with hand-held cameras, they are shaking them, while dollies and tripods are getting rusty . . . and the joke was on the press too, they swallowed the bait and the hook. All those articles on Underground movies! What's more, some of the filmmakers themselves got hooked on the scheme! They really believe, some of them, what the press tells them. . . .

Intoxicated as some of them might have been by all the hype, the majority of those filmmakers belonging to the New American Cinema were deeply enmeshed in a distinctly underground milieu. They were working outside institutional channels, financing their films with money from day jobs and editing the raw stock in makeshift attic studios. The "authorities" were generally against what they were doing and considered some of them subversives. Films were seized by cops and customs officials and on occasion theaters were raided and filmmakers and projectionists were jailed. They were sworn enemies of the system, of the official culture, the "official cinema."

Three decades later and an ocean away the definition of the term "rebel" has been turned on its head.

The four original Dogme brothers—today's rebels—are by contrast very much products of the system as it exists in Denmark. The System is thrilled with them, the State is thrilled them. Politicians are thrilled with them and love to be photographed with them. They are the products of everything that is institutional about filmmaking in Denmark. They were no drop-outs, they went to school. Six of the first seven Dogme films were made by graduates of the Danish Film School. Many of them then went on to make good money shooting commercials. *Commercials!* Others cut their teeth on TV series work. All have received grants from the Danish Film Institute and expect to receive more, and they complain loudly when the grants are not big enough. They enter their films like mad in film festivals and win prestigious awards right and left and bask endlessly in the glory.

By contrast the young Americans were not products of film schools, which by and large didn't even exist in the '60s. They received, with very few exceptions, no grant money and they considered film festival competitions to be a travesty and a joke. A corporate ruse.

Of course they were not competing in the same arena. The New American Cinema filmmakers were overwhelmingly engaged in the making of short (hence non-commercial) films while Dogme is exclusively concerned with the production of commercial feature films, however experimental some of them might appear.

The New German Cinema

Counterparts to the New American Cinema existed in Europe as well. On February 28th, 1962, 26 German short-film makers, including Edgar Reity and Alexander Kluge, issued "The Oberhausen Manifesto." Inspired by the example of the American underground, it proclaimed the conventional German cinema to be in a state of collapse and declared that a new cinema now had a chance to grow.

> *The collapse of the conventional German film finally removes the economic basis for a mode of filmmaking whose attitude and practice we reject. With it the new film has a chance to come to life.*
>
> *German short films by young authors, directors and producers have in recent years received a large number of prizes at international festivals and gained the recognition of international critics. These works and these successes show that the future of the German film lies in the hands of those who have proven that they speak a new film language.*
>
> *Just as in other countries, the short film has become in Germany a school and experimental basis for the feature film.*

We declare our intention to create the new German feature film.

This new film needs new freedoms. Freedoms from the conventions of the established industry. Freedom from the outside influence of commercial partners. Freedom from the control of special interest groups.

We have concrete intellectual, formal and economic conceptions about the production of the new German film. We are as a collective prepared to take economic risks.

The old film is dead. We believe in the new one.

Oberhausen, February 28, 1962

The Oberhausen manifesto is seen today as the starting point of what would eventually blossom into the New German Cinema of the '70s.

Following the Manifesto, nothing much happened until 1966 when Kluge's first feature, *Yesterday Girl*, won eight awards at the Venice Biennale. That same year several other German films were acclaimed at Cannes and Berlin. The hype had begun and suddenly the arrival of New German Cinema was being hailed far and wide. Packages of German films were showcased at European festivals throughout 1967 and the popular German weekly, *Der Spiegel*, even dedicated a cover page story to the subject in their final issue of the year.

But nothing came in the wake of all this. In an effort to encourage the production of more fresh new films, film funding guidelines were changed in 1968 via the Film Promotion Law, but due to political maneuvering it had the opposite effect and German audiences just got more of the banal, trivial, and "safe" films that had previously dominated. It was not until 1976–1977 that the New German Cinema became a reality on the strength of work by filmmakers such as Rainer Werner Fassbinder, Wim Wenders, and Werner Herzog.

Lars von Trier was at that point in time a 20-year old neophyte attending film classes at Copenhagen University. He was very much obsessed with German culture and this new German film wave effected him deeply—not just the films themselves, but the whole allure of the thing, the way it turned the film world upside-down. Now *this* was a revolution.

Years later he would pay Fassbinder something of a tribute by casting one of his actresses, Barbara Sukowa, in *Europa*. She looked beautiful in it. Fassbinder would have approved, had he not died nine years before, in 1982.

Other Danish Film Movements

Denmark itself had a few of what could be called "underground" film groups in the 1960s.

Film-group 16, founded in 1964, was one of them. This associ- ation inhabited an equipment-packed cellar in an old villa in the town of Hvidovre, south of Copenhagen. Their goal was to raise the technical and artistic standard of non-commercial cinema in Denmark and to encourage the use of the 16mm format.

By 1974, the group had lost their cellar space and had become more of a coffee club that met once a week at the house of one of the members.

In 1977, while he was attending University and planning to make his own films, Lars von Trier became a member of the club. It was with Film-group 16, using their equipment and employing them as cast and crew, that he made *The Orchid Gardener* in 1977 and *Menthe—The Blissful* in 1979. By then, however, they had lost the revolutionary zeal that had originally given them such hopes for the medium. And in any case, von Trier was only using the group to make his films. He wasn't buying into anything and he wasn't signing on to any philosophy.

He was really in fact very much a loner and never a part of any "wave" or "movement." He couldn't be a part of the New German Cinema; he was Danish and living up here in this little unimportant country where there was no revolution taking place, where nothing was happening to which anyone was paying particular attention. Perhaps, then, Dogme was to a great extent the product of nostalgia, a belated attempt to be a part of a real wave. Maybe that is why all the Dogme talk about solidarity and purity sounds a bit exaggerated, the way that nostalgic tributes are often a bit exaggerated. Almost satirical.

ABC Cinema was another important underground Danish film group, a collective founded in May of 1968 that counted a lot of painters and artists among its members. It was the largest film collective in the country and a very active and productive one. It made itself (in)famous in February of 1969 when it forcibly occupied the Danish Film School and declared that it was now a "film commune" which was being "liberated from the vultures." The ABC'ers demanded "free access to the means of production," and made a lot of other bold demands, but ended up clearing out the next day before the cops arrived.

While no Dogme brother was a member of ABC cinema, the artist, poet, and documentarian, Jørgen Leth, was one of its leaders and front figures. Leth is today a pal of von Trier's and a kind of unofficial Dogme brother. Together with von Trier he recently completed the Dogme-esque experiment, *The Five Obstructions*, and was one of the four founders of the previously noted "Dogumentary" movement founded on May 6, 2000 (see section on Jørgen Leth).

The French New Wave

The previous film "revolution" that has most closely been associated with Dogme is the French New Wave, and this is due to the fact that it is referred to at some length in the Dogme manifesto. Yet what the manifesto has to say about it is highly ambiguous. To repeat the relevant passages:

> *In 1960 enough was enough! The movie was dead and called for resurrection. The goal was correct but the means were not! The New Wave proved to be a ripple that washed ashore and turned to muck.*

> *Slogans of individualism and freedom created works for a while, but no changes. The wave was up for grabs, like the directors themselves. The wave was never stronger than the men behind it. The anti-bourgeois cinema itself became bourgeois, because the foundations upon which its theories were based was the bourgeois perception of art. The auteur concept was bourgeois romanticism from the very start and thereby . . . false!*
>
> *To Dogme 95 cinema is not individual!*

What exactly did the two original Dogme brothers, or rather Lars von Trier, whom we can safely refer to as the guiding force behind the Manifesto, mean by this apparent swipe at the French New Wave?

This question was heatedly debated in Danish film circles in the Spring of 2001 with the publication of the book, *Barnet og Idioten—Danske Dogmefilm i nærbilleder (The Child and the Idiot—Danish Dogme Film in close-up),* by Hans Jensen.

Jensen had, in the opinion of *Politiken* book reviewer, Bo Tao Michaëlis, committed an unforgivable error by claiming that the two movements were closely related, and not just because von Trier was apparently disparaging the Frenchmen in his manifesto:

> *If one can in base estimation say that Dogme is a rejection of Hollywood's technical and melodramatic hardware, readers of* The Child and The Idiot *will be startled to learn of its kinship to Truffaut, Chabol and Godard . . . How can a group of filmmakers who championed concepts such as the genre film and the* auteur *theory and who loved the American B-movie with its music, CinemaScope and all—films made by idolized professionals such as Howard Hawks, Alfred Hitchcock, Sam Fuller and Douglas Sirk—at all be seen as the fathers of Dogme? . . . Directors who looked upon film as their 'personal pen' and used actors as their pawns . . . can hardly be said to be inspiration for the kind of filmmaking that revolves around*

*a loose story and a handful of talented actors placed in inti-
mate focus via modern digital shooting techniques. One could
reluctantly live with Jensen's definition if he also called attention
to the fact that film artists such as Cassavetes and Fassbinder
are also obvious fathers of Dogme.*

*And is it not probable that Dogme has been influenced as
much or more by recent works of Danish film realism, created
by directors such as, among others, Nils Malmros, Christian
Braad Thomsen and Helle Ryslinge, than by . . . film waves
that happened 40 years ago?"*[9]

Jensen fired back in *Politiken* on April 20th that Michaëlis had
failed to register or appreciate the von Trier-esque irony that permeated
the Dogme manifesto:

> *. . . It is precisely that irony which characterizes, in par-
> ticular, the part of the Dogme manifesto that is conveyed with
> typically bombastic Marxist phrasing . . . for example: 'The*
> auteur *concept was bourgeois from the start and thereby false!
> . . . Discipline is hard, we must dress our films in uniforms
> because the individual film will be decadent by definition!'*
>
> *Dogme* resembles *a definitive rebellion against, and a
> 'father killing' of, the French New Wave directors,"* main-
> tained Jensen, *"but it is in reality an homage to them and
> their great contribution to a modern breakthrough for film.*

While Michaëlis is certainly correct about the contradictory
nature of the two movements, Jensen's point is also well taken. Von
Trier *is* being ironic, he *is* being over-dramatic. Just look at all the
exclamation marks that litter the Manifesto. One can almost hear the
exaggerated stridency in his voice. And the fact that the Manifestos
were printed on sheaths of *red* paper. It's a bit too obvious.

Von Trier's accusation that the New Wave directors sold-out or
betrayed some revolution—"they were up for grabs"—rings hollow if

we look at the facts. To start with, the New Wave, unlike the British Free Cinema of the late '50s, never was about social or political change, never was about solidarity with the downtrodden or the working classes—never was "red." To claim as von Trier does that "the anti-bourgeois cinema itself became bourgeois" is erroneous, and he knows it, because the French New Wave never was anti-bourgeois to start with and never laid claim to being so. It is furthermore curious that a filmmaker like von Trier who never made a political film in his life and states he never will make one should feel so betrayed by the New Wave directors for selling out "the revolution," even if they had.

Von Trier was clearly role-playing. He was acting the part of the angry rebel, making impassioned demands and levelling accusations dramatized in socialist phraseology. This was a conscious, on-going satirization of his own youthful involvement in the Communist party in the '60s and '70s, which he had joined at a young age at his mother's behest. He knew the lingo, he knew the attitude. He had turned against all this communist ideology at University and was continually thereafter gripped by a certain reflexive anti-leftism, but he would return to it in his manifestos for ironic/dramatic effect every now and again.

How serious was von Trier about Dogme?

That's the question many ask. If reports were true that he and Vinterberg had drawn up the manifesto in a mere 25 minutes amid gales of laughter, *he*, at least, wasn't taking it seriously. In retrospect one has to wonder how seriously he might have taken it if he could have known how successful it would become. Would they have copy-righted the term Dogme 95? Would he have taken more care with it, made the manifesto longer? Made it more *coherent*? It would have been a mistake had he done so, since it is the inscrutability of the manifesto statements ("We must put our films into uniform, because the individual film will be decadent by definition!", etc.) if not the actual rules of the Vow of Chastity, and von Trier's subsequent ambiguous behavior in regard to the whole thing, that has given Dogme impact and longevity. Had everything in the Manifesto been objectively, clearly and concisely laid out, nobody would still be taking about it and debating it today. It can be dismissed—all the better if some hate it!—but it can't be disproven because it isn't "real" to start with, and because for all the specificity of the rules they are constantly held up as being only voluntary guidelines.

The nuances of von Trier's intentions and sense of humor aside, the actual relationship between the two movements is relevant and merits a closer look if only because the ghost of the French New Wave hovers so closely over Dogme's shoulder.

In truth the New Wave was a confederation of several different groups and included a great number of filmmakers. Ninety-seven debut feature films were released during its heyday from 1958 to 1962. Denmark on the other hand is a much smaller country with a much smaller film market and production capacity, and has produced on average between 16 and 20 feature films a year over the last decade. And out of that only 12 Dogme films have been completed or are in some stage of production as of mid-2003.

Taking the numbers into consideration, one must wonder how the Danes, or anyone, could have the temerity to compare Dogme to the New Wave. One might also wonder if, when using the New Wave as a measuring stick, Dogme is a fake or constructed wave. Unlike the French movement or New German Cinema, Dogme was not a spon-taneous movement in any sense, born as they typically are from a confluence of favorable creative and economic conditions that already exist and lead to the release of expressive urges that are seeking outlet . . . born from a chemistry that is already starting to bubble. The Dogme Manifesto was not the result of or a response to such forces, not an expression of any situation or condition at large in Danish film. Not a sign of things stirring below the ice. Things started stirring below the ice *after* Dogme was launched, but there were no such broader forces at play in the conception of Dogme. There was just Lars von Trier, who in any case had always been angry. It's true that a new generation of Danish filmmakers came of age in the '90s, but Dogme did not instigate that.

A rebellion it might legitimately be called, but a wave . . . ? Dogme gave voice to dissatisfactions and frustrations that already existed all over the world, and it purported to give some answers as well if one just *believed*. Dogme served as a catalyst and was adaptable and easily translatable. It was a one-size-fits-all portable revolution all packed up and ready to go, the perfect kit with glue and decals included. But from a strictly Danish perspective, there was no obvious need for Dogme. There was no obvious need for a wave of cheap, low-budget, honest little films in a country that didn't make "big" films to start

Jean-Luc Godard and unidentified friend in transit in the mid-'60s.

with. And Danish directors hardly needed to go "cold turkey." What were they addicted to? They hardly ever used special effects anyway, and Danish studios weren't even capable of staging big scenes. Of course there were false, insincere films being made in Denmark, too, but generally speaking, the Danish Dogme films, whatever their merits, were not born of a wider necessity but rather were born of a personal necessity—Lars von Trier's. Probably in no other country could a single filmmaker have had such overwhelming sway.

There are other prominent differences between the two movements. The most visible and energetic faction of the New Wave was composed of a number of writers such as Chabrol, Truffaut, Godard, Rohmer, and Rivette who had contributed to *Cahiers du Cinema* in the early '50s. Despite their antipathy for the "official cinema," they were not attempting to erase all that had come before and return to "year zero" as Dogme apparently was. They were dyed-in-the-wool cineastes and their heads were full of a thousand favorite films. They had a genuine sense of film heritage and culture.

In that sense, von Trier was their spiritual brethren. He was an indefatigable cineaste whose films were as full of homages to all of his heroes as surely as Godard ever paid homage to Bogart. Yet Dogme seemed to be a subtractive, not an additive process, a set of limitations rather than a set of possibilities. What kind of picture can you paint, asked doubters, if all your brushes are taken away?

In this regard, one has to question von Trier's commitment to Dogme as anything more than just a temporary fling. His pre and post-*Idiots* films flagrantly violate all the Dogme rules, and he's never expressed any desire to make another Dogme film.

If the New Wave guys were "up for grabs," what was he? Just a slumming tourist? Where did he measure on the scale of revolutionary purity?

Pretty low, it would appear.

One might say for the sake of argument that *The Idiots* was not a "necessary" film for him to make, not a natural film for him to make or a film he *had* to make. It was a film he made as an act of solidarity, as a commitment to his Dogme brothers. Rather than using the possibilities that Dogme provided to make the film he wanted to make, the case can be made that he was merely making the film to advertise Dogme, to fulfill commitments. A letter he wrote to the Danish Culture minister, Jytte Hilden, in December of 1996 to complain about lack of funding for Dogme, read in part; "If I should make more films, as I hope to, the stupidest thing I could do would be to denigrate the relative commercial success I've achieved by throwing myself into a Danish-spoken, low-budget film project . . . and that was also not the intention." In other words, *The Idiots* had in and of itself no reason to exist, it only had value for him as a part of Dogme, a part of the wave. It is unlikely that Fassbinder felt the same about New German Cinema or Godard about the French New Wave. They considered their films all-important, they did not think of them as mere components of some greater philosophical order. They made the films they had to make, and if afterwards somebody said they were part of this or that wave, fine. . . .

In that both Dogme and the French New Wave were rebellions against the status-quo, they of course shared similarities. As Roy Armes writes in *French Cinema*,[10]

> *The New Wave aimed at change on virtually every level of film style . . . a work could be directly personal . . . and could reflect a direct and immediate response to a particular time and place, filmed on location, not constructed in a studio. All the rules of conventional 1950's narrative continuity editing, with its careful establishing shots, patterned use of close-ups and its total rejection of any trace of spontaneity or improvisation could be questioned.*

In these and other respects the similarities between the two movements are clear, despite the fact that they are separated by culture and almost half a century.

There are other parallels as well. Both movements received their public unveiling at the Cannes Film Festival, the New Wave in 1959 when Francois Truffaut's *The 400 Blows* won the prize for best direction and Marcel Camus' *Orfeu Negro* won the Palme d'Or. Additionally there was Alan Resnais' *Hiroshima mon Amour*, which was shown outside competition. Almost 40 years later, in 1998, Cannes' director, Gilles Jacob, invited Lars von Trier and Thomas Vinterberg down to introduce Dogme to the world with somewhat less spectacular results. *The Celebration* did win the Jury's special prize, but *The Idiots* won nothing. As von Trier's business partner, Peter Aalbæk Jensen, would later remark, nobody really gave a hoot about Dogme at that point.

The influence of the French New Wave was also felt in Denmark, most notably with the 1962 film, *Weekend* (not to be confused with the Godard film from 1968), which came to be known as the first Danish New Wave film. Another von Trier connection surfaces here, as it was written by Klaus Rifberg who would go on to become good pals with von Trier and to engage in a number of projects with him.[11] *Weekend* was a bold stab at realism and was clearly an inspiration for *The Idiots* (although in structure it rather calls to mind *The Celebration*). Both films dealt with a disaffected group of "velfærdsdanskere," a term that might translate into "average middle-class Danes," and both were ensemble pieces that supposedly contained some amount of improvisation.

Weekend is set in a Danish summer house where three married couples and a bachelor mingle for a weekend of discussion, drinking, beach-going and angst-ridden soul-searching. They are educated, articulate, and they own things and they perceive themselves to be free, and yet they are dissatisfied and frustrated. But they continue forward in this kind of spiritual fog because in spite of everything their existence is secure. The film came as a shock to viewers; its narrative structure was episodic and unorthodox and its treatment of sex was frank and "adult." The director, Palle Kjærluff-Schmidt, was young and so were the actors. Non-actors were also used, and it was shot on location. No staging, no sets.

Perhaps the most important lesson Dogme learned from the French New Wave was the value of bold declarations, the value of self-promotion. The value of creating buzz and allure around a set of ideals and a body of work that would go on to generate its own momentum.

"The great achievement of the young French (New Wave) film-makers of this period," writes Armes,[12] "was to accomplish this within the mainstream of production, so that their low-budget features were not marginalized but competed in the same cinemas and on the same terms as the major productions of Clement, Cayatte or DelAnnoy.

A scene from the 1962 film, Weekend, *directed by Palle Kjærulff-Schmidt and hailed as the first Danish contribution to the French New Wave.*

Their breakthrough not only opened the way forward for themselves, it also allowed such innovative older directors as Tati and Bresson to work with the assurance of an audience and with new possibilities of raising funding for ambitious and unorthodox works."

Dogme did for Danish cinema this and much more. It has been repeatedly credited for giving a massive boost to the entire Danish film industry. It has given all the Dogme brothers, excepting von Trier, their big breakthroughs and other Danish directors have been pulled along in its slip stream. In another country and another film milieu, such a concept of primitive, low-budget films shot on video would have been ghettoized, would have been tagged an "underground thing" and relegated to the film festival circuit, but thanks to von Trier's clout in the Danish film world and his financial muscle as co-owner of Zentropa studio, it has become positively mainstream. Perhaps too mainstream. But more on that later.

IV

Lars von Trier's Pre-Dogme Films

The Element of Crime, Epidemic, and *Europa*

Ultimately, in spite of all the parallels that are drawn between Dogme and foreign movements, the story of Dogme starts inside the brain of Lars von Trier.

The "prehistory" of Dogme, that is to say the set of conditions that gave birth to the movement, naturally predates March 22nd, 1995, when von Trier threw a clutch of red flyers over the edge of the stage in Paris. In fact the very personal desires and compulsions that gave rise to the need for Dogme go back to the start of his career as a commercial filmmaker, for however much Dogme is accused of being a publicity stunt—and in whatever sense it might have *been* a publicity stunt—it was born out of some very hard experiences and the emotions they produced. It was born out of all the frustration, impatience, exhaustion, and pure misery that the filmmaking process had been for him. It was a product of all the films that had been a torment to finish and all the projects that never came to be. It was a reaction to all the scripts that were never funded, all the producers who just weren't interested. As he described it in his third manifesto, bringing a film to life was nothing less than pure "hell."

Lars von Trier shortly after his graduation from The Danish Film School.

But it was not just a rebellion against the process, rather it was, for the most part, Lars von Trier rebelling against *himself.* He hungered for simplicity because he himself was so prone to making things complicated, in his relations with people and his relations with the medium. He was a man who naturally wanted to continue his craft and maintain his mental health at the same time, and this is what gave rise to the invention of Dogme, the will to survive—even if his Dogme film, *The Idiots,* ironically almost killed him. And even though he has since left Dogme behind, he has taken with him a few grains of what he learned to help him survive. In this sense Dogme was more of an internal rebellion than the noble battle waged against the superficiality of Hollywood as it is so often depicted.

Lars von Trier was fresh out of Film School when in 1983 he embarked upon his first commercial feature film, *The Element of Crime.* He had aroused some controversy with his student films and had won a few prizes, yet the mammoth self-confidence he possessed hardly corresponded in any way to his actual accomplishments up to this point. Nonetheless he was ready to make a masterpiece. He was already good enough; of that he had no doubt.

He approached the task as an uncompromising perfectionist, as a craftsman obsessed with every detail. Every shot was story-boarded, every camera movement was exhaustively diagrammed, planned and rehearsed and every location was thoroughly scouted. "I am convinced that rarely has so much basic research been done before the shooting of a Danish film," he noted at the time. "We knew precisely every single camera position before we began."[13] It was a six-week shoot done mostly at night through the fall of 1983, in the cold and rain and in all manner of bizarre locations from the claustrophobic sewers of Copenhagen and the subterranean passageways of Kronborg castle to the gloomy open spaces of abandoned factories and chalk pits.

His diligence paid off in visual terms and the film was roundly praised for looking much more expensive than it was, but his inexperience was also in evidence as many of the locations proved too difficult to work in and this, in turn, caused delays that sent the shooting over-schedule and over-budget.

This was his first encounter with "The Apparatus"—all the money, demands, pressures and deadlines that commercial filmmaking entailed . . . the dependence on crews, producers, accountants, and erratic stars, all that makes filmmaking a hell for creative, sensitive souls. For directors who still had much to learn about communicating with their actors.

Police detective Fisher, played by Michael Elphick, on the trail of mass-murderer Harry Grey in The Element of Crime.

Although it was accepted "in-competition" at Cannes, it won only a technical prize and was largely ignored in Denmark. For all his work, the film was acclaimed no masterpiece. It earned him the tag of "promising," but in retrospect it really wasn't much of a career boost.

Following *The Element of Crime*, von Trier attempted to get several projects off the ground, but due to various reasons they all imploded on the launching pad. He worked on some until he was simply sick of them and abandoned them, all the while searching in vain for a foreign producer who would allow him to make his next film in English.[14] His legendary insistence on having total artistic control might have had something to do with his inability to find such a producer.

It has been said that when a writer or painter wants to create a work, they sit down with a pen or brush and start working, but that when a filmmaker wants to create, he has to sit down and start calling up producers and financiers on the telephone. He was at this point surely a victim of this situation and it was a frustrating three year period for him (1984–1986). He found it painful that with all his energy and ideas he was prevented from making another film simply because he couldn't raise the money or get a producer interested. And look at all the lousy films that *could* get funded!

It was this frustration and impatience that led him to his next film, *Epidemic*, which was every bit as much a rebellion against this situation as it was a movie. With *Epidemic* he would escape this eternal waiting game, this torment of developing scripts until he couldn't stand the sight of them while he waited for some producer to sign on. This hell of being at someone else's mercy.

The film actually originated as a wager between he and his pal, Claes Kastholm Hansen, who happened to be one of the two consultants at the Danish Film Institute who were responsible for approving support for film production.[15] Von Trier bet him he could make a commercial feature film for a mere one million Danish kroner (130,000-plus USD in current exchange). Kastholm Hansen accepted.

On paper, *Epidemic* was a novel conception, a kind of fantasy about how a film could be created at the last moment.

It opens with two filmmakers (played by filmmakers Lars von Trier and partner, Niels Vørsel) who have five days to complete their manuscript and submit it to a consultant—played by none other than Kastholm Hansen—for approval. But the whole thing, a tawdry drama called *The Cop and the Whore*, is accidentally erased on the computer. They still have five days and decide to write a completely new film and submit that instead. The new film will be about the onslaught of a deadly plague that takes place in the near future and it will be called *Epidemic*. Fictional passages from their film-in-progress soon begin to appear on the screen, interweaving with "reality" as the two of them struggle to complete the script. In something that resembles a case of psychic transference, the filmmakers begin to evidence symptoms of the plague themselves. Five days later they have dinner with Kastholm Hansen and hand over the script. He is not impressed, and so to demonstrate the dramatic potential of the story, they bring in a hypnotist and a teenage girl who is hypnotized "into the film" and back to 14th century London to experience first hand the horrors of the Black Death.

A scene from the carefully staged fictional line of Epidemic *where a powerful coterie of elderly doctors meet to discuss the approaching plague.*

The film was a marriage of diametrically opposed aesthetics. The fictional line was filmed by Henning Bendtsen, the acclaimed cinematographer of Carl Theodor Dreyer's last two films, *The Word* and *Gertrud.* These scenes were carefully composed and shot in monocolor. The acting here was underplayed and stylized. The dialogue was dubbed in a rather stiff English to give it a real "movie" feel and to play up the fictional nature of this plot line, setting it in contrast to the "reality line," which was shot in 16mm black-and-white film in unstaged locations. Here the non-actors wore their own clothing and engaged in long scenes replete with the casual boredom of real life.

Here in the reality line everything *would* be reality—no studios, crews, make-up or costumes, etc. The film would tell itself and even shoot itself, literally speaking in the latter regard, for as von Trier wrote in the manifesto booklet he published to accompany its release:

> *During much of the filming of* Epidemic *no film techniques were used. Thus for almost one-third of the film, the camera rolled unmanned. This provided the film with its intimate atmosphere and most important of all—* ease of mind.

To obtain "ease of mind" was von Trier's primary goal with *Epidemic* as he sought to escape both The Apparatus and his own perfectionist nature.

It was an experimental film and it was a schizophrenic film. Von Trier was running in two opposite directions at once: the fictional half of the film was an exercise in creating the kind of ultra-stylized and consciously staged atmosphere that would come to characterize his next picture, *Europa* (which Bendsten would also shoot), while the reality line was both in technical style and in principal the same kind of rebellion against filmmaking orthodoxy that Dogme would be. It has in fact been called the first Dogme film.

While *Epidemic* in some respects is the antithesis of Dogme, the similarities that do exist are uncanny. A closer look at these similarities can serve to shed light on the evolution of von Trier's thinking and reveal how some of the basic concepts of Dogme were rooted in his earlier work. (Note: in the 4 points below, references to *Epidemic* apply to the "reality line" of the film.)

1. *Epidemic* was, like Dogme, an attempt to achieve spontaneity and to find the space to breathe in the normally suffocating environment of a film shoot. Improvised acting existed to some degree, or rather one might say "improvised non-acting," since von Trier didn't want acting. Von Trier's Dogme film, *The Idiots*, in comparison, was rumored to be largely improvised, but in fact was not. Like *The Idiots*, *Epidemic* was a very "naked" film stripped of special effects, glossy production values, and artificial plot mechanizations.

2. In *Epidemic* there was no post-production manipulation (Dogme rules #2 & #5). It was a "rejection of aesthetic" beyond what even Dogme demanded, an even *more* primitive film—straightforward and for long passages uneventful to the point of not being anything that resembled a movie. Deadpan and "everyday" to such a degree that a large segment of viewers and critics could hardly stand it. For many von Trier-haters (and even some fans), it is a point of fierce debate as to whether *The Idiots* or *Epidemic* is his most unwatchable film.

3. *Epidemic* largely conformed to Vow of Chastity rule number one, "Shooting must be done on location. Props and sets must not be brought in." Gitte, the teenage medium brought in at the end of the film to travel back in time to the Middle Ages via hypnosis, is a possible exception. One is tempted to say that if she really *were* hypnotized, then she was no prop. In *The Idiots*, von Trier hired professional porno actors to fornicate in the background in a single scene and was roundly accused of breaking the "no props" rule. If Gitte *was* faking hypnosis, then she was a prop, brought in just to provide atmosphere, and yet she was a central character in the film—not a decoration—whether or not the hypnosis was genuine. The porn actors, however, even

though they were engaging in actual intercourse, were props by almost everyone's estimate, brought in to decorate the set.

Which leads us to the "bodily fluids issue." They must be genuine as well, goes the wisdom of Dogme. No fake tears or blood, etc. In *Epidemic*, Gitte, we assume, breaks the rule when at the end she goes amok and lances her buboes (pustular swellings in her armpits that are symptoms of the plague) and blackened bile squirts out.

So much for bodily fluids.

4. *Epidemic* also conformed to rule #5—"optical work and filters are forbidden," and rule #6, "The film must not contain superficial action." The film contained precious little action, superficial or otherwise. The only thing resembling action that took place in the entire film was the hypnosis of Gitte Lind who, as noted, breaks out with symptoms of Plague in the end and goes berserk. One can argue that this wasn't superficial action, in that it was central to the plot and was, according to all present, *real*, an assertion they have maintained to this day. In that case, if she really had been hypnotized back to 14th century London, it would have violated another rule, #7: "Temporal and geographical alienation are forbidden (That is to say that the film takes place in the here and now)." One might even say that applying the Vow of Chastity rules to a film made before Dogme existed is a violation of rule #7.

There were of course some obvious breaks with Dogme. *Epidemic* was not (always) in color and set lighting lamps were used. And consider vow #3, "The camera must be hand-held." There were the aforementioned scenes in *Epidemic* when *nobody* was running the camera, and at this point it was of course fixed on a tripod. Getting rid of the cameraman is certainly taking the concept of a "primitive" film even further than Dogme does. What's next? Getting rid of the camera? Getting rid of the actors? Getting rid of the movie?

Finally, if one can say that Dogme was an attempt to force the director to renounce his own ego (as per the manifesto passages: "I am no longer an artist . . . my supreme goal is to force the truth out of my characters and settings," and Rule #10—"The director shall not be credited") then *Epidemic* was in direct opposition to this. Here the film was at the service of the director, not the other way around. With von Trier writing the script and playing the two lead roles in a movie about himself as he attempts to make a movie, *Epidemic* was hardly an act of self-repudiation. It was no attempt to achieve the state of supreme humility that Dogme so encouraged. It was instead vanity incarnate, the film a "vehicle" for von Trier. He has long claimed that of all the films he has made, this is his personal favorite, and that might well be because he looks good in it. He's fit and relaxed and enjoying himself. He looks to be in harmony with himself, and that was not always the case with him according to many observers.

Ultimately it would be a stretch to call *Epidemic* "the first Dogme film," but it was the same kind of take-no-prisoners attack on film orthodoxy as Dogme, the same kind of search for simplicity and spontaneity conducted in the hope and assumption that when the artist has peace of mind, he or she can create their best work. After all, why are other kinds of artists allowed to go off into the country to create their works in soul-refreshing peace and solitude while a filmmaker must battle on under the most hectic and pressurized production conditions?

As for "the bet" between Kastholm Hansen and Lars . . . no money ever changed hands.

Europa (1991), von Trier's next film, was the culmination of the visual style he had first employed in *The Element of Crime* and the acting style he had experimented within the fictional line of *Epidemic*. And it was, like all of his films, a radical rebellion against the previous film.

It would also be another very complicated production. Again he ran over-budget and over-schedule. Unpredictable problems, characteristic of relatively big-budget films, arose. At one point the low-paid "walk-ons" in Poland, where all the exteriors were shot, went on strike in demand of higher pay. At other stages the complicated rear-screen projection processes needed adjustment, etc.

Europa was von Trier caught in the jaws of The Apparatus again, but it was a trap of his own making. It was the man in his own ele-

Lars von Trier on the set of Europa *(released as* Zentropa *in the U.S.).*

ment: creating complicated visual effects, solving arcane technical problems and planning and story-boarding every shot to the ninth degree as well as keeping an eye on production details.

In Cannes he once again had to be satisfied with a technical prize, but many reviewers now hailed his film as a masterpiece. Perhaps because von Trier had quite consciously intended it to be one, or in any case to visually resemble one. As he explained at the Cannes premiere, "This film is made as a masterpiece. I decided that beforehand. It was conceived big and contains clarity of thought. It is un-Danish to set out with premeditation to make a masterpiece and furthermore to concede that."[16]

Although *Europa* was the recipient of considerable international praise, it was no hit in Denmark.

The Kingdom and *Breaking the Waves*

In 1992, von Trier and Aalbæk Jensen founded their own studio in an old tobacco factory and called it Zentropa. If their little company was able, it would produce von Trier's next film which he was already now working on and which would end up being called *Breaking the Waves*. In this way he would be sure to maintain total artistic control over the project.

Over the next couple of years, von Trier earned enough money making commercials to keep the company afloat, but only just, and when Danmarks Radio asked him to make a TV series for them, he couldn't refuse.

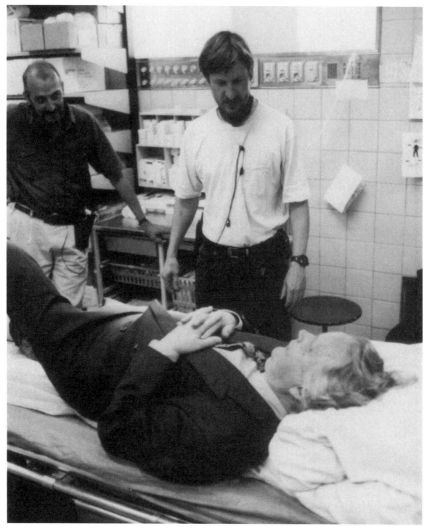

Morten Arnfred, a relaxed Lars von Trier (L to R), and
Ernst-Hugo Järegaard (reclined) on the set of The Kingdom.

That series would be *The Kingdom*.

One of his primary inspirations was the American TV series, *Twin Peaks*, by David Lynch. While he found Lynch's feature films to be "rubbish,"[17] he found *Twin Peaks* to be "brilliant and different." In his view the switch from feature filmmaking to television had given Lynch the freedom to experiment, to relax and exhale. He had made a "left-handed" masterpiece, as von Trier termed it, that was both spontaneous and delightfully unpredictable.

After all the tensions and pressures involved in *Europa*, von Trier thirsted for the same freedom.

The Kingdom would stand as the first obvious forerunner to Dogme.

It pioneered the kind of shaky, hand-held camera work which utilized available light only and which is today considered a trademark of Dogme. The photographer, Eric Kress, a Film School graduate (class of 1991), deserves much of the credit for that. He would go on to become one of Denmark's most sought after cinematographers, and von Trier would again employ him as second-unit cameraman on *Breaking the Waves* and *Dancer in the Dark*, but *The Kingdom* was to remain his most groundbreaking work.

Unlike *The Element of Crime* and *Europa*, which had been carefully choreographed, here in *The Kingdom* Kress didn't even know beforehand where the actors would be positioned when the action started, just as the actors did not know where he would be standing. He was given minimal guidance by von Trier and co-director, Morten Arnfred, and just told to shoot what he found best. Scenes were shot from start to finish with no cuts, and four or five re-takes were done in which the actors were encouraged to improvise. He covered the action from all four corners of the room with full mobility, since there were no cables, sometimes spinning 360 degrees and prompting the sound-man and an assistant to dive to the floor. "The experience," noted Danish critic, Ebbe Iversen,[18] "was liberating for both Kress and the actors, and was at the same time a kind of kick-off to Dogme."

The Kingdom was, of course, in some important ways in violation of the Vow of Chastity. While rule #3, "The camera must be hand-held," was followed by Kress as he covered the actors, at other points in the production steady-cams and tripods were employed when the camera needed more fixed positioning, for example with the special-effects shots—special-effects themselves being in violation of the spirit of Dogme. The Vows that prohibited post-production processes (2 and 5), were violated with a vengeance, as there was actually quite a bit of color tweaking and filtering, not to mention the fact that Kress' 16mm footage was transferred and edited on video, giving the images a very grainy "TV reportage" look. This was surely indulging in an aesthetic, which was forbidden by Dogme, but in fact it was von Trier's favorite *modus operandi*.[19]

And von Trier's Alfred Hitchcock-esque appearances at the beginning of each episode surely were in discord with rule #10—"The director must not be credited"—or, we can assume, deified, glamorized or fetishized. Finally, to sum up breaks with Dogme, all shooting was not done "on location," and one might venture to say that the character, Mary, a child murdered by a doctor in the hospital a century earlier, but whose ghost now roams its subterranean passages, is a break with rule #7, which, to repeat, states that "Temporal and geographical alienation are forbidden."

Most important, though, was that *The Kingdom* succeeded in liberating von Trier. He had managed to escape The Apparatus, to find a freshness in the working process. He could breathe again.

There were a number of secondary factors that no doubt helped to lighten the burden. The hospital itself, which served as a location, was only a ten minute walk away from where Zentropa's studio stood at that time on Ryesgade. The company didn't have the headache of being sole producer for the series, and there were no great expectations weighing von Trier down this time. He had little to lose and described the series as a lark, done for the hell of it.[20] Finally, he had the key assistance of Morten Arnfred as co-director. Arnfred was good at working with actors, which suffice it to say was never von Trier's strong point, and his contributions to *The Kingdom* were immeasurable.

All the while *The Kingdom* was in production, von Trier had the previously mentioned project, *Breaking the Waves*, in development. That film would have some tentative resemblance to Dogme, such as the shaky, hand-held camera work and some degree of semi-improvised acting, most apparent in Emily Watson's performance, but in almost all its other essentials it would be Dogme's polar opposite. It was a major production with all the planning and personnel that implies. It was not set in the "here and now" (taking place in the '70s) and it employed a mass of special effects and post-production lab processes. The Apparatus was back in all its clanking, grinding glory.

"I think von Trier had a hard time with *Breaking the Waves*," Søren Kragh-Jacobsen remarked to an *L.A. Weekly* writer in March 2000 while promoting *Mifune* and Dogme in America. ". . . he said, 'I want to rediscover spontaneity.'"

While the launching of Dogme came, in fact, before any shooting had begun on *Breaking the Waves*, one can well imagine that von Trier was already exhausted by the film, having begun work on it back in 1991.

It would be his costliest and most complicated movie to date, an international co-production with 26 investment partners from all over Europe. And there were casting disasters: Helena Bonham Carter, who was signed to play Bess, quit on short notice after rethinking her participation in the sex scenes and was replaced by Emily Watson, who only had live-theater experience to that point. The film didn't keep to its schedule, and the last 15% of the budget wasn't secured until the last minute. Little Zentropa had really bitten off a bigger mouthful than it could chew. As the studio's producer, Vibeke Windeløv, warned, they should really think twice before over-extending themselves in the future on such big productions.

And again it was an ordeal for von Trier. The ability to delegate work was not one of his strong points as he like to involve himself on every level of a film he made. "He takes on way too much of the load," Aalbæk Jensen would state several years later in reply to a question as to why it was so hard every time for Lars von Trier to make a film. "He has to be director, photographer and producer all at once."[21]

Finally, this time everyone seemed to be hailing his film as a masterpiece. It was tipped to win the Palme d'Or at the 1996 edition of Cannes, but once again it got beaten out for the Festival's top prize—a crushing blow for von Trier, who was forced to watch the ceremony at home on television after an attack of travel phobia had prevented his journey down to the festival.

V

Dogme Unveiled

Creation and Initial Reaction

By the time *Breaking the Waves* appeared at Cannes, von Trier already had Dogme 95 in the pipeline, having launched the concept almost a year before in Paris at a symposium held in March 1995 to mark the Centennial of cinema. Von Trier and a select group of other film notables had been invited down to participate in a seminar on the future of motion pictures. On March 22nd they would meet for a panel discussion at the Odeon Theater.

Von Trier rarely accepted these kinds of invitations, but this time he had a reason. This time he was a man on a mission. What that mission was would become clear to Danes when prior to his departure he issued a press release (on March 14th) declaring the establishment of something called Dogme 95. The declaration contained some fiery back-to-basics rhetoric and a "Vow of Chastity" that contained ten rules (see pages 21–23).

By March 18th, reaction was already starting to surface in the Danish press.

Von Trier and Aalbæk Jensen have in subsequent utterances on the subject nurtured the perception that Dogme 95 was written off, scorned and attacked from the get-go in Denmark, but this was in reality not the case. Such claims are rather the product of their desire to portray themselves as rebels who achieved success in spite of every-thing, but in truth von Trier had always been given special treatment. The March 18th spread in *Politiken*, which sought out the opinions of a couple of prominent Danish film figures, can for example be characterized as at worst cautiously positive.

"Dogme is," said Danish Film School headmaster, Poul Nesgaard,

> *something we work with a lot at the school since it is necessary to give students a specific frame. . . . We do have use for films that contain a simplicity and lightness, also in a technical sense. Today it seems everything in the studio must be updated in accord with the latest technological developments. More focus is placed on the technical aspects than on whether the studio is infused with an inspiring and positive atmosphere, and that is wrong.*

Veteran director Nils Malmros, who had once employed a young von Trier as a student intern on his 1983 film, *The Tree of Knowledge*, took a dimmer view. He found it odd that von Trier would subject himself to a set of rules that would have made it impossible for him to shoot so much as a single frame of his earlier films. "If it was anyone other than Lars von Trier, I'd say it's a stupid joke, but if he has use for a straitjacket, then he'll probably get something out of it."

On March 21st, Morten Piil of the daily *Information*, speculated in somewhat more depth on von Trier's potential motivations.

> *A month has gone by without von Trier appearing on the front page of any newspaper, and now he has apparently calculated that the time is ripe for a return. . . . The unique success he has harvested with* The Kingdom *has prompted him to reevaluate his aesthetic and turn to a more primitive style. . . . von Trier's problem is that already before the start of* The Kingdom *he had set a big, expensive, international and frightfully 'unchaste' project in motion,* Breaking the

Waves, *which is scheduled to become a reality in the Fall. This manifesto can be read as an attempt to revisit the experience of* The Kingdom *and disarm eventual criticism of his relapse into old, bombastic bad habits with* Breaking the Waves.

Piil's ruminations raise an interesting question: Was Dogme among other things the product of cold calculation? Seen in retrospect we can dismiss his inference that von Trier wanted to or felt he should "return" to any specific aesthetic or adopt any kind of permanent style, since his film style has always been in a state of flux anyway. But the insinuation remains: Was Dogme possibly a calculated career shift rather than just the lark it was portrayed to be from the start? A jovial, half-serious attack on the status quo christened by more than just a single bottle of red wine? Von Trier could have had his career in mind. He wasn't above thinking in career terms, however frequently he seemed to commit premeditated "career-icide"—*Epidemic* and *The Idiots* being just two examples. Down in Cannes in May of 1991 to

Lars von Trier during the filming of The Idiots.

present *Europa*, hadn't he aroused some amount of antipathy by stating that this film was a conscious attempt to be more—perish the thought—accessible? He could be calculating and could make very wise career decisions when he wanted to. He had done it in the past, and, seen in retrospect, Dogme did turn out to be among other things exactly that, a brilliant business decision. On the other hand, the Dogme film von Trier would make as a result of all this, *The Idiots,* was anything but a brilliant business decision.

Piil continued:

> *Lars von Trier has a habit of publicizing manifestos at regular intervals to the delight of himself and his fans, and this delight is quite innocent. On the other hand one can be a bit apprehensive when the Vow of Chastity is used to handcuff other directors as well, such as Thomas Vinterberg, the promising young director of the two short films,* Last Round *and* The Boy Who Walked Backwards. *This means that Vinterberg has pledged to honor the Vow of Chastity even before he has started to make his first feature film. He is quoted as saying that he is happy to live in a state of chastity. These are in truth strange words from a man who is still a feature film virgin!*

On the 21st, von Trier left for Paris.

On the 22nd, the panel discussion took place as planned. Von Trier, dressed in a plaid flannel shirt, was seated amongst esteemed colleagues such as Jean-Jacques Beniex and Costa Gavras, many of whom were clad in formal wear.

When it came his turn to speak he asked permission to depart from the agenda: "It seems to me that for the last 20 years—no, let's say 10 years—film has been rubbish." Nervous laughter spread among the panelists and audience as he continued. "And what can we do about that? I've done a bit of paperwork—it's called Dogme 95."

He now pulled a sheath of red flyers out of his satchel and tossed them out over the edge of the stage into the audience. They contained the manifesto and the Vow of Chastity which he then proceeded to read aloud to a mixture of laughter and applause.

He then left the theater. Later, when queried further by reporters, he refused to elaborate, saying only that he had the group's permission (a group of two) to present the text but not to discuss it.

And thus Dogme was born.

The Growing Controversy

Von Trier had always been fond of manifestos. He had studied the Surrealist Manifesto as a mere boy and was familiar with all the great manifestos of film history, such as those, for example, issued by Dziga Vertov in the Twenties. As an ex-member of the Danish Communist Worker's Youth Party, he, as noted earlier, had become familiar with this kind of socialistic sloganeering that characterized the leftist milieu in Denmark in the '60s and '70s. He remained fond of this kind of overblown revolutionary rhetoric, and these kind of puritanical proclamations—purposely obtuse and yet flush with what appears to be a passionate idealism—can be found in the first three manifestos he wrote to accompany the releases of *The Element of Crime*, *Epidemic*, and *Europa* which comprise his "Europa Trilogy" (see Appendix). Manifestos to which no one paid much attention.

When seen in this light, as the continuation of his manifesto output, there was no reason to think this one would change the world. And the other manifestos were at least accompanied by a film. This one was pure theory. One might reasonably assume, since his manifesto mentions the "100 years," that his invitation to the Paris seminar prompted Dogme, for here was the perfect opportunity to make a splash with it. The splash it was already making in the Danish press before he left was more than anyone could have reasonably expected. Then again Lars von Trier was now a figure to be reckoned with, and his words carried more weight. Particularly when spoken up on a big stage in Paris.

Reaction to Dogme in the Danish press continued apace after the "Paris Proclamation." On March 25th a full page spread surveying the opinions of a range of film people ran in *Politiken*.

Although he voiced some modest apprehension about certain details, Mogens Rukov praised the initiative in no uncertain terms. He maintained that all filmmaking involved a kind of chastity, a kind of discipline, and went on to elaborate on the sexual metaphors of Dogme. (The bearded, wiry, chain-smoking Rukov was a colorful personality in the Danish film milieu and was not shy about pontificating about his sex life in the Danish press.)

Rukov was hardly an impartial voice: he had sat on the selection committee that had accepted von Trier into the Film School in 1979, and von Trier and Vinterberg had been students in his manuscript class. He had often supported young von Trier during his time at the institution and the two had stayed in close touch since then. Rukov would quickly embrace Dogme and go on to co-write scripts to many of the Danish Dogme films and to provide on-going advice to the Brotherhood. His role as a kind of mentor to the Brothers is evidenced in the Jesper Jargil documentary about the movement, entitled *The Purified* (2002), in which he lectures his former students from a video monitor in von Trier's house in November of 2000.[22]

In addition to Rukov, seven other figures from the Danish film world weighed in on Dogme in the March 25th piece. Three of them, Ib Monty, Christian Braad Thomsen, and Ole Bornedal, were flat out critical.

"I can't take it seriously," scoffed Monty, boss of the Danish Film Museum. ". . . it's completely comic. They feel they have to sell themselves under a pretext and create attention, and then the media hops on the bandwagon."

"I'll take lecherousness over chastity," opined Bornedal, who had directed *Night Watch* which had battled von Trier's *The Kingdom* for movie of the year in 1994 (and lost). "I would rather fuck than live in celibacy. . . . I'll take Dogme seriously the day I sit in a cinema and get floored by a great film—until then I consider it to be a concept, and one can always spend time on concepts if one can't manage anything else."

Filmmaker and author, Christian Braad Thomsen, had first encountered von Trier as a student who had attended a lecture of his at the Film School. He noticed that one of the boys wore a fascinated or transported expression while he lectured. At first this seemed flattering until he realized the lad, von Trier, was wearing a Walkman.

"I perceive Dogme 95 as an ironic comment on decades of state-supported, social realist Danish films that lack fantasy," wrote Thomsen. "It is a rebellion against this type of film which has outlived its usefulness. From that perspective I'm in agreement. On the other hand every single one of the ten vows of chastity is complete nonsense filmicly speaking. There is neither meaning nor sensibility in them and I believe that Lars von Trier in every single case means the opposite of what is written."

Others were more amenable to Dogme, such as director Niels Gråbøl, who was cautious but optimistic and viewed it as a healthy challenge.

Peter Aalbæk Jensen was also queried and was predictably positive and predictably ironic, noting that if shit was the result once in a while, at least it would be cheap shit.

Veteran director Søren Kragh-Jacobsen, ten years von Trier's senior, was very positive about Dogme, as was Anne Wivel, a director of documentaries and a fellow Film School graduate who had sat on the selection committee (as student representative) that had accepted von Trier into the school.

Both Kragh-Jacobsen and Wivel would soon become official "Dogme brothers" themselves! Another graduate of the Danish Film School, Kristian Levring, would join the Brotherhood soon thereafter, bringing their number up to five.

The Funding of Dogme

Dogme was now a thoroughly Danish phenomenon, although that hadn't necessarily been the original intention. Only von Trier and

Vinterberg know how many directors they asked to join at the start and who refused, but at least one and probably more were not Danish. The tabloid *Ekstra Bladet* had reported that Finnish director Aki Kaurismäki had been invited to join and had "given Dogme the finger."[23] It is very possible that Dogme was not conceived as a Danish concept, but became so by necessity. Thereafter, perhaps out of a sense of patriotism and/or perhaps for financial reasons, its Danish pedigree was loudly trumpeted. Later on it became "internationalized" as foreign directors started making films, but the core and the profile of Dogme was and is as Danish as black bread and schnapps, and its biggest successes have been the Danish films—an issue to be treated in more depth later.

The Brotherhood now planned to make five Dogme feature films in 1996 for a total budget of 20 million kroner (2.6 million USD)—4 million kroner (533,000 USD) per film. Very cheap indeed by normal standards.

That summer of 1995 "The Five" agreed with handshakes that they would set the plan back a year and reserve 1997 for their Dogme films. The delay was mostly due to the fact that financing was not yet in place, and in any case they all had other projects in the works. Von Trier was sweating out *Breaking the Waves* while Vinterberg was at work on his first feature, *The Greatest Heroes* (1996), and Kragh-Jacobsen was working on *The Island on Bird Street* (1997).

Anne Wivel, for her part, as previously noted, quit the Brotherhood approximately a year later and it became a true boy's club.

A lot of folks thought Dogme was a fascinating concept, including the Minister of Culture, Jytte Hilden. Allegedly she gave von Trier a verbal promise that he could count on 15 million kroner (2 million USD) for the Dogme project. He assumed this would be outside the Film Institute's normal consultant-approved channels, and figured that he could find the rest of the money through those consultant channels and through his own studio where he reckoned he could raise 3.75 million kroner (500,000 USD).

He penned a letter to Hilden on August 14th (1995) to remind her about the deal, stating that the 15 million Kroner she had promised "outside the normal DFI channels" sounded fine. Aalbæk Jensen wrote to Hilden on February 14th and asked about the status of the 15 million. He got no reply. The two of them were shocked to learn four months later that the DFI had received a new pool of money for the making of "low budget films."

Hilden wrote to Aalbæk Jensen that the funds would be allocated via normal procedures and signed off by wishing them good luck. This meant that all five filmmakers now had to apply for funding individually and that their films had to be evaluated on their individual merits and in competition with anyone else who wanted to apply.

Von Trier was livid. This was after all supposed to be a wave, a group thing done in the spirit of solidarity. Otherwise from his perspective there was no reason to continue. He had no doubt he could get his own film funded but it seemed unlikely that all four of the other films would be approved, not least because they didn't *exist* yet, having no scripts or even titles. As he wrote back to Hilden, "If I should make more films, as I hope to, the stupidest thing I could do would be to denigrate the relative commercial success I've achieved by throwing myself into a low-budget Danish-spoken film project . . . and that was also not the intention."

He also chided her on her use of the term low-budget. "That Dogme films in highest probability can be produced cheaply has nothing to do with the original idea . . . Dogme 95 is an artistic concept, not an economic concept." (By contrast, Aalbæk Jensen would go on to portray Dogme as a fiendishly clever financial ploy.[24]) Von Trier was also annoyed that this so-called "low-budget" craze was catching on, thanks to him, and that he was getting nothing out of it.

Hilden claimed at some point that she "meant" that the money should go to Dogme, but that the DFI had misunderstood. But in fact money for film production could *only* come from the DFI, never from the Ministry of Culture as such.

In any case, the DFI, which would catch a lot of flack for this over the years, was not budging. The low-budget pool would stand. There were obvious political sensitivities involved: the DFI felt themselves reduced to the role of bank clerk, doling out cash to Zentropa pursuant to what seemed to be a personal deal between Hilden and von Trier conducted through the press.

The DFI had three principal objections:

(1) Jytte Hilden was a politician, not a film professional, and her interference in this manner violated the "arms length" principal. She was not being employed and was not competent to evaluate film projects. (2) As noted, none of the films had scripts or titles yet, thus they could not be evaluated, much less approved. (3) The DFI could not and would not automatically approve funding for a "package" of films for a specific production company sight unseen. This would inevitably draw charges of favoritism from other companies and undermine the very foundations of the consultant system which had sustained the production of films in Denmark since 1972. The DFI was not, as they would repeat over and over again, a self-service buffet for the producers.

So the 15 million went to five other films, including one by Dogme-doubter Christian Braad Thomsen, *The Blue Monk* (1998). He had publicly aired his scorn for Dogme and now he was reaping the benefits of von Trier's idea in cool cash. In hindsight, though, from a Dogme perspective, the 15 million was not completely wasted since one of the films funded by the low-budget pool was *Dem Fra Døgneren*, the working title of a film that would go on to become known as *The Pizza King*. It was directed by a young man named Ole Christian Madsen who would go on several years later to make the very well received Dogme film #7: *Kira's Reason—A Love Story*.

The funding issue simmered on through to the start of 1997.

In the February 12th issue of the tabloid *B.T.*, headlines screamed that Dogme was dead. Aalbæk Jensen, speaking on behalf of von Trier who was not talking to the press anymore, declared that since the DFI had refused them the money, Dogme was dead. He claimed that he could have easily secured foreign funding for the project but that "the Dogme brothers were in principal committed to the idea that the project should be Danish."

Surprisingly, by April 9th Dogme was alive again. Bjørn Erichsen, the boss of the country's main broadcasting company, Danmarks Radio (DR)—and whose wife was then head of Zentropa's publicity department—had managed to put together the 15.5 million kroner in funding from various Scandinavian TV stations and film funds. In exchange, DR would be allowed to broadcast the films a mere three months after their theatrical premiers (a highly unusual arrangement since normally there is a 24 month "hold-back" period to allow films to exploit second-run theatrical and video rental and sell-through).

The rebirth of Dogme was celebrated at the cafe Bananrepublikken in the Nørrebro neighborhood of Copenhagen on April 8th, 1997— over two years after the launch of Dogme. And a very frustrating two years it had been for von Trier and company.

Thomas Vinterberg was the only Dogme brother to show up for the festivities, but von Trier sent a tape of himself reciting a poem he had composed to convey his feelings about the situation. Translated into English by the author (and taking creative liberty to make it rhyme), it reads thusly:

> *First it was on, then it was off*
> *And the tears had by now run dry*
> *And even though it was probably fine*
> *Nonetheless it still wouldn't fly*
>
> *Yet that was likely all just as well*
> *For it was rightly and truly a mess*
> *For why make a film that's really the dregs*
> *Instead of one that is simply the best*
>
> *We don't want to be jerked around*
> *To get money that's from our own pockets*

They've already taken enough of our dough
And for far too long, on top of it

Now we must let time heal all wounds
And so will this plague soon be past
They'll forget everything in a very short time,
So never mind all we've said, at last

Let down by many and missed by few
So now finally Dogme has something to do
And most important for us
is to re-find the joy that we knew

Apart from whatever Dogme meant as an aesthetic, this package-funding arrangement was unique in Danish film production history and gave a great deal of freedom and peace of mind to the filmmakers themselves. The value of that alone, as Mogens Rukov would point out years later, was immense:

> *That was certainly the first time in recent film history that four directors and four crews could start a project secure in the knowledge that it was guaranteed to be produced. The shooting dates were set—and already before a single idea about the films had been formulated. It was that simple. And that gave the project an enjoyment and lightness. One had to simply find something that could be made within these frames. The whole thing became a pleasure cruise. Hard work, but work carried out with a feeling of freedom.*[25]

Various people would take the credit for Dogme's success over the years, not least Danmarks Radio director, Bjørn Erichsen. As Jakob Høyer reported just after the 1999 edition of the Berlin Film Festival, where *Mifune* won a Gold Bear:

Denmarks Radio gradually exploits every opportunity to advertise that the TV station saved the Dogme concept by granting the 15 million kroner of support which the Film Institute denied it. . . . Last week it was Announced that DR was the only Danish media outlet that would get permission to interview Thomas Vinterberg if his film, The Celebration, *won an Oscar nomination. The explanation his studio, Nimbus, gave was that DR had after all financed the film and therefore had special status over the other media outlets.*[26]

And now, as Høyer reported, DR was making the most of Kragh-Jacobsen's triumph to blow its own horn:

With only 2 to 3 days notice, Erichsen ordered that a special direct-transmission broadcast be made from the Dogme reception at the Berlin festival. Mette Fugl (the best known female reporter in Denmark – ed.) was, with only hours warning, re-routed from coverage of European Union issues to host the gala event where she interviewed film stars and in all seriousness asked Bjørn Erichsen: 'What else do you have up your sleeve?'—as if it was the TV director himself who had formulated the 10 Vows of Chastity, written the manuscripts and directed the films.

The Danish Film Institute itself would belatedly jump on the bandwagon and attempt to buy its way back into the good graces of Dogme by co-financing the Dogme gala celebrations at both the 1998 Cannes and 1999 Berlin Film Festivals, where in the case of the latter the director of the Institute himself, Hening Camre, and 20 Institute functionaries deemed it necessary to come to Berlin and join the merry-making in-person. Dogme had set in motion an orgy of partying and self-congratulation in Danish film circles—parties that von Trier himself would apparently do anything to avoid. It seemed almost everybody in the Danish film world was pumped with pride over Dogme and claiming some of the credit.

"All in all," concluded Høyer, "both TV-director Bjørn Erichsen and the Film Institute's leadership could learn something from the artistic humility which characterizes the rules of Dogme as laid out in the Vow of Chastity: that the film work alone should explain the story to the public—without disturbances of artificial light and sound from self-promoting officials."

VI

Danish Dogme Films

Note: In Denmark, Dogme is charted by two sets of numbers—the overall international count which takes into consideration all Dogme films (see the "Plot Synopsis" section in the Appendix), and a purely domestic count which includes only films made in Denmark. The numbers in this chapter refer to the Danish system only.

#1—*The Celebration*

Raised in a liberal collective in north Sealand, young Thomas Vinterberg's dream of being in a rock band never materialized and instead, at 16, he joined up with a pal to make a movie called *Snowblind*.

It took them four years to make and, according to Vinterberg, it turned out to be a horrible film, the whole experience a great humiliation. Today he can't even bear to re-see the film, and any request to screen *Snowblind* in a Vinterberg retrospective is met with a flat and immediate "no."

So much for the perception that everything has come easy for Denmark's proverbial fresh-faced, golden-haired boy.

In any case, he emerged from the experience now knowing what he would do with his life; he would make films. And it was with an edited-down version of *Snowblind* that he applied to the Danish Film

School. He was accepted (at 19, the youngest student ever admitted to the director's line) and in 1989 he began attending classes.

His graduate project, a short film entitled *Last Round,* was broadcast on TV in 1993 and received some amount of praise. The following year he made *The Boy Who Walked Backwards,* considered by some to be the best Danish youth film of the 1990s.

And then came Dogme.

But first he had to finish a film called *The Greatest Heroes,* a kind of a road movie which he had already set in motion. Written together with Mogens Rukov, it was the story of a bank robber named Karsten who is out on parole when he runs into the 12-year-old daughter, Louise, he never knew he had. He liberates her from an abusive stepdad, meets up with a pal named Peter, and the three of them flee to Sweden in an old Ford to find freedom and adventure. Actors Thomas Bo Larsen and Ulrich Thomsen are excellent playing Karsten and Peter, respectively, the two lovable losers. And as in *The Boy Who Walked Backwards,* the film involves a child caught between the pull of adults who don't have their own lives in order. *The Greatest Heroes* was not

Left to Right: Ulrich Thomsen, Mia Maria Black, and Thomas Bo Larsen in a scene from Thomas Vinterberg's feature debut, The Greatest Heroes.

necessarily a "youth picture," but definitely a youth-friendly picture in the Danish tradition, and while there was no happy ending here, it was heavy on the "warm hearted." (Interesting to note that Dogme directors Søren Kragh-Jacobsen, Åke Sandgren, Natasha Arthy, and to some degree, Lone Scherfig, also had roots in this tradition.)

In spite of a somewhat constructed plot and a host of one-dimensional characters, *The Greatest Heroes* was popular with critics and audiences alike upon its release in 1996, and beat out *Pusher*, a much grittier and more realistic depiction of criminality, for the Bodil prize that year (the Danish equivalent of the American Oscar).

Vinterberg kept many of the elements in place for his Dogme film, *The Celebration*. He had a producer, Nimbus, that gave him creative freedom, a co-writer, Rukov, that gave him ideas, and a very capable cinematographer in Anthony Dod Mantle. And actors Thomas Bo Larsen and Ulrich Thomsen, not to mention Paprika Steen and Trine Dyrholm, were also sticking with him on this next picture.

Vinterberg stumbled upon a story for his Dogme film when a friend told him about a fellow who had made a startling confession on a radio program. The man, Allan (a pseudonym), told of the sexual abuse he and his twin sister, Pernille, had suffered as children at the hands of their father—traumatic events that eventually drove Pernille to suicide. At the father's 60th birthday party, held in the old hotel of which he was the proprietor, Allan stood up and, surrounded by his extended family, told all.

It was a powerful piece of drama with obvious potential. "I could feel that this was an important story in many ways," Vinterberg commented in *Politiken*. "Not specifically because it dealt with incest but because it dealt with the secrets repressed inside a family." And yet for some time he kept the source of his story a secret.

Vinterberg and Rukov brought their characters to life with emotional pyrotechnics and by imbuing them with quirky mannerisms and behavioral eccentricities, eschewing the use of prologues, flashbacks, and voice-overs, all of which were anti-Dogme in nature. They made the patriarch's 60th birthday celebration into a sleep-over arrangement that would stretch out over an 18-hour period and come complete with all the traditional Danish trappings and atmosphere. (The fact that the film takes place in one location and much of it around banquet tables made it ideal for live-theater adaptations, and through the years over 36 productions of *The Celebration* have been staged.)

It took seven weeks to write the script. Allan becomes Christian, who returns from success abroad—he owns several restaurants in Paris—to attend the family reunion, and, on behalf of his dead sister, to confront the evil secret that has left the family fractured and dysfunctional. A bleak tale indeed. Rukov would later recall that no one was particularly wild about the finished script.[27]

Vinterberg found an old mansion to shoot it in, and it was made to pass for a hotel. Prohibited from using sound-stages or sets, the primary locations in all Dogme films became that much more important, and no location functioned better than this. It infused the picture with a marvelous atmosphere and gave it credibility. But even more essential to the authenticity of the story were the actors. They were among the very best Denmark had to offer and spanned the generational divide. More than anything else, this film is referred to as a triumph of good acting.

Shooting with small hand-held video cameras and with no cables, tracks, or tripods to litter the set, the formal separation between cast and crew melted away. They were all in motion, all caught up in the spirit of the story, all in the field of action. The older more traditionally schooled actors discovered there was no single camera to "play to" and reportedly found this liberating.

Six weeks later, shooting was finished and they had themselves a pungent little family melodrama.

Due to its small size, relatively homogenous racial composition, and the rather inbred nature of its customs and traditions, Danish society is in fact often described as a "family," and the film seemed to be as much about the Danish family as about the fictional film family. The parallels to broad societal norms, Danish and otherwise, are quite striking.

The father, Helge, can be seen as "the establishment," the corporation in all its power and arrogance. The mother, Elsa, is the loyal and trusting "silent majority," her impervious smile repelling all doubts in the cause of preserving the status quo. Oldest brother, Christian, is the dissident expatriate who has renounced his citizenship and left the country. And then there is the younger brother, Michael, who owns a "bistro" (probably a ratty bar) in Sydhavnen—the little Brooklyn of Copenhagen. He assumedly works hard and is the only one with a functioning family (after a fashion). He wants to be "in the club," but is disdained by his parents and suffers from a weighty inferiority complex. He represents the lower classes. His sister, Helene, is the politically correct intellectual. She represents the educated classes and gives the impression of being independent, but has not managed to free herself from the dark karma that shrouds the family. Instead of acceding to her parent's wishes and studying law, she studied anthropology instead, but has not dared to really break from them aside from small rebellions like having a black boyfriend, and she heatedly counsels Christian to behave when it becomes clear that all this unpleasantness won't just blow over.

Denmark is allegedly a "classless society," and *The Celebration* is no class drama in the traditional sense. And yet as we see, the family is riven with class antagonisms and a kind of class structure has imposed itself on the family. This is so often the way that class manifests itself in Danish society, internally, so to speak.

Class oppression usually leads to revolt and so it does here. Michael, Helene, and the mother must all in different ways finally make a decision and act on it. No more denial, no more hoping that it will all just pass, no more complaisant silence. No more collaboration with the enemy in the black tuxedo for the sake of appearances and convenience. In their own ways they all finally stand up to him and disown him.

They stand up to him and acknowledge the true history of the family in the same way that, for example, Danes in general have in recent decades stood up and acknowledged that most painful chapter of their history, the chapter that took place during the Second World War when a policy of appeasement, and in some cases, collaboration, with the Nazis quietly ruled the day. The film is all about appeasement and collaboration as well. The desire to hush things up and get along as best possible is a Danish character trait both in the collective and individual sense, and Vinterberg plays upon it with an almost sadistic glee. This determination to keep a lid on things, to keep up the traditions and conviviality and avoid open conflict, these are qualities that both the film family and the Danish family have in common.

Secondary characters also represent archetypes. The blond Master of Ceremonies, so proud of his German heritage, represents the EU. He is smooth, friendly and efficient; he wants to take over the family, to act as spokesman for the family. Helene's black boyfriend is the immigrant, the proverbial outsider crashing the family party. He doesn't understand or speak the language in any sense, doesn't know the history or the customs, doesn't even really know how unwanted he is. (He seems to be a flat character, accused by some critics of just being thrown in to show how awful these people are, but it's appropriate that he is flat. We don't need to know anything about him, he is the stranger.) And Michael's blonde sun-tanned wife is the prototype of the classic feisty Danish gal, every bit his match as they argue and fight. Their relationship seems destructive but has an equilibrium about it. He never *hits* her, although he shows himself capable of hitting other women. The servants function as a Greek chorus, although they sometimes involve themselves in the action.

As pure melodrama, the film works. A great collection of well-honed characters have been brought to life by some truly outstanding performances submitted by some of Denmark's very best actors. The film has verve, energy, and chemistry. Raw, but at the same time carefully crafted if a bit overdrawn in spots. As noted, it is a very Danish film, firmly rooted in a specific place and mentality, and yet its theme of darkly repressed family secrets bubbling to the surface is universally recognizable and made it very exportable.

Yet while some maintained it was courageous of young Vinterberg to deal with a topic as charged as incest, it was really anything but. For all its supposed transgressiveness, it was an easy choice. Incest and the controversy over "recovered memories" had been hot-button issues throughout the 1990s, and in 1998 alone several other high profile films were also using incest as grist for their dramatic mills. Incest was being hauled out as predictably and conveniently as the terminal illnesses that had been hauled out to slowly kill off the beautiful heroines in tear-jerkers like *Love Story* and *Terms of Endearment* and a thousand others.

In *The Celebration*, people were instead being spiritually killed off, but the mechanics of the dramaturgy were the same—this was a "tear-jerker in reverse" with a villain so horrible that nobody could cry for him, a villain without any glimmers of humanity or moral complexity. No attempt was made to explain this figure or to make him realistic or in any way ambiguous, and when judged as the kind of unvarnished realism that the movie lays claim to, this makes it a shallow, flawed film. On the other hand, if the film is considered strictly as a piece of story-telling, the father is not really important. He is merely a catalyst, a stone cold historical fact and is not really relevant as a living, breathing character. The other characters undergo transformations while he remains inert and one-dimensional. In a purely narrative context, fine.

When key personnel were finally able to view a print of the film at a private screening, they were left cold. Who would want to go see such a dark and depressing film? And when Nimbus approached a major Danish distributor to take it on, they passed, claiming the picture was just too strange. So much for Dogme #1. Everybody's entitled to at least one mistake.

As everyone knows by now, these initial impressions proved completely wrong.

The Celebration went on to win the Jury's Special Prize at Cannes '98 and thereafter took Europe and America by storm, attracting huge interest on the international film festival circuit. It would go on to rack up grosses of 90 million kroner (12 million USD) world-wide on a 7.5 million kroner (1 million USD) investment, and collect a pile of prestigious award nominations and trophies in the bargain, not least both the Robert and Bodil (the two major Danish film awards) for best film. It would prove to be clearly the most popular and money-spinning of the first four Dogme films. And the most influential. Many young filmmakers today point to *The Celebration* as a main source of inspiration. It was influential both as a working process and as a piece of dramaturgy: Here was the first little DV movie that conquered the world, a little ensemble piece with no sets, props, or tricks. Pure story, pure acting—Presto! It gave Dogme the best possible launch.

There was some critical dissent. Some said it was not a particularly original film, not as brave as *The Idiots*. It could have been set in any country where traditions existed for these types of extended family gatherings. And it could just as easily have been told in a more orthodox style. The stylistic conventions of Dogme had given it a certain edge, but it was not a film that had to be told in Dogme. Some even thought the shaky camera was a distraction. And in Denmark there was a hard-core segment of the public that simply hated the picture.

But qualitative debates aside, no one could deny that *The Celebration* was the proverbial "right film at the right time," the kind of gutsy little low-budget wonder that was like nothing else you could see just then. Apparently the cinema-going public needed a twisty little melodrama at that point in time. And it gave foreign viewers a sense of discovery. People were intrigued by this strange little country that wasn't afraid to put its worst face forward. "I went to Denmark on a vacation that had nothing to with Dogme," notes Kimberly Shane O'Hara, producer and screenwriter of the American Dogme film, *Reunion,* "and saw *The Celebration* and fell in love with the whole country." All thanks to this dark little movie with a very sharp edge and some really potent psychology behind it.

Yeah . . . the psychology.

Who *was* this Allan guy after all?

In 1996, Kjeld Koplev, host of the radio program "Koplev's Krydsfelt" ("Cross Field") came in contact with him via the Support Center Against Incest. The arrangement was that Allan would talk about his past, but nobody knew he would launch into this whole story about his father's birthday celebration. That came as a surprise to everybody.

For a long time Vinterberg was silent about where he got the idea for the film. He was afraid Allan's father would take him to court for millions. Therefore it was important to maintain that *The Celebration* was pure fiction. "I was forced," said Vinterberg years later in a November 24, 2002 *Politiken* interview, "to lie about where I got the story from, which makes it appear that I was the kind of person who would steal a story and then refuse to admit where I got it from."

The fact that Vinterberg heard the confession on a radio program (he was first told about it and later heard a recording), eventually became known, sans specifics, and in 2000 a journalist unsuccessfully attempted to track Allan down. One rumor had it that Allan had died of AIDS. Others suspected that Allan might just be in reality an actor that Vinterberg had planted on the radio show to create attention around his upcoming film.

Finally in 2002, broadcast journalist, Lisbeth Jessen, in the process of preparing a radio program entitled *After the Celebration*, managed to track down the real Allan. He was gay and had lived for many years in Copenhagen. He had been active in the more flamboyant extremes of the city's '70s gay scene, but had some years previous moved to a small village in south Jutland. He was now suffering from full-blown AIDS, but was willing to be interviewed.

He'd never seen *The Celebration* nor had he any inkling that Vinterberg had based his film on his confession. Jessen played some cuts from the film's soundtrack and Allan's amazed reactions can be heard over the dialogue, all of it aired on the November 23, 2002 broadcast.

"It was *just* like that!" he exclaims.

"Yes, now I can see my father's face!" he says during the dramatic scene where actor Ulrich Thomsen, as Christian, stands up and reveals his father's heinous acts.

"A toast to the man who killed my sister," says Thomsen . . . "A toast to a murderer."

"Exactly my words!" Allan declares.

Very moving stuff, this. Great radio.

Jessen later brought Thomas Vinterberg down to Allan's little village and recorded the encounter.

"You must know that I have allowed myself to be celebrated on the basis of your tragic story, your very brave story, I would add," Vinterberg tells Allan. "The story has meant a lot to people all over the world . . . It gets people to think about their own families and the secrets, not necessarily of the same character, that families have. So when you once smashed the glass and stood up . . . that act had reverberations that still resonate. You should know that. And I must say that I am deeply grateful."

And Allan thanked Thomas. He was happy they had finally met. The circle had now been closed.

Before he departed, Vinterberg asked to see a picture of Allan's twin sister, Pernille. Allan said he had no photo of her on hand, but promised to send one later.

Fine, said Vinterberg. But something was not right.

After traveling to the small town where Allan had said his sister was buried, journalist Jessen could find no grave. His father was dead enough, having passed away two years before. And true enough, he had worked at a hotel, although he had been a cook, not the proprietor.

Christian, played by Ulrich Thomsen, disrupts his father's birthday and is ejected from the party in The Celebration.

No big deal there, but a lot of things weren't adding up. Jessen talked to Allan's uncle and his story was completely different. Apparently the twin sister, Pernille, never existed.

Jessen confronted Allan who all but admitted the story had been concocted. His childhood *had* been a misery—three children growing up in a leaky old house with a toilet in the cellar. The parents were frequently gone and when they were home, they constantly fought. But no twin sister . . . no incest.

But why the fabrications? Possibly because his partner had died of AIDS in 1995, just prior to the radio show, and at that point in his life he was suffering from great sorrow and was very possibly deranged to some degree. (Shortly after his radio appearance he had moved out of Copenhagen and ended up in the psychiatric ward of a hospital near the town in which he now lived.)

"I simply believe," said Allan, "it was all the negative stuff, all the sorrow, all the bad in my life that simply tumbled out."

A confession? Maybe.

Kjeld Koplev, for one, had doubts. The new stuff he was now saying could just as well be the lie.

Vinterberg was unmoved to learn his movie was probably based on the fantasy of a demented individual, a lie told by a man that he still, however, thought was a nice guy. "It doesn't make any difference in relation to the film," he said to *Politiken* after hearing the whole story unfold on Jessen's radio show. "It makes no difference to the many people who have come up to me and told me about their parents and what they themselves have experienced . . . all of that interplay with his sister and stepfather is simply so psychologically correct. . . . Well at least now I know who I should call the next time I need a good story."

Postscript—Thomas Vinterberg

Thomas Vinterberg put all further film work on hold while he traveled the world for a year and a half to hype *The Celebration* and bask in the adulation. As noted, it took almost five years before he got another picture into theaters and he looks back at that period as a waste, a mistake. A mistake that he didn't have other projects in development and didn't immediately plunge into another film. But he was young and it was easy to get caught up in all the hoopla . . . hundreds of reporters and festival functionaries hanging on your every word, everybody telling you how handsome you were, how brilliant you were.

Finally, back in Denmark, he took a year off to help support his wife, the theater director, Maria Wallbom, with whom he has two daughters and who at the time had three plays to stage.

Now, in the wake of the success of *The Celebration*, offers were pouring in. There were stacks of scripts to read, lots of them from Hollywood . . . most of them awful! It was flattering to be asked to go to Hollywood and it might have been a real boost to his career, but first and foremost he could not bear the thought of moving to Los Angeles. It was no place for his family, no kind of life.

After a period of paralyzing uncertainty, he decided to make another one of his own films again. Mogens Rukov was again brought on board to help him write it. *It's All About Love* would be the title. It would be set in the near future, a dark romantic drama about a couple being pulled away from each other in a world where careers and success meant all, where people lost their ability to relate, to identify, to love. It was the kind of world he had encountered while jet-setting around promoting *The Celebration*, a world of people constantly in motion, people who had become un-grounded.

It's All About Love was filmed in various foreign cities, a major production of 85 Million kroner (11.3 million USD) with fairly big American stars like Joaquin Phoenix, Claire Danes, and Sean Penn.

Unable to get the 10 million kroner (1.3 Million USD) they had expected from the DFI, who ruled that it was not a "Danish Film," Nimbus turned to other Scandinavian funding sources where they could get money without making creative concessions or having to compromise on rights or casting issues. (The DFI did, however, step in with an emergency grant of 2 million kroner (266,00 USD) after a French investor pulled out at the last minute.)

Everybody reckoned that *It's All About Love* would premiere at Cannes 2002 and Vinterberg was shocked by the previously noted rejection.

This gave him more time to work on the film, and it was subsequently re-edited so radically that according to reports it almost became a completely new film. Whether this re-edit was prompted by the Cannes rejection or whether the film, as Vinterberg claimed, had not been properly completed in their rush to submit it to the festival is uncertain.

In any case it had its long awaited Danish premiere on January 10, 2003 and, as noted in the beginning of this book, Danish critics were disappointed.

Shooting is slated to start on his next film, *Dear Wendy,* in September of 2003. It will be about a group of Caucasian gun-lovers living in Harlem. This is a film that von Trier wrote and had planned to shoot, but he talked Vinterberg into taking over the project in order to "blow some life into the story." It's expected to premiere in November of 2004.

In the meantime, another version of *The Celebration* is in the works, to be directed by none other than Nicolas Cage. "I promise to make a film that isn't soft and harmless," Cage told a Norwegian paper in September of 2002. "I am very fascinated by Dogme films and the simple way they are made. Lars von Trier is, for me, a master, a true artist."

In the future, Vinterberg doesn't intend to dwell on a film the way he did with *The Celebration,* or to spend years talking about it if it's a hit. If he learned one thing from that experience it is to always have another project waiting to throw yourself into.

#2—*The Idiots*

In the spring of 1997, after two years of battling through recurrent bouts of apathy and despair wrought by the constant on-again-off-again status of Dogme, it was finally time for Lars von Trier to put up or shut up—to make his Dogme film. It was essentially his concept and now it was time for him to deliver the goods. Whatever that might be.

Legend has it that he checked into a hotel, wrote the script in four days, gave it to the actors, and told them to read it and then throw it away and forget everything that was in it.[28] In fact there was a script; Mogens Rukov advised on it and it was largely adhered to during the shoot and was later even published. The film was in this fashion a product of its own myth-making. There was the "bold experiment" and then there was the film that had to be completed on schedule, marketed, and sold, and somewhere in-between these two extremes, *The Idiots* was born.

The story centered on a group of young Danes who inhabit an old villa in a well-to-do suburban town north of Copenhagen. It is a kind of collective run by a malcontent named Stoffer who leads his little band of merry pranksters on raids into the community which are designed to bother, offend, and play upon the misplaced sympathy of the town's good citizens. Under his loose guidance, the gang indulges in absurdist behavior in public places, "spazzing out" and pretending to be retarded. At Stoffer's behest, they attempt to find their "inner idiots." In so doing they are not only ridiculing up-tight bourgeoisie social norms, but also challenging themselves and pushing their own borders into the process. But ultimately they have to wonder if they are any better or freer. They know the limits of the townspeople, but how far can *they* go in their attempts to break free from the sacred Danish concept of "the group?" After all, they are all originally fairly normal, well-functioning people in their own right, and always have the option to go back to the straight world.

In the end, this experiment proves to have different effects on them as individuals. The collective disbands in turmoil, leaving behind a host of unanswered questions. The idiots go their own ways while the viewer is left sitting in the theater to ponder the result of this somewhat obtuse experiment.

Von Trier cast the film with fairly young Danes, all of whom had professional acting experience behind them except one last-minute replacement by the name of Knud Romer Jørgensen. He was an under-paid factotum in an ad agency who, by a twist of fate, picked up the phone one day and was offered the role that had been meant for his boss, a tough-talking gangster-like character. To survive at the agency, Jørgensen had adopted the Marlon Brando-meets-Al Goldstein manner of his employer (a persona completely at odds with his true nature), and he was deemed a fitting last minute replacement. He quit his job to make the film and became, for 15 minutes, famous. At the opposite end of the spectrum, actors like Nikolaj Lie Kaas and Bodil Jørgensen were already well known to Danish cinema-goers. Von Trier wanted real actors for the most part, but there were no big stars on board, no unwieldy egos down in the hold to tip this fragile vessel. All energy was to be focused on the film, on the task at hand.

In any case, von Trier didn't want great "performances" from actors playing "roles." Rather he wanted the actors to reject the conventions of acting, to open their minds. And that required that they comply with this very personal pact he was asking them to enter into. He was not asking them to learn lines, but to *unlearn* lines, all the lines they had ever put into their heads. Actors that had their heads full of memorized lines would just clutter up the set . . . the great actors, the great technicians laying cables and tracks, and the diligent camera operators choreographing perfect pan shots would have ruined this movie, would have crowded all the room out of it and sucked all the energy and oxygen from it. All these great people had a strange tendency to make a lot of very bad movies.

The Idiots would be a great challenge for the actors, but also a great personal challenge for von Trier himself. Cast and crew were one on this film, a small and mobile unit. Von Trier's original idea was that everyone would live together in the villa, and while his actors nixed the idea, a sense of solidarity was nevertheless essential. They had to work out this film together, to figure out on the spot what was working and what wasn't.

Shooting began in June of 1997, and there was a feeling of solidarity in the beginning, particularly on the "all naked days" when cast and crew stripped down together. These sessions proceeded in a relaxed and non-sexual atmosphere. Von Trier wanted to do an ensemble piece with lots of improvisation, something vaguely in the mold of favorite films like *Weekend* (1962) and *The Grand Bouffe* (1973), Marco Ferreri's perverse and oddly effective tale about four men who lock themselves into a villa and proceed to eat themselves to death.

The script, as noted, was not just read and thrown away, but it was never intended to be a script in the traditional sense. In all of von Trier's idealism, it was meant to be just a blueprint, or not even that. It was more like a window frame without any glass and not attached to any wall. One that could be carried around. It was all about being ambushed by the moment. . . . "Let's just *do* it!" one can almost hear von Trier say, "Lets just go out and see what happens."

Something always happens, the world is full of fascinating things happening, just go out on the street and look around. And in the middle of all these interesting things happening you have people making movies where nothing is happening. Groups of people locked into some artificial bubble, blocked off from all the vibrations and karma that makes life interesting and exciting and strange. Break this bubble,

A bunch of Idiots take a nude romp in Lars von Trier's The Idiots.

get rid of the paralyzing apparatus of movie-making, the mental and physical baggage, and things can happen again. But it also takes guts and courage to depart from a script, and it is even more important to have and be able to use *instinct*—the instinct to know when something fresh and new is happening and to go with it wherever it leads, to capture it without crushing it under the weight of the obvious. To leave room for the unexpected.

Phrased in endless variations, this was the basic idea.

Nice theories and principles, but the trouble with this approach was sometimes one was left with nothing *but* room. And this was also not the way that control-freak Lars von Trier liked to work, giving up control to unknown forces.

Not too far into the shooting of *The Idiots,* he found it hard to get the improvisation to function. The actors had no base, no building blocks to work with, as he observed in his diary, and nothing created nothing. Or as his Dogme brother, Ole Christian Madsen, later expressed it, "Like anything else, improvisation requires that you act according to a particular set of rules."[29] Thereafter, he changed back to a more scripted approach, and, as noted, most of the finished film followed the script or rewrites done "on the run." And the great and bold experiment became somewhat less great and somewhat less bolder than intended (or advertised).

As author Peter Schepelern writes, "*The Idiots* is at heart just as formalistic as *Europa* where every single shot was planned down to the last detail. If this proves anything, it is that von Trier cannot completely break from his own nature. He apparently acknowledged this fact himself when he wrote in his diary that 'it is of course a film that is not nearly as calculated as *Breaking the Waves,* but nevertheless much, much, much more calculated.'"[30]

Eventually the positive atmosphere that characterized the first weeks of shooting became somewhat poisoned by a growing sense of hostility and paranoia that spread between von Trier and his actors. Although they credited him for being honest with them—no small virtue for a director to possess—his icy blasts of sarcasm and almost daily temper tantrums were starting to wear. The fact that he had fallen in and then out of love with one of the actresses, Anne Louise Hassing, further complicated relationships on the set, and his idiots began to exclude him. He was making a movie about outsiders and becoming one himself.

Ironically, he had invented Dogme to re-find the joy in film-making, and *The Idiots* experience was turning out to be hell. It was, in many ways, the toughest film for him to make, and by the time shooting wrapped in August, everybody was happy and eager to put this behind them.

And yet, film being the supremely self-aware medium that it is, the experience was to be eternally preserved in the diary and in a documentary about the making of *The Idiots* entitled *The Humiliated*, by Jesper Jargil, who culled through the collective footage that he, von Trier, and two assistants had shot with mini DV cameras. Von Trier's mercurial mood swings were now preserved for posterity.

The diary was the result of sporadic rendezvous von Trier had held with a dictaphone throughout the shoot, mostly at night when he couldn't sleep. He wanted to record the birth of a film. He had always voiced a desire to see this kind of thing from other filmmakers, to see the filmmaking process rendered transparent, to unveil the creative mechanisms that were glossed over in the finished product.

His ruminations into the dictaphone touched on all possible sub-jects and survives as an interesting—if not always earth-shaking—slice of life from this period. It demystifies the creative process if nothing else. If there is genius at play here, it certainly disguises itself well, hidden amongst the welter of mundane observations from a man who seems given to anything but grandiose gestures. Von Trier is certainly not without vanity, but if he *is* a genius, then genius is all too human. We share the banal domestic joys and satisfactions of a suburban family man, a father of four who likes to tend his tomatoes and paddle in his kayak. We find out what books he is currently reading. We look on as a grade-A hypochondriac stews over the possibility of getting cancer of the esophagus, and last but not least we get progress reports and tech-nical notation from a filmmaker and artist whose daring pet project has finally been set in motion, a man still full of doubts and apprehensions. This diary was published in almost completely un-edited form in French to coincide with *The Idiots* premiere at Cannes 1998 and later that summer in Danish in conjunction with the film's domestic release.

It aroused no small amount of controversy in Denmark, largely thanks to the raw honesty von Trier brings to bear on his relationship with Hassing during the shoot. One gets perhaps more than one wants to know about the platonic (from all indication) affair between the two. The gentle reader finds out exactly how many times von Trier masturbated at night thinking about her (five, reduced to two after acts of great self-discipline). To some, the diary seemed like a tawdry piece of trash and reportedly put some amount of strain on his marriage, earning him lots of space in the Danish yellow press in the process.

Lars von Trier totally naked.

The Idiots was test-screened at the start of January 1998. It seems rather amazing that a film that was supposed to be the essence of spontaneity and experimentation would be subjected to that most cold-blooded of Hollywood marketing strategies, but so it was.

Idiots Knud Romer Jørgensen and Anne Louise Hassing sing chorus on von Trier's single,
"You're a Woman," released in conjunction with The Idiots.

The Idiots and *The Celebration* had both been selected to participate in-competition at Cannes that year by festival boss Gilles Jacob,
who had been a champion of von Trier's work going back to 1984
when he had selected his very "difficult" feature-film debut, *The
Element of Crime*, to participate in-competition. This would be the
unveiling of Dogme to the world.

Von Trier and a pal drove down to Cannes in his camper while
some of the idiots followed shortly thereafter, driving 28 hours
straight down in an old handicapped bus and ending up sick and
exhausted in the process. They staggered out into a sea of flashbulbs
to find their tuxedoed director waiting for them.

The Cannes screening of *The Idiots* polarized critics and public
alike, and the film won nothing while Vinterberg's family drama was
roundly applauded and took home the Jury's Special prize. Von Trier
claimed beforehand that he did not expect to win the Palme d'Or, but
it had to be a disappointment. It was the fourth time he had failed to
win the top prize.

The Idiots went on to split critics and audiences all over the world.
It was considered by many to be a jolting bump in von Trier's career
path, a bizarre and pointless detour. A big come-down from his previous film, *Breaking the Waves,* which had been hailed as a masterpiece.
To some it was a sign of his cynicism and laziness, to others proof of

(Most of) the Idiots *assembled in Cannes.*

his courage. In any case it could not be ignored. It was, after all, a Lars von Trier film. And it had the whiff of a scandal about it, testing censorship statutes in many countries thanks to a mere few seconds of hard-core footage. Whether this helped it in any sense is debatable.

The film was not a particularly big hit in Denmark, but did well in the other Scandinavian countries and played well in France. Its U.S. release was held up for two years for some reason, possibly because the American distributor had no idea how to market it, and it did poorly. To a lot of American critics von Trier had shown in spades that he was too erratic and self-absorbed to be a true "great," too undependable to ever make movies in America where he had vowed he would never come anyway. In any case, he had violated Hollywood's main unwritten rule with a vengeance: "Once you go big, you never go small again." Let him stay in Europe, scoffed detractors. To them he was the epitome of the arrogant European film "artist" who cared nothing about the audience, who made films just for himself. (A suspicion with more than a grain of truth to it.)

Others saw it as proof of his genius and independence, his determination to question the status quo, to relentlessly experiment. Here was a man not just interested in having a career, but a filmmaker (and, yes, an artist) dedicated to provoking, challenging, and re-inventing film language, and pushing beyond his own borders in the process. A man who was not afraid to fail. In a world where films were increasingly made by corporate hirelings devoid of any courage, rebelliousness, or imagination, he was setting himself apart.

Purely in the context of Dogme, *The Idiots* was something of a red herring, not in any way indicative of what had come before or what would come after. But at least he had challenged himself. He had not made just another "Lars von Trier movie" (whatever that was). He had not turned out just another piece of product.

Postscript—Lars von Trier

Von Trier continued his attempts to distill the filmmaking process down to pure acting and pure story with his next picture, *Dancer in*

Lars von Trier (center) in the midst of the Cannes circus.

the Dark, primarily through his very intimate and intense focus on his lead actress, Björk. This gave the film an aspect of Dogme, but the story and setting and his preoccupation with technical processes—like the installation of 100 video cameras for the shooting of the musical numbers— were as far from Dogme as could be. It was a constructed story set in another time and in a country, the U.S., to which von Trier had never been.

Following that, in May of 2003 he released what many consider to be his most experimental film to date, the almost three-hour long *Dogville.*

Set in the Rocky Mountains of 1930's America, the story centered on Grace (played by Nicole Kidman), a young woman who is pursued by gangsters. She finds refuge in a squalid backwoods hamlet called Dogville whose inhabitants offer her protection and acceptance. But gradually, as the price on her head increases, the townsfolk want more in exchange for their silence and begin to abuse and exploit her, finally chaining her up so she can't escape. In the end she takes revenge on them all in an extraordinarily violent turn. It was a narrative set-up which had some obvious parallels to Thornton Wilder's classic play, *Our Town,* but the degradation melted out to the frail and trusting Grace was 100% von Trier and recalled the tormented fates of the heroines from his "Golden Hearted" trilogy.

The entire movie was shot on a sound stage in Trollhätten, Sweden, where the little village was re-created out of nothing more than chalk lines marked out on the floor, together with a few random facades, doorways, and fences. For this audacious mixture of live theater and film, von Trier drew inspiration from John Caird's version of Charles Dickens' *The Life and Adventures of Nicholas Nickleby,* performed in 1982 by the Royal Shakespeare Company and broadcast on Channel Four (UK). The influence of Bertold Brecht is also credited frequently by von Trier in connection with *Dogville.*

While employing very few props and no special effects in the Hollywood understanding of the term, those few props that were present, and the extensive use of sound and lighting effects, assumed a central importance in bringing the fictional setting and characters to life, and in this sense it was the antithesis of Dogme. The artificiality and nostalgia of the setting was purposely pronounced, almost exaggerated. For lack of any authentic locations, the film became all the more dependent on these visual and audio clues—a bit like a museum exhibit, what with all the period costuming and antique automobiles that rolled onto the stage and down the imaginary main street. And stereotypes abounded, particularly the gangsters and the Aunt Jemima-like cleaning lady.

This was von Trier's world, his story. No need for the actors to supply their own characters since the characters came courtesy of Lars von Trier. They would act out the story he had written or, in the case of some of the secondary actors, decorate the story. Like mannequins made of flesh and blood.

The control-freak von Trier was back, if he had ever left. As his friend, Stellan Skarsgård, who also acted in *Dogville* put it, "Lars von Trier is a super-intelligent, easily disturbed child who sits and plays with his dolls and cuts their heads off with scissors."

Here was the ultimate "staged" film, staged not only in a mechanical sense, but also in the physical and verbal communication between the actors. Most of their exchanges had a measured, deliberate, theatrical feel, and were devoid of any spontaneity. By this point nobody had put Dogme further behind them than von Trier. There was no talk here of the actors forming their characters from their real-life experiences, no attempt to "force the truth out of characters and settings." There was only one truth and it was Lars von Trier.

Following *Dogville*, he launched into *Manderlay*, the second part of this so-called "U.S.A. Trilogy," or as sometimes referred to in the Danish press, the "U.S.A.—Land of Opportunity Trilogy." This film was to be set in the deep South and according to von Trier would deal with slavery.

He has stated that the story will pick up with Grace and her father three days after *Dogville* ends. But *Dogville* is set in the 1930s! Von Trier is obviously playing loose with the facts in the cause of his stated desire to deal with the "idea" of America rather than the reality. As such, actually going to America to find out what it is all about would be counter-productive.

This approach of exploring one's impression of a place rather than the reality of it was a concept actually manifest in his work as far back as *Epidemic*. Although this was mid-point in his "Europa Trilogy," when his fascination for all things German was predominant, the film contains a self-standing episode in which his co-writer and collaborator, Niels Vørsel, talks about a voluminous correspondence he struck up with teenage girls from Atlantic City, New Jersey—all in an attempt to get a *second-hand* impression of America. After all, Franz Kafka, never having stepped foot in the U.S., had written an amazing novel, *Amerika*, solely based on impressions culled from letters his uncle had written to him. Now, in similar fashion, von Trier was demanding the right to give free reign to his own admittedly subjective impressions.

But von Trier's American critics, who railed against his negative depictions of the country's legal system in *Dancer in the Dark* and the spiritual and moral bankruptcy that was at the heart of his small

American town in Dogville, remained unconvinced. With *Manderlay*, von Trier seems determined to give his critics not less but more ammunition—a lot more. He feels provoked to do so, he says, after the criticism he fielded for *Dancer in the Dark*, and the fact that he got swindled out of the Palme d'Or in Cannes 2003 where *Dogville* was the talk of the festival and the overwhelming favorite. But no, the French wanted to curry favor with the Americans again after splitting with them over the war in Iraq, and so, perceived as anti-American by some influential voices, *Dogville* could not be allowed to win. It was a victim of pure politics, or so went the conspiracy theories back in Denmark.

Following *Manderlay*, von Trier is scheduled to take a break from filmmaking while he stages the Richard Wagner opera, *The Ring of the Nibelungen* in Bayreuth in 2006. After that he'll launch into the concluding installment of the "U.S.A. Trilogy," *Washington*, expected to premiere sometime around 2008. The story doesn't yet exist at this early stage but he reveals that it will take place in a government ministry.

Another Dogme film doesn't seem to be on the agenda. In fact, he will probably never make another one, and in most of his comments he refers to it in the past tense. But it is also clear that he has incorporated elements of Dogme in his subsequent work.

And if Dogme had never happened, Lars von Trier probably never would have survived.

#3—*Mifune*

Søren Kragh-Jacobsen, the director of *Mifune*, is kind of the odd-man-out of the four original Dogme brothers, being a generation older than his fellow directors and by far the most experienced.

Unlike Vinterberg, he was not a child prodigy. He was not particularly good in school and at 16 he dropped out. His father decided that he should get himself a proper trade and he became an electrician and got a job at the huge Transmotor plant in Copenhagen. He spent the next five years of his life there, on call all over the plant. He adapted well enough to the working world, but quietly nourished hopes of becoming a teacher or an architect, and spent his free time strumming a guitar. From the age of 13 or 14, he had been into rock and roll music, occasionally performing in a band and singing Cliff Richard covers and the like.

Kragh-Jacobsen was also into film from an early age, spending many leisurely hours in the cinema. He and his older brother bought a 16mm camera and shot short films whenever they could afford it. One of his uncles was even a film reviewer for a leading Danish daily.

By the end of the 1960s, Kragh-Jacobsen had decided he would become a documentary filmmaker, and he applied to and was accepted at FAMU, the esteemed Czech national film school in Prague which his brother was already attending. It was a happy time for him, finally out on his own and away from Denmark and the various pressures and expectations.

He claims in an interview with Richard Kelly that he was "thrown out" of the school in 1971, but his departure owed rather to the more prosaic fact that the school had raised its tuition fees beyond what the brothers Jacobsen could afford.

Back in Denmark, he turned to music to make some money, working gigs as a professional nightclub musician, dressed in a tux and knocking out covers of standard lounge fare. On his own time he wrote songs . . . cut his first record in '73 and continued to make his own music sporadically over the years, forging a part-time career for himself as a singer-songwriter somewhat in the troubadour tradition. In 1975, he had a big radio hit with "Kender Du Det?" ("You Know the Feeling?"), the chorus of which—"Mona, Mona, Mona . . . ," just about every Dane of a certain age can hum in their sleep.

Not long after his return from Prague he was hired by Danmarks Radio. The broadcasting conglomerate was at the time looking for young filmmakers to give radio and TV programming in their children and youth department a new edge. Kragh-Jacobsen worked there making radio and television quiet successfully and productively for many years.

He made his feature-film debut in 1978 with a coming-of-age picture entitled *Do You Want to See My Beautiful Belly-Button?* It was part of a new wave that was happening in the mid-'70s as young Danish filmmakers rebelled against established norms and made new types of youth pictures that were aimed at the 15-to-18-year-old age group and employed young actors. The movie was popular with both critics and public alike. Kragh-Jacobsen clearly had an affinity for the subject matter and an ability to tell engaging stories about the trials and tribulations of youth, stories wherein difficult or bittersweet situations were resolved with life-affirming conclusions.

Over the next two decades he continued to make features that were not necessarily exclusively aimed at the youth market, but which were "youth friendly" in this manner. The most popular of these was *Rubber Tarzan* from 1981. It was a huge hit with ticket buyers across the age spectrum and it also caught the attention of Danish film critics who praised it to the skies and awarded it a Bodil for best Danish film of the year.

It also caught the attention of a young Lars von Trier who had just graduated from the Danish Film School and was embarking on his own career—and who was less amused. In one of the first pieces of press on the young von Trier, a profile in the November 23, 1982 issue of *Politiken* headlined "Danish Film is Totally Harmless," he lashed out at what he considered to be the anemic state of Danish cinema.

"Danish film is so dainty in its style that no one could ever be offended by it. They are harmless stories told in a harmless style. Only topics which everyone can agree on are taken up. Like for example, *Rubber Tarzan*. 'Ah . . . that's a shame for the boy,' we all say in unison. This is precisely the kind of (preconditioned response) I will go against." Von Trier was taking no prisoners. He wanted his films to be "like a stone in one's shoe," to provoke, to challenge. He claimed proudly that the premiere screening of his graduate project, *Images of a Relief,* had caused people in the audience to faint. He no doubt had Kragh-Jacobsen's films in mind when he soon after declared in his first manifesto that, "We will no longer be satisfied with well-meaning films with humanistic messages. . . ."

Thirteen years later, upon the founding of Dogme, von Trier had softened up considerably and was hardly the angry young man of yore. To the contrary, he was about to start churning out melodramas. And Kragh-Jacobsen was by now in tight with the Zentropa/von Trier crowd who were ascending to a position of dominance in the Danish film world. It seemed natural for Kragh-Jacobsen to sign on to Dogme, and though he would always remain the most restive about strict adherence to the Dogme rules, he was ready to give it a go.

First, however, he had to finish work on a previously committed-to project called *The Island on Bird Street*, a film about the survival of a Jewish boy in the Warsaw ghetto of World War II. This would tie him up through 1995–1996. It was a big and relatively complicated co-production shot in Poland (in English) with British, American, and German producers who made a multitude of demands upon him. The production was such an ordeal that he vowed he would never make another movie.

But *Mifune* got him back into the flow. At that point in time the simplicity of Dogme was just what the doctor ordered.

He wrote the script with Anders Thomas Jensen over the course of two months. From the outset he had three actors in mind: Anders Berthelsen, Jesper Asholt, and the fetching Iben Hjejle. He tailored the script for them, keeping their faces in mind as he wrote.

The story began to flesh itself out. An attractive Copenhagen call-girl, Liva (Iben Hjejle), pursued by a mysterious stalker and slapped around by her heartless pimp, wants to flee Copenhagen and answers an ad for a housekeeping job out in the country, down on Lolland, a southern Danish island crisscrossed with fields and wooded groves. She gets the job and finds herself in a weird situation, living out in the boondocks with two brothers, one of whom, Rud, (Jesper Asholt) is retarded. The other, Kresten (Anders Berthelsen) plans to quickly return to his wife, job, and upscale lifestyle in Copenhagen once he gets Rud committed. Nobody is laying their cards on the table and things only become more complicated when Liva's troubled younger brother, Bjarke, is kicked out of school and joins them to make it a foursome. Their existence is made none the easier by the harassment of some local hillbillies who have noticed the good-looking Liva. Kresten's problems pile up when his wife divorces him and he loses his job. And yet, nursing their own secrets and wounds, they all end up coming together to find a certain harmony and salvation in this temporary alternative family.

It was a kind of social-realist fairy tale in the classic Kragh-Jacobsen mold. And although it could be said that this was his first official "grown up film," he still managed to include one of his familiar youth picture themes via the sub-plot that involves the troubled teen, Bjarke, who finds redemption by being needed.

With its small cast, gentle pace, and beautiful visuals courtesy of cinematographer Anthony Dod Mantle, *Mifune* was a jolting departure from the psychological tension and tumult of *The Celebration* and the austerity of *The Idiots*. For one thing, there was no shaky camera, already a trademark of Dogme. "I asked Tony many times to stop moving the camera," Kragh-Jacobsen told author Richard Kelly, "because I don't believe intensity and energy are in the restless camera. I think they are between the actors."

Søren Kragh-Jacobsen confers with Iben Hjejle during the shooting of Mifune.

Mifune was a triumph of craft and subtlety. Here was a Dogme film that didn't scream "Dogme!" in every frame. Kragh-Jacobsen had combined concept and story in such an organic way that it was quite possible to watch the film without even realizing it was Dogme. And yet its (for the most part) faithful adherence to the Dogme dictates clearly shaped it in tenor and tone. For example, the prohibition against laying on music later contributed to its often languid feel. The rhythms, so to speak, were provided not by music, but by the sounds and feels of the countryside in high summer, the wind, for example, blowing through fields of grain. Here was the healing refuge in which the two wounded souls from the city found solace. And yet when music is present, as it is in a couple of spots—a silent visitor suddenly flailing away at a guitar with passion and skill, or the small combo which serenades Kresten and Liva as they dance slowly at the end—it is all the more effective. Less *is* more.

In Denmark, *Mifune* did extremely well, selling approximately 350,000 tickets, about the same as *The Celebration*. This was not surprising since it was every bit as grounded in a native aesthetic, if a very different one, and connected with Danish viewers. Its city-vs-country dynamic, and the promise of sanctuary and renewal in the idyllic bosom of nature, were both very traditional themes in Danish film and literature. The picture's pastoral tone would have met with the approval of one gentleman by the name of Morten Korch (1876–1954), Denmark's most beloved and prolific post-war novelist. His rustic melodramas, rich in faith and morality, epitomized the idealized notion of the Danish countryside as the vessel of the Danish soul. Almost all his novels were made into films.

Mifune might be called "Morten Korch with an edge"—with just a smidgen of *Straw Dogs* or *Deliverance* thrown in. We were in Lolland, after all, weren't we? Hillbilly country, Danish-style as it were, *sans* the hills, gorges, and Appalachian accents. The local shit-kicker who plagues them and finally, with his gang in tow, attempts to rape Liva, is, moreover, the personification of a distinctly negative Danish archetype;

the jealous neighbor or associate who begrudges your success or good fortune and will not countenance your desire to be different.

Situating the old farm on Lolland had very pointed implications for Danish viewers. This was not just "out in the country," but a very *declasse* piece of country. To be from Lolland and have to go back there to sort out messy family business was, for any self-respecting Copenhagen yuppie like Kresten, the most embarrassing of dark secrets. His wife was horrified not just to discover that his fine "country estate" was little more than a broken-down farmhouse, but that it was a broken-down farmhouse on Lolland, and that he was still connected to the area.

Danish audiences, for their part, connected to *Mifune,* but this avidly awaited third Dogme film caused some confusion and disappointment with a large segment of Dogme's new legion of fans outside the country and was no huge success. It sold, for example, more tickets in Denmark than in Holland, Italy, France, and Germany combined. To many, *Mifune* just didn't look and feel like a Dogme film, and it had an altogether different spirit. It lacked the transgressiveness and subversiveness of the first two films—it was too sweet, too warmhearted. Where was the black humor? The cutting edge? Instead we get a predictable happy ending! Kragh-Jacobsen had attempted to give the film some sharp edges, but he just didn't have the touch for that kind of thing. The audience at no point in the film felt they were out in uncharted territory. He was just too good at his craft and too self-assured. He knew exactly what kind of film he wanted to make and he made it. For all of its undeniable attributes, he hadn't managed anything really new, and certainly hadn't challenged himself the way von Trier had with *The Idiots.*

Postscript—Søren Kragh-Jacobsen

Back in the beginning of the '90s, shortly after he'd released *The Boys From Sankt Petri,* Kragh-Jacobsen had come up with the idea of making a trilogy that featured women in the lead roles. Women who trade in some way with their bodies or with their sexuality. *Mifune,* with Iben Hjejle playing a call-girl, had been the first installment of his "Girlie trilogy." Now with *Mifune* behind him he was ready to make the second part, *Skagerrak*. This was what Danes called the North Sea, but he just liked the ring of the word and in the film it passes for an old auto garage. (The third part he planned to entitle *The Irish Geisha*. It would be a "simple story with a Chinese woman in the lead role playing opposite Willem Dafoe."[31])

He sat down to write it with the omnipresent Anders Thomas Jensen, then took a couple months off in the spring of 2001 to cut a record and tour with it, and then applied finishing touches. There was no hurry, in any case, since his studio, Nimbus, had their hands full at the time producing Vinterberg's mammoth *It's All About Love*.

Iben Hjejle would be back in the lead role, playing Marie, a restless Danish gal who travels the world working odd jobs with her Irish girl-friend, Sophie. After working a stint on an off-shore oil rig, they arrive in a small Scottish town and go out with their wad and party and drink and end up getting ripped off. Now broke and desperate, Marie is forced to accept the offer of a wealthy lord who needs an heir to his estate, and she becomes a surrogate mother. She gets a big check and drives with Sophie to Glasgow to celebrate, but in a giddy moment loses control of the car and her friend dies. Now completely a mess, she gets to Glasgow and ends up moving into the ramshackle car garage where Sophie's boyfriend worked, which had been their original destination.

The film was intended as a kind of cross between Barbara Cartland and *Trainspotting*, a wry and poetic comedy that would con-tain elements of both fantasy and bleak social realism and feature the kind of class antagonisms that figured in most of Kragh-Jacobsen's work. But why set it in Scotland? In his opinion a story that dealt with such desperate, lower-class characters could never be made credible in Denmark, "since in Denmark Marie would have been suffocated in a forest of social aid workers."[32]

The script was run past a Scottish script-doctor to make sure local cadences were in place, and by Spring of 2002, Kragh-Jacobsen, cin-ematographer Eric Kress, and crew were on the streets of Glasgow shooting all the exterior scenes. Scottish financial backing had come with the stipulation that it be shot in Glasgow, while Swedish backing necessitated that the interior scenes be shot in Trollhätten, Sweden. Hence there was never any possibility, or talk of, shooting "in chronology," something never mentioned in the Vow of Chastity, but which could be considered a Dogme-friendly approach. This would certainly be no Dogme film, but neither would it be an anti-Dogme film. Unlike the other four original Brothers, Kragh-Jacobsen had backtracked and now said he would eventually make another Dogme movie—at some point.

#4—*The King is Alive*

Generating all the hype and attention that it did, Dogme was a chance for a lot of directors to break through to a higher level of visibility, and the long-haired Kristian Levring, maker of Dogme #4, *The King is Alive,* needed exactly that kind of opportunity. He was without doubt the most anonymous figure in the brotherhood, although he wasn't in any sense a newcomer.

At the age of 23 he was accepted into the Danish Film School, in the editing line, class of 1980–84. Two years after he graduated he made his first feature film, the low-budget *A Shot from the Heart,* a futuristic fable set in a ruined and war-ravaged northern Europe. Without access to special effects or elaborate sets, this would-be thriller was obliged to resort to symbolism. It was a product of the consultant system and was backed by the same consultant, Claes Kastholm Hansen, who had stood behind von Trier's *Epidemic.* And like *Epidemic,* this "film experiment" was a flop with critics and public alike, selling only 3,354 tickets. Following *A Shot From the Heart,* Levring busied himself editing documentaries and features, and in 1988 he began to make commercials of which he has to date between 300 to 400 to his credit. He lived for extended periods in London and Paris.

A decade later, Dogme was his ticket to a comeback.

His first attempt to write a script fell apart because he couldn't get form and content to hang together. And then he had an idea. "I thought about an English acquaintance of mine who lives in the Mojave Desert in California. He lives in a small town called Johannesburg that has about 60 to 70 inhabitants, and he's grown a proper lawn right there in the middle of the desert, since that's what you must have when you're an Englishman. When he gets homesick, he arranges a 'Shakespearean Evening' with the locals, and so maybe it's Chuck from the gas station who plays Hamlet. I considered making a documentary film about that, but I'm not a documentary filmmaker so instead I used it in *The King is Alive*."[33]

Levring sat down and wrote the screenplay with Anders Thomas Jensen. They moved the story to the Namibian desert where 11 foreign tourists and a bus driver, guided by a faulty compass, end up stranded in an old mining town that is completely abandoned save for one very old man no one can understand. They move into several of the deserted dwellings, living on canned carrots and waging a losing battle against boredom and a merciless sun. As the supplies dwindle and their desperation increases, the elderly sage of the group suggests they perform an off-the-cuff production of Shakespeare's *King Lear* as a kind of therapy to keep their minds occupied. They agree to participate and it helps in some way, but as nerves wear thin and tempers explode, the relationships between characters take some very strange twists and turns. Several die.

Despite his modest budget, Levring managed to assemble an impressive cast that included the likes of Bruce Davidson, Janet McTeer, and Jennifer Jason Leigh. After seeing *The Celebration*, Leigh had reportedly told her agent to "get me a Dogme film!"

"For me, as a completely unknown director," commented Levring to *Berlingske*, "it was a great experience to work together with established actors who gave as much as they did. I was very moved. We did a lot of basic preparation and were together for 6 to 7 weeks before the shooting. We held collective meetings that were a bit hippie-like—all the actors were completely into it at these meetings. We came so close

A lost busload of tourists searches in vain for a road to civilization in Kristian Levring's The King is Alive.

to each other that after the shooting it took many months before we landed again."

Like *The Celebration* and *The Idiots, The King is Alive* was another classic ensemble piece, but in the estimation of many the true star of the film was the Namibian desert itself in all its spectacular desolation. The shooting, all done on location, had a been a true adventure and in conjunction with the film's Danish release, a gallery exhibition was held where still photos, taken by the cinematographer, Anders Overgaard, were displayed along with "sound pictures" from the shoot. It must be said, though, that for all the freedom and convenience that shooting in DV afforded Overgaard, it's a pity *this* Dogme film wasn't shot on 35mm. The desert locales would have been all that much more striking.

As for upholding the Dogme rules, "It was impossible to maintain them all," stated Levring.[34] "And it would be a lie to say that you've done that, but what it's all about is to push yourself as much as possible in the direction of the rules. I especially had a problem with the command in the Vow of Chastity that stipulates that one must refrain from expressing personal taste, since as soon as you shoot a close-up, it's the result of personal taste. . . . the rejection of an aesthetic is after all in reality an expression of personal taste."

The King is Alive premiered at Cannes 2000 in the *Un Certain Regard* section and aroused interest and some amount of critical praise. Several reviewers, including the Variety reporter, deemed it superior to Lars von Trier's *Dancer in the Dark* which was "in-competition" and would go on to win the Palme d'Or. Its Danish release was long delayed, however, reportedly because key figures in the trade judged it to be too "non-commercial" and it was hard to find a Danish distributor willing to take it on.[35]

Peter Aalbæk Jensen figured it to be a film for egg-head intellectuals, not a general public, and in a strategic move postponed its release until a month after *Italian for Beginners*—the latter released in 60 prints while *The King is Alive* was released in a mere 4 prints! Box office reports soon proved his judgments to be correct: *Italian for Beginners* went on to become a monster hit at 800,000 tickets sold while *The King is Alive* racked up a far more modest 13,000.

Perhaps, in seeking to realistically depict the boredom and aimlessness that plagued his characters, Levring had succeeded all too well, managing to turn off average ticket-buyers who went to the movies to experience other emotions, to cry or to laugh or to feel excitement, the kind of reactions this film did not provoke. However ground-breaking it might have been as a piece of film art, as an emotional experience it was bleak and hopeless. It could also be said that the characters were not well formed enough to really engage the viewer, and that they were at once both trivial and pretentious, although in reality people and their problems are often just that. In any case, if the filming had been an adventure, the film itself was not one. It was almost an "anti-adventure," an exercise in doom and existential nothingness. The characters did go from point A to B and were transformed in some way, but the journeys were all of the inward variety, and in the end the film was perhaps too severe and barren to appeal to the general public.

Danish critics had mostly kind words for the picture and several ranked it as the most unique and in many ways compelling of all the Dogme films. In the context of Danish film in general, it was deemed something unusual. Very un-Danish. "In contrast to the three previous Dogme films," wrote Anders Rou Jensen, "*The King is Alive* is completely without humor or irony . . . To the contrary, it dares to confront the viewer with a harshness and mercilessness which can perhaps pass for Dogme but which certainly cannot be said to be particularly Danish."[36] Being "un-Danish" could get a filmmaker recognized, though—that was how Lars von Trier had come to be.

Outside Denmark the film had considerably better luck with the public, particularly in Great Britain, and it continued to intrigue critics. Levring accompanied the film on the festival circuit and was heartened by the general audience response and by enthusiastic reviews in papers like *The Guardian* and *The New York Times*. And by encounters with fans of the film, like, for example, one Al Pacino who approached him after a festival screening in America to heap praise on the acting.

The King is Alive provoked different reactions in different countries. In Japan, some saw a religious dimension to the film and Levring was asked if he was a Buddhist. In England, many were intrigued by the Shakespearean connection, although ironically his distributor had him under strict orders not to talk too much about Shakespeare and theater because they figured that would turn off *movie*-goers!

Postscript—Kristian Levring

Following *The King is Alive*, Levring put Dogme behind him and began writing his next picture, *The Intended*. The cast included Janet McTeer, who co-wrote the script with Levring, as well as Olympia Dukakis and Brenda Fricker. Inspired by the Joseph Conrad novel, *The Heart of Darkness*, it was filmed in the jungles of Borneo and centered on

a young surveyor and his lover who end up stuck at a bleak trading out-
post in the middle of the jungle in 1924. It was yet another story of people who suddenly find themselves in an alien environment with their
backs against the wall. As Levring commented shortly before the film's
July 18, 2003 domestic release, "I am driven by a curiosity which also
prompts me to make films in the desert and the jungle, even though it's
wildly impractical. Where there is too much control, I lose interest."

#5—*Italian for Beginners*

With the arrival of Lone Scherfig's Dogme #5, *Italian for Beginners*,
the Brothers now had a sister.

While a few foreign journalists tried to make something of this
fact, it aroused scant attention in Denmark where women are well
represented in most trades and professions, including film. And yet,
while gender didn't seem to be relevant as an equality issue, it would
emerge as a legitimate point of debate in regard to the content and
approach of the later Dogme films, more and more of which would
be made by women directors.

Scherfig was not new to the Danish film scene, but like Levring
was in need of a breakthrough.

She had attended Sorbonne University in Paris in 1976 and later
studied film at Copenhagen university. Subsequent to that, she applied
to and was accepted at the Danish Film School, in the director's line,
enrolled in the same class as Levring (1980–1984).

She went on to make short films and commercials and to direct TV
series episodes. *The Birthday Trip,* from 1990, was her feature film debut.
It was about a fried sausage vendor whose pals take him to Poland to
indulge in cheap liquor and women for his 40th birthday, but things get
complicated when a girl who has mistaken him for a wealthy car dealer
gets serious. The film, driven by Scherfig's trademark bittersweet mix of
satire and melancholy, got great reviews but audiences stayed away. (It
actually did somewhat better outside of Denmark.)

Her second feature, *On Our Own,* from 1998, was a kind of family comedy/adventure film about three kids who get the apartment to themselves after their criminally-prone mother suddenly ends up in jail. The mix of comedy and lacerating social realism didn't quite jell and this film was no great success either.

It was Scherfig's television work that would be most enthusiastically embraced by the public, particularly the several episodes of the hugely popular series, *Taxi* (1997–99), that she directed, and to a lesser extent her work on the later episodes of Lars von Trier's peculiar pet project, *Quiet Waters,* a series based on the writings of Morten Korch.

After her work on *Quiet Waters* she was asked by Zentropa if she wanted to make a Dogme film. The offer came with a certain amount of pressure attached, for although Kristian Levring's Dogme film #4, *The King is Alive,* was not yet out, the first three Dogme films had all, in different ways, been very successful. And there was already a backlash developing against Dogme. Would Scherfig drop the ball? Would she confirm suspicions among doubters that Dogme was beat, worn-out, exhausted? A hoax?

She wrote the script herself. She had displayed a precocious writing talent at a young age, already at 12 penning short stories and commercial jingles for weekly magazines and papers, and entering contests with them. She specialized in dime-novel, melodramatic stories about people with horrible lives and even gloomier destinies. She wrote like this until her teenage flights of literary fancy were brought crashing to earth by a high school writing teacher. "He taught me what *trash* was," she recalls, "and after that I became almost afraid to set pen to paper again! . . . But it didn't stop me from making mistakes again once in a while. And today, in fact, I use many of the same narrative tricks that I used in the stories I wrote as a child."[37]

Narrative tricks that found their way into *Italian for Beginners,* which deals with a loose circle of lonely individuals who come together in a language class and find strength and hope in the experience.

She assembled a cast largely drawn from her previous films and began shooting in Film Town and on locations in the nearby environs of Avedøre and Hvidore. This is a kind of down-at-the-heels suburban area south of Copenhagen, and one never sees anything "city like" in the film. Yet that fits the melancholy tone of what was billed as a romantic comedy but was more like a "romantic tragedy," and jibes well with the fact that the story presumably takes place in a small town where people can continually bump into each other by accident, although the setting is never really clarified. The setting, in fact, is very much secondary to the characterizations, and the locations are all rather neutral and dreary looking. (This wouldn't stop busloads of eager location-hunters from later ferrying around between the quite unremarkable bakeries, restaurants, and churches where the film had been shot.)

There wasn't much buzz around the shoot, and nobody had particularly great expectations for the film. It was an unknown commodity and, as noted, Scherfig was no big star in the Danish film world.

"It's quite apparent we're talking about a Dogme film here," noted *Politiken* reporter, Per Dabelsteen, on a visit to a shoot in Film Town on February 27, 2000. "There is scripted dialogue but there is no artificial lighting, and for example, there is no detailed plan for how the cinematographer, Jørgen Johansson, will move around to shoot the scenes. He runs up and down the stairs, is up on a ladder (which 'accidentally' stands in the vicinity), runs into actors and almost trips over a chord, but just keeps the camera running. All for the sake of getting a sense of spontaneity out of the situations and a mass of footage to work with later in the editing stage. Things are so wild that as a visitor on the set you get worried that you're getting in the way."

"Am I in the way?"

"No, I don't think so," replied Johansson, "but this is after all Dogme, so if we get a glimpse of you in the film, so be it."

Who would have guessed at this point that the movie would become one of the five most-seen films *ever* in Denmark, or that it would go on to break records in a string of foreign countries? Who could have predicted that it would over-shadow all the other Dogme films put together and go on to create its own worldwide cult? ...That it would even end up as a political football? (Why, asked Pia Kjæsgaard's ultra-right nationalistic Danish People's Party (DF), should Danish taxpayers give so much money to Lars von Trier to make English-spoken films when modest little Danish-spoken films like this could have such great international success?[38])

Why *this* little film?

To begin with, it was, unlike the earlier Dogme films, not particularly Danish in any sense. Although the Danishness of Dogme had always been considered an attribute, the absence of any such local color in *Italian for Beginners* rendered it more easily translatable and exportable, a film boiled down to its universal emotional elements. And it followed the same formula that had made other "romantic tragedies" big hits in the past: The viewer is introduced to a group of characters oppressed and/or abused by ungrateful family members, employers, or by simple unjust circumstance, good people who don't deserve such fates . . . lovable losers whose groping attempts to connect and find love in a dysfunctional world evoke sympathy and melt the hearts of many a viewer as the plot winds on, assisted by several characters who conveniently drop dead.

Sounds simple (and formalistic) enough, but what exactly was *Italian for Beginners*? It was sold as a light comedy, but had a bleak and barren feel to it and wasn't much of a comedy. A love story, then? Romance or at least attraction is involved since everyone comes together in the end, but it is hardly about the transcendent power of love. It is not about love as any kind of obsession or overwhelming compulsion and it is not about star-crossed love. To the contrary, it is a very conformist film about safety in numbers. In the end, matchmaker Scherfig has everyone paired off not only in couples but also as part of a larger group. The Danish sense of coziness triumphs. Things are finally as they should be and nobody has to worry about being alone anymore.

The film's message seems to be that the state of being single implies a perpetual pathetic quality, and that anyone can find happiness with whomever happens to be available if one just has the courage and gumption to engage them. Then everyone can be pathetic together.

It's about "love the one you're with" . . . or the one you work with, or go to language class with, rather than the one you dream about, dreams being totally absent here in a film that makes average life seem exceedingly average indeed.

Are female viewers more inclined to sympathize or connect with these lovable loser characters than male viewers, who might rather tend to think of them as mere pathetic drips? Was it a film that *pandered* to its audience? These are open questions, but in any event *Italian for Beginners* was clearly an example of what is called in trade parlance,

Ann Eleonora Jørgensen (left) and Anette Støvelbæk in Italian for Beginners.

a "women's picture," for all the sentimental excess that implies. Even Lars von Trier, who has made some of the most shamelessly manipulative melodramas on earth, reportedly could not swallow what he deemed the saccharine sweetness of its ending.[39] Had Danish film, then, simply come full circle? Back to pumping out the kind of harmless and predictable films with sweet happy endings that he had raged against back in 1982? And was his company, in fact, not producing most of them?

But something didn't compute. If it was just sentimental sludge, just a weepy women's picture, why all the across-the-board critical praise? Aside from Steven Simel of the American *TV Guide*, who found the death toll far too high for a "light comedy," it was hard to find a critic who had anything bad to say about the film. This simple little picture had clearly seduced the critics too. They could not call it pretentious or bombastic or grandiose because it hadn't tried to be any of those kinds of things, particularly not within the spartan confines of its Dogme structure. It was just what it was, and it had gotten the critics to accept it as that. It did not in any way offend them. It was not guilty of the crime of vanity and they were prone to be at least sympathetic to it.

If Scherfig had loaded the film with all the narrative "tricks" she had learned in her youth, she had also demonstrated some strengths that could only come from experience. She had gotten great acting from actors who had been perfectly cast, and their performances managed to breathe life into a group of characters otherwise cut out of cardboard. And there were several well written and effectively staged scenes. Her TV experience had come in handy here. She knew how to make things work on a budget. It was pure story and pure acting, even if the story did reek of drugstore novel.

So there it was, a nice modest little movie all wrapped up and ready to conquer the world, a humble little film that managed to tap into the potentially huge market for women's pictures. A masterpiece no one was calling it, but so what? The great immortal masterpieces born out of pure genius—that was von Trier's department.

Postscript—Lone Scherfig

The dimensions of the success of *Italian for Beginners* completely overwhelmed Scherfig as well as just about everyone else. It was hard to keep your feet on the ground in the wake of all this success. But now it was time for Scherfig to get to work on her follow-up, *Wilbur Wants to Kill Himself,* another romantic tragedy with a bittersweet-happy ending. The story, set in Scotland, centers on two brothers who have inherited a second-hand book shop, the good-hearted Harbour and the younger, suicidal Wilbur. Into their lives comes Alice, a struggling single mother who marries Harbour, but then falls for the smoldering passion of Wilbur and has to deal with all the emotional pain that results.

Originally the film was to be Danish-spoken and employ pretty much the same cast from *Italian for Beginners,* actors Scherfig knew, trusted, and had worked with before. Actors who had accepted a lower-than-average wage to work on a Dogme film which had gone on to conquer the world and make millions. Actors who now wanted a pay raise for this non-Dogme picture, *Wilbur Wants to Kill Himself.* . . . Actors who Zentropa said "no" to. They instead moved the film to Scotland where they had contacts, and shot it in English with a largely Scottish cast who were, for the most part, not well known (or expensive). Mads Mikkelsen, proven draw with the ladies back in Denmark, was one Dane kept on board.

Wilbur Wants to Kill Himself opened in Denmark in mid-November, 2002. It was top of the charts for a few weeks, got generally very good reviews, and even ended up ranked as "Best Danish film of the Year" according to *Politiken.* "Danish film does it again!" one could easily read between the lines. There were, however, a few chords of dissent amidst this chorus of praise. Johannes H. Christensen, writing for *Jyllands-Posten,* called it "carefully calculated," while *B.T.*'s Brigitte Grue scored some of the scenes for their sugary sentimentality.

In any case, Danish critics generally found *Wilbur Wants to Kill Himself* to be a step beyond *Italian for Beginners,* darker and heavier, but tighter, more intense, and availing itself more fully of the expressive tools of film art.

And yet, despite the fact that the plot of *Wilbur Wants to Kill Himself* was very different, basically a *menage a trois* rather than the ensemble play of *Italian for Beginners*, Scherfig had used the same narrative tricks to tug at the viewer's emotions.

Once again we meet a poor, suffering character in the person of Alice. Alice works as a cleaner at the hospital, down on her knees scrubbing up bloody tissue in the morgue after autopsies have been performed . . . all to make a home for her little daughter. To add to the indignity, she is sent packing by her mean boss, fired for being late. He tells her she was never any good at the job to start with. In all her frail and girlish vulnerability, and equipped with an apparently endless capacity to suffer on behalf of other people, she very much echoes Emily Watson's "Bess" from *Breaking the Waves*.

There is plenty of pain, death, and guilt to go around in Scherfig's story. Not only is one brother suicidal, but the other suffers from terminal cancer. We sit in with Wilbur as he attends group therapy sessions for the chronically suicidal. All of it set in the murk and gloom of Scotland. Bleak stuff, this, but Scherfig managed, at least in the estimation of most Danish critics, to redeem it with infusions of wry humor and a very humanistic approach. In fact, the film never manages to be really disturbing or sad because the characters prove too flat to be plausible and the psychology behind it all is too half-formed. Wilbur's transformation from human wreck to a loving, functioning person is as formalistic as it is inevitable. No twists or surprises here.

Wilbur Wants to Kill Himself attempts to deal with life's most profound issues, and here Scherfig is clearly out of her depth. She never manages to get the otherwise promising mix of atmosphere and pathos to jell in a believable fashion. This was not a problem in the more superficially plotted *Italian for Beginners* where basically average characters were not asked to bear up under the dramatic weight of such profoundly tragic situations. To make such a story function, the characters would have to be incredibly well-drawn, and this is clearly not Scherfig's strength. An additional drawback is the presence of overplayed and ill-conceived secondary characters. *Wilbur Wants to Kill Himself* remained oddly inert and ended up as a tear-jerker that didn't jerk.

Scherfig's next project is reported to be the English language, *Moments of Clarity,* adopted from a manuscript by the Danish-American writer, Mikael Colville-Andersen, which is based on a true story.

More suicide, death, and depression from one of Scandinavia's most promising female directors? Who knows, but as Zentropa ballyhooed in a May 12, 2001 press release, the film would first and foremost be a showcase for "Scherfig's talent for creating characters one can relate to."

#6—*Truly Human*

After the shocking amount of success achieved by *Italian for Beginners,* Dogme was plunged into something of an identity crisis. The four original Dogme brothers had all made their films and put the experience behind them to a large degree, and although more films were in the pipeline, no real thought had been given to officially expanding the Brotherhood. Now suddenly the beginning of a whole new chapter was being written.

Frankly it was never the intention that Dogme should be so, well . . . successful. There was supposed to be equality, but *Italian for Beginners* was not being equal! Now the danger was that Dogme would be measured by such success, defined by numbers like ticket sales, nets, and grosses. God forbid that Dogme should come to be seen as part of a formula that spelled sure-fire popularity. Something one simply added to a film to make it a hit. Another blurb to print on the poster, another tag-line for the ads.

But revolutions have a habit of falling victim to their own success, especially revolutions that lay claim to such purity of intent. Would that success now defile the purity of Dogme, or perhaps even kill it?

These issues all hung in the air as the April 27, 2001, premiere of Dogme #6, *Truly Human,* approached.

The film was directed by Åke Sandgren who had been born and raised in the north of Sweden. He had originally applied to the Swedish Film School in Stockholm, but was rejected. Later he applied to, and was accepted by, the Danish Film School, and found himself in the same class with a peculiar but promising young student named Lars von Trier. After graduating, he would go on to act as assistant director on a number of pictures, including von Trier's feature debut, *The Element of Crime.*

Sandgren directed his own first feature in 1985, *The Secret of Johannes.* The film was about a nine-year-old boy who questions the meaning of life and gets answers from, among others, a spiky-haired girl with a backpack who emerges out of a toilet bowl, and is, in fact, Jesus. Søren Kragh-Jacobsen advised on the picture and the two would remain good friends.

His next film, *The Miracle in Valby* (Valby being a somewhat *declasse* working-class Copenhagen neighborhood), from 1989 was an effective mixture of everyday realism and fantasy. It dealt with a 14-year-old boy who accidentally constructs a time machine out of a shortwave radio and travels back to the Middle Ages with two pals. The element of fantasy remained central to all of Sandgren's subsequent films as well, most notably his fifth feature, *The Beyond,* made in 2000. Here a young diver discovers a sunken submarine that contains the answers to the mystery of life.

For Sandgren, by now a respected figure in the Danish film world and a member in good standing of von Trier's inner circle, it was only a matter of time before he would be asked to make a Dogme film.

He had been working on the core idea of *Truly Human* for quite a few years. "It was originally intended as a documentary," he told reporter Claus Christensen, "about a mythological creature, the *Vitra,* that lives in Norrland, Sweden, but really only resides in people's imaginations. Later on it occurred to me to make a feature film about a creature that travels around and experiences the evils of the world. But it got too pretentious, too grandiose, and I had trouble making the story credible. Something was missing. Then I was asked to make a Dogme film and I knew at once that I'd found my form, a form that would never allow me to make the plot pretentious. The Dogme rules generate a reportage-like atmosphere that is a productive counterpart to my fable-imbued story."

The story began, as did so many of Sandgren's earlier films, in the fantasy world of a child. Here the seven-year-old Lisa, neglected by her yuppie parents and starved for a soul mate, fantasizes that the older brother she would have had (had he not been aborted) is, in fact, alive—inside the walls of her bedroom. But tragedy strikes: Lisa dies in a car accident. Soon after, her parents move out and the house is demolished, freeing the imaginary brother that Lisa has willed into existence, so to speak. He now comes to life in the real world. He must now become a genuine person, must become truly human. He has to learn everything from scratch, how to function both mechanically and spiritually, how to understand what people mean. How to read their signals. Having no apparent identity or language, he is taken to a refugee camp.

As the shooting script developed, Sandgren began deleting all the special-effects shots upon which the film had been to a large degree dependent. He had to figure out how to adopt his fantasy fable to the severe dictates of Dogme.

This in turn put more demands on the performance of Nikolaj Lie Kaas, who played the imaginary brother. He had to convey the finely nuanced development of a character who knows absolutely nothing but who can feel and whose senses and instincts sharpen with time. Kaas had to be able to play "blank," so to speak, to act without acting.

It was a challenge, but he was an actor up for challenges. His breakthrough had come in Søren Kragh-Jacobsen's 1991 film, *The Boys from Sankt Petri*, for which he'd won both the Robert and Bodil for best male supporting role. Later he had been one of von Trier's "idiots," in the estimate of some the best idiot. So he already had some experience with Dogme, but unlike von Trier's film experiment, here there would be no freedom to improvise.

As noted, the limitations imposed by Dogme forced re-shoots and re-thinks. In one scene, for example, Kaas' naive and childlike character was to stand outside a cafe and ponder some torches, coming too close and catching his hair on fire. But now, without recourse to special effects, such a scene was impossible and simply dropped, as were others.

One scene they didn't drop involved Kaas being dragged under a moving automobile. He needed something to grab on to so a bar was attached to the vehicle, although this probably technically violated the "no props or sets" rule. Stunts were also decidedly anti-Dogme in spirit if not letter, although this (physically quite impossible) scene was accomplished by editing.

"For our sound people, Dogme could be hell," remarked Sandgren to *Film*. "The second Dogme rule states that all sound must be recorded on location and sometimes that feels like carrying water from a river and pouring it into the sea. For example, in one car scene we needed the sound of a boys choir in the background, and because everything had to be recorded on the spot we had to take the boys choir along in a special car and pass their singing over to the other car—which had to be of the same make and have the same engine so the sound wouldn't be any different!"

Dogme forced Sandgren to reconsider the film from the ground up. What was it really all about? And how to convey that?

In the early drafts, the fantasy character of the brother, dubbed Ahmed at the refugee camp, had supernatural powers, but Sandgren began to realize that it would be far more interesting if the character was totally ordinary, and in the end the only supernatural quality he possessed was his almost instant ability to learn languages.

Ahmed would remain the central character, but he would function in a more reactive manner. Good natured and totally agreeable to the point of being (apparently) thoroughly gullible, he becomes a profoundly neutral presence, and the people he encounters see in him what they want to see, for the good or bad, and act accordingly. In this way he becomes the catalyst that sets the story in motion. He effects people not with supernatural powers, but with an almost Jesus-like supernatural innocence, and the fantasy element is reduced almost completely to metaphor.

Like Kasper Hauser, Ahmed must learn everything from the beginning. To most adults he appears to be a good-natured and malleable idiot, somewhat in the mold of Steinbeck's Lenny (*Of Mice and Men*), and he is exploited and ridiculed for it, but others react to these qualities in a positive way. For example, he becomes friendly with a teenage girl who connects with his innocence and ability to have fun. He prefers the company of children, for he himself is a child—the spiritual reflection of the boy who would now be 10 had he not been aborted.

To Lisa's parents, whose lives have come unraveled after the accident—and in whose apartment building Ahmed is coincidentally given his own flat by the social authorities—he is a mystical and inexplicably positive figure. He is, after all, the spirit of their lost son, and also a kind of link to their deceased daughter, although they never learn the hows and whys, and Ahmed himself seems incapable of enlightening them. It is a film content to let some mysteries linger.

Finally Ahmed is targeted by paranoid neighbors who suspect his attraction to children is pedophiliac in nature and he is beaten up. Now his time as a "real" person is over; he has become tainted and

Man-child Ahmed, played by Nikolaj Lie Kaas, finds some fun and female companionship in Truly Human.

infected by all the hate and suspicion of the adult world. He has lost his innocence and retreats back into the cloistered security of an existence inside walls.

The film is equal parts existential fable, satirical comedy, and psychological drama. It plays out on several levels and deals with a host of profound issues like spiritual development and the roots of identity. Its basic premise, a child trapped in the body of an adult, has striking similarities to the 1988 Tom Hanks' vehicle, *Big*, but is in every other way very different. *Truly Human* only uses this device to reflect further upon the spiritual drift of modern family life, and it takes a much more uncompromising position on the dangers that await the naive in an "adult" world. Indeed, no mainstream American movie would incorporate issues such as homosexuality and pedophilia into their plot the way that *Truly Human* does. And although Sandgren's film has occasional deft touches of absurd humor, its deeply introspective tone goes against the grain of the kind of warm-hearted entertainment that Hollywood has turned into a money-spinning formula. The distinctly "thoughtful" feel of the film is no doubt one reason why it was a disappointment at the box office in Denmark.

On another level, *Truly Human* critiques various aspects of modern Danish society with a deadpan humor. (In fact, most Danish Dogme films double as essays on the modern social condition.) With Lisa's parents standing in as the typically insensitive, career-obsessed couple, Sandgren depicts modern-day Denmark as a place rife with stress, self-absorption, and materialism. And that's exactly how he sees it in real life. "If you look at Denmark today, we live in the classic bourgeoisie manner where people first and foremost look out for themselves, and where there is hardly any room for those who are different, for foreigners, the mentally ill, the addicts. . . ."[40] Being an outsider himself, the Swedish born-and-raised director was perhaps ideally positioned to comment on these social issues—issues as dramatic as the recent pedophilia witch-hunts that have swept Denmark (and Sweden to an even greater degree), and issues as subtle as the Danish tendency to treat asylum seekers (and everyone) like "clients."

The film is no hard-hitting political attack on Denmark's treatment of foreigners. After all, the social authorities give Ahmed a big apartment in the heart of Copenhagen of the type that few hard-working Danes can manage to get their hands on! But Ahmed does start life in a refugee camp, and while Sandgren depicts his treatment there as well-intended if institutionalized, many Danish critics read the film as a negative comment on the country's treatment of foreigners—a viewpoint certainly also at play in the foreign media. This is perhaps more a reflection of current Danish sensitivities (or guilt) about the subject than anything directly conveyed in the film. Danes have long considered their society to be a just and exceptionally human one, and to many the recent government policies on immigration seem coldhearted and xenophobic. This suspicion that Danish society is becoming more isolationist was confirmed to many by the results of national elections six months after the release of *Truly Human*, when on November 21, 2001, a right-wing coalition government was voted into power and quickly set in motion a series of measures aimed at foreigners that appeared to advance the "politics of exclusion." Real-life events were putting focus on the film's political dimension.

In any case, *Truly Human* was an ambitious film operating on many different levels and it was a challenge to bring all these elements together into an organic whole and make it function.

Most critics thought Sandgren succeeded and deemed it an intriguing work that was both witty and troubling. And it made a moderate splash on the international festival circuit, winning, among other awards, first prize for best direction at the International Art Film festival in Teplice, Slovakia. Kaas' performance was invariably singled out for praise, and he won the Bodil for it.

But the Danish public, as noted, didn't get swept up by the film, and it sold only a modest number of tickets. And not every critic agreed that the story was suitable for Dogme treatment. Writing in the May 2001 edition of *Night & Day*, Eske Troelstruup opined that "the Dogme concept here seems a bit misplaced . . . this is after all a genuine adventure story, but it is poorly served by the Dogme brand of realism and the magic stays away. *Truly Human* is a courageous low-budget version of a film that was originally conceived with more boldness."

Postscript—Åke Sandgren

Shortly after *Truly Human*, Sandgren was employed as a producer at Nordisk studio. There, together with fellow producer Lars Kjeldgaard, he created a Dogme-like concept called "Director's Cut," and unveiled it to the press in August of 2001. Like Dogme, it is based on a firm set of rules, but it exclusively focuses on the production process and addresses logistical issues which Dogme had never directly engaged. Its intention is to streamline and shorten the production process so directors don't have to exhaust themselves spending years to raise money, so they can get stories and ideas on to the screen while they are still fresh.

The five rules are:

1. The budget is 8.5 million kroner (1.15 million USD) per film. (Ed: this makes it about the same as the average Dogme film. A normal Danish feature film costs between 12 and 15 million kroner —1.6 to 2 million USD).
2. Films are to be shot on location with small crews of 10 people maximum.
3. The shooting time will be short, typically six weeks.
4. Editing can, however, take considerably longer.
5. The decision to make a "Director's Cut" film will be made solely on the basis of a synopsis and not, as it happens today, on the basis of a manuscript.

The DFI immediately expressed an unwillingness to go along with point five, but in any case four directors, including frequent von Trier collaborator, Morten Arnfred, signed on to make the first four "Director's Cut" films.

"Son of Dogme," as it might be called, scored its first breakthrough at Cannes 2003 where a young Film School grad by the name of Christoffer Boe won the prize for best debut film, the Camera d'Or, with his experimental love story, *Reconstruction.* Boe has come to be known as "the new Lars von Trier," in Denmark, and ended up stealing the spotlight from the old Lars von Trier whose *Dogville,* heavily favored to win the Palme d'Or, was shut out at the awards ceremony. In his public utterances, Boe has shown himself to be every bit as outspoken and controversial as his role model.

#7—*Kira's Reason—A Love Story*

Ole Christian Madsen, the director of Dogma film #7, *Kira's Reason—A Love Story*, was typical of the kind of young director that was being called upon to carry the banner of Dogme (and Danish film in general) forward. O.C., as he is known, came to Copenhagen from a small provincial town at a young age and worked as a bartender for three years before gaining admittance to the Danish Film School. On the basis of his subsequent film work he became typecast as the maker of hard-hitting, streetwise action/crime films, largely on the strength of his 1999 movie, *The Pizza King,* which was set in an immigrant milieu racked by crime, violence, and drugs. (The film had similarities to Nicolas Winding Refn's 1996 picture, *Pusher,* and some pundits saw them as indications that a contemporary variant of the hard-boiled Danish gangster film was about to be born, but it remained pretty much just these two films, with the overwhelming bulk of new releases continuing to be comedies, romantic dramas, and warm-hearted children's pictures.)

Madsen's real breakthrough with the Danish public came with his wildly popular TV series, *The Spider,* a historic criminal drama.

Kira's Reason—A Love Story, which he wrote with Mogens Rukov, would be a radical departure for him, "a real love story," as he termed it, an intimate drama about a modern married couple, Kira and Mads, who lead a seemingly picture-perfect existence before the death of their baby causes Kira to suffer a mental breakdown and almost destroys their marriage.

Dogme veteran Mads Mikkelsen (Left) and Kim Bodina star in Pusher *from 1996, which was seen as the start of a Danish wave of realistic crime pictures.*

The material had inherent dramatic potential and could easily have been over-played, but to Madsen's credit he never allows the drama to overshadow the psychology, and Kira's emotional and mental transformations are conveyed with credibility and poignancy by Stine Stengade, who submits a remarkable performance. Kira has been blessed by beauty but damned by fate and possibly also by heredity, since her mother also went mad and insanity may lie in their genes. Foregoing the use of special make-up to roughen and defile her classically chiseled features, Stengade resorts to facial ticks and nuances of gesture and behavior to convey the fragility and instability of her mental condition. She remains perfectly beautiful throughout her ordeal, almost imperviously pretty, and though this could certainly strike some as unrealistic, her performance still convinces, and soon we do not envy or desire her, but just pity her. Her beauty is of no value, it cannot help her in any way to become well or happy and just becomes a kind of cold fact.

Mads, benumbed by a feeling of helplessness over Kira's growing irrationality, still loves her and tries to hold the family together by devoting himself all that much more to his job. Yet his insistence on keeping up appearances and small inconsiderations—like refusing to dance with her at a formal business dinner—only drive them further apart. Sex won't rekindle their relationship; Kira apparently lacks desire or the necessary powers of concentration and it is just more proof of their mutual failure.

They feel increasingly separated and alone. They trade angry accusations, lunging out and trying to hurt each other until finally it seems there is nothing left to salvage. But there is still love between them, and when they dance together at the end of the disastrous business dinner, Mads, for Kira's sake, lets go of the one thing he has clung to so tenaciously, his control, his rationality, and they dance wildly and rudely around in a kind of shared spasm of madness and joy, casting off all pretenses and concern for the opinions of others.

It was no happy ending, just a small victory, and the future still looks mighty uncertain. It was not an easy film; there were no heroes or villains. Nor was it an "issue movie." It was not about the repressed status of women in a materialistic society—although it was open-ended enough so that those issues could be found if one was predisposed to look for them. It was a bleak, but not totally hopeless, slice-of-life, and did not pull its punches with convenient dribs and drabs of humor. It was light-years from the kind of feel-good films that Danish cinema seemed swamped with at the moment, and was also very different than the love stories that Dogme sisters Lone Scherfig and Susanne Bier had or were in the process of offering up.

Madsen was primarily inspired by John Cassavetes, and particularly by his 1974 film, *A Woman Under the Influence,* which starred his wife, Gena Rowlands, as a housewife coming apart at the seams. O.C. followed suit, casting his wife, Stine Stengade, in the role of Kira, another woman who has come unraveled. Unlike his previously improvised films, Cassavetes wrote a script for this one, but his general knack for improvisation clearly impressed Madsen, and according to reports, *Kira's Reason—A Love Story,* was 70% improvised—improvised to a far greater degree than any other Dogme film thus far. "Even so," noted Madsen, in an interview in issue #15 of *Film,* "it is intriguing that the finished film is very much like the script." His thoughts on improvisation bear repeating: "Contrary to what many people think, improvisation, like anything else, requires that you act according to a particular set of rules."

And this suited him fine as a working method. As he went on to comment, "Many intuitive decisions were taken at the last moment while we were shooting. I work best under pressure. Then I don't have time to feed the fear of failure that anyone who works in cinema is familiar with. If you start thinking about the amount of money riding on a film and the number of awards the other Dogme films have won, it wears you down."

In common with the other Dogme films, long takes were favored. Each scene lasted at least 15 minutes, during which the actors underwent at least half a dozen emotional transformations. Shorter takes would have disrupted the momentum of a scene. Here the actors could improvise and play off each other as they went along. To do scenes in long takes supposedly was more like real life where there are no takes at all. Unlike other Dogme films, there was very little "shaky camera." One can easily watch the film and forget for long stretches that it is Dogme.

Stine Stengade plays Kira, a mentally disturbed housewife and mother in Kira's Reason—A Love Story.

Nimbus, which had backed all of Madsen's previous films, produced the picture for 7 million kroner (just under 1 million USD), the average Dogme budget. Three million of that was granted by the DFI which never again would be caught dragging its heels on Dogme. For O.C. this was like a breather, to be able to make a film not just for the sake of selling tickets. He was dead tired of hearing about Dogme being described and quantified as a commercial success. In his opinion, that wasn't how Dogme should be measured.

Opening in Danish theaters on October 26, 2001, *Kira's Reason—A Love Story* garnered rave reviews across the board. No other Dogme film had been or would be praised this highly by Danish critics. It went on to win five Robert Awards and two Bodils—all the "biggies." The Bodil awards ceremony was held at the huge Imperial theater in central Copenhagen, and the statuettes were given out by none other than Lauren Bacall, who had just finished shooting von Trier's *Dogville* in Trollhättan, Sweden and had been persuaded to stop over in Copenhagen on her way back to the States. Called up on stage to receive his Bodil for "Best Film of the Year," the shaven-headed Madsen dropped to his knees in front of the diva as if praying to Mecca. "I should be doing that to *you,*" she gamely quipped.

No doubt about it, in critical circles, *Kira's Reason—A Love Story* was the Danish film of the year.

It wasn't such a big hit with the public, however, selling a very modest 70,000 tickets. That was marginally better than the 50,000 tickets *Truly Human* had sold, but minuscule compared to the numbers *Italian for Beginners* was still racking up.

Postscript—Ole Christian Madsen

Following *Kira's Reason—A Love Story*, Madsen returned to the mean streets of Copenhagen's foreign quarter to complete his trilogy on the life of second-generation immigrants—*Sinan's Wedding* (1996) and the aforementioned *The Pizza King* being the first two installments. With these pictures, O.C. was attempting to realistically depict the immigrant milieu in a way that was not beholden to the accepted wisdoms of politically-correct orthodoxy, and in a way which did not look at the immigrant situation as a social welfare issue. Sharp edges intact and no apologies offered. Films that had "street cred."

Maybe he succeeded all too well with *The Pizza King*. The release of this action-packed tale of crime and double-dealing, shot in a raw hand-held style and set to the beat of a pounding hip-hop soundtrack, was delayed for a year by nervous cinema owners who feared that gang violence would erupt in their theaters. To Madsen's irritation, the film came to be seen as a straightforward contemporary crime/action picture, when in fact he had tried to put more weight on realism.

In any case, he forged new ground with his treatment of foreign cultures in modern urban environments. That is rarely dealt with in Danish cinema. Why? According to Madsen, "it owes to a combination of different factors: Danes have always been hesitant to engage in new milieus and have a great fear of either coming across as too prejudiced or pedagogic. It is hard to break through with a film that deals with these things."[41]

His next film will be an adaptation of Jakob Ejersbo's novel, *Nordkraft*, to which he recently purchased the rights. The book is based on three young characters whose drug abuse has led them to the brink of the abyss. Madsen plans to cast the film with young and relatively unknown actors and to move the action to the provincial Jutland city of Aalborg. Brave choices, both.

#8—*Open Hearts*

Dogme film #8, *Open Hearts*, arrived toward the end of the summer of 2002. It was directed by Susanne Bier. Like most of her Dogme brethren, she was a graduate of the Danish Film School, class of 1987, same as Aalbæk Jensen. In fact he had worked with Bier on her graduate film, *Island of the Blessed*, which had gone on to win first prize at the Munich Film School Festival.

Her first feature film was *Freud Leaving Home* (1990), a highly praised Swedish-language drama about a family in Stockholm forced to come to grips with their mother's fatal illness. She made her next film, *Family Matters* (1993), for the just-established studio, Zentropa, and followed that with *Like It Never Was Before* in 1995 and *Credo* in 1997 before scoring a massive breakthrough hit in 1999 with the quirky romantic comedy, *The One and Only*.

Bier favored domestic dramas highlighted by farcical elements and off-the-wall dialogue in the screwball mold. In 2000, she returned to Sweden to shoot the musical comedy, *Once in a Lifetime*, the story of a struggling mother who wins the Eurovision Song Contest, and this time the humor was mixed with some gritty realism.

While none of these films had been of Spielbergian proportions, Bier was the kind of director for which Dogme had been made—an experienced veteran seeking a new challenge and a new way to tell and film a story.

The raw manuscript to *Open Hearts* was written in 10 days in a summer house in Sweden with Anders Thomas Jensen who, as noted, had already scripted two previous Dogme films, *Mifune* and *The King is Alive*. Bier laid out the scenes as she saw them in her mind's eye and Jensen scribbled away and the story, about a star-crossed love affair, took shape. In a nutshell, the plot involves a doctor who finds himself consoling the wife of a man who has been hit by a car and who now lays paralyzed in his hospital—a car that was driven by his own wife. Both couples see their marriages crumble as the doctor and the injured man's wife find their relationship turning physical.

Bier felt her collaboration with Jensen provided a good balance: "I came to the project with my sentimentality and he brought a certain cynicism."[42] Dogme dictates and a modest 8 million kroner (1-plus million USD) budget necessitated that the story be told in a bleak, realistic style which was very much a departure for her.

The shooting, much of it in a rented house north of Copenhagen, lasted from November 2001 to the end of that December.

On December 9th, *Politiken* scribe, Dorte Myhre, visited the set and Bier shared a few thoughts about shooting her first Dogme film. "It's a little Laurel and Hardy-like with all these limitations. I can easily see the goal in being prohibited from laying music on afterwards, but in any case there are certain things one can do without violating the concept." That rule, #2 ("The sound must never be produced apart from the images, or vise versa."), was the toughest for her to abide.

"We shoot it all in long sequences," added male lead Mads Mikkelsen. "In part because that way you can play full out, and in part because then one doesn't feel one is wasting someone else's money." To Mikkelsen, there was nothing noticeably different about shooting a Dogme film. Although he had never done Dogme before, he had launched his acting career in 1996 with *Pusher*, which is often described as "Dogme like."

Bier worked with editors Pernille Bech Christensen and Thomas Kragh throughout the winter and spring of 2002, and Aalbæk Jensen was able to show some sample footage to perspective buyers that Spring at a number of European film festival markets. It attracted huge interest, he claimed. Of all the horses in the Zentropa stable, Bier was one of the easiest sells. It was often easier to sell her films than von Trier's.

In June a funny thing happened on the way to the next Dogme victory party—Dogme was canceled. The reasons were outlined in a press release (reproduced in full in the Appendix) which stated that the causes were aesthetic as well as financial:

> *The manifesto of Dogme 95 has almost grown into a genre formula which was never the intention. As a consequence we will cease to mediate or interpret how to make Dogme films and will therefore close the Dogme secretariat. The original founders have moved on with new experimental film projects, as we have moved on. Additionally, we do not have any economic foundation to continue our work, which has indeed been a broadening journey . . ."*

Mads Mikkelsen and Sonja Richter in a scene from Susanne Bier's Open Hearts.

No problem for *Open Hearts*—its papers were in order. It was the 8th Danish Dogme film and #28 on the international chart. (Curiously, however, its title is never listed with its number—possibly out of a desire to play down its Dogme connection?—and this has caused some confusion in the numbering of Danish Dogme films to follow.)

Finishing touches on the film were completed that summer as it awaited its September 16th Danish release, with festival appearances scheduled shortly thereafter in Toronto and San Sebastian. As for its domestic reception, there was still a fair amount of uncertainty as to how much enthusiasm Danish ticket buyers would show. Although it had top Danish stars on the roster, a bleak "everyday" drama wasn't what they expected from Bier. How would they react?

They flocked to the film, as it turned out. The response was a surprise to everyone. *Open Hearts* set the record for opening weekend grosses for a Dogme film, exceeding the phenomenal numbers *Italian for Beginners* had posted almost a year and a half earlier. It was the "feel bad hit of the year" and Danes loved it.

Four Danes, at least, were not so enthused: The Brothers. They had a bone to pick with Bier and it came in the form of a press release soon after the film opened. In an interview, Bier had dismissed criticism that she had broken rule #2 by laying music on the track. The music, she explained, was coming from a Walkman that one of the actresses went around in, going on to add that

> *furthermore I find this discussion about possible broken rules uninteresting. After all, there is talk that one should voluntarily be in philosophical accord . . . of course one should try to abide by and not cheat the rules. All this talk about rules is, though, in my opinion navel contemplation and distracts from what the film really deals with. But if that can generate publicity and give the film some extra buzz then it's okay by me.*

The four Dogme brothers hardly agreed that it was navel contemplation, responding in their press release:

> *When we experience, in connection with the premiere of the Dogme film,* Open Hearts, *that there has been doubt cast on the need to comply with the Vow of Chastity, thereby causing a dilution of the concept, we feel called upon to repeat the principal for issuance of Dogme certificates. It is impossible for The Brothers to concern themselves with the maintenance of the rules in specific incidents. It is thereby very strongly recommended that the directors exercise self discipline, and that, most importantly, the media and the public exercise vigilance. Dogme is still meant as an unambiguous set of rules which first obtain their proper effect the moment the rules, and not least, the intention, is taken at face value.*

The rule breaks, notably the use of music, were noticed by critics, but it didn't dissuade them from showering the film with superlatives. "Bravo Bier!" headlined *Ekstra Bladet's* rave, penned by Henrik Queitsch, who doled out six out of a possible six stars. "An intense and moving film," declared Ebbe Iversen. Kim Foss wrote that despite some amount of "Dogme fatigue" he had noticed in the media lately, here was proof that Dogme was alive and well. Danish critics unfailingly lauded the film's "shining revelation," a newcomer from the theater world named Sonja Richter who played one of the two female leads.

Apart from Richter, the other leads, Mads Mikkelsen, Paprika Steen, and Nikolaj Lie Kaas, were all very well-known faces. Perhaps even a bit too well known. The problem wasn't so much that this was Steen's fourth Dogme film and Kaas' third, but rather the fact that these actors had all starred in a lot of recent Danish hit films, several of which even bore a strong resemblance to *Open Hearts* in tone and plot mechanics. A general pattern was discernible in films like *Minor Mishaps, Okay, Mona's World* and the last three Dogme films (#5, #6, and #7).

The basic recipe seemed to call for a serious illness or tragic accident that ended up putting relationships under strain and marriages through the grinder. Men cheated on their wives. People became bitter. There were lots of arguments and fights and awkward and embarrassing scenes as the futility of life was brought home in a train of usually bleak and washed out images. A new wave of "Danish realism" some called it. Even Bille August, with his critically praised return to intimate drama, *A Song for Martin* (2001), was part of this pattern.

Could Danes ever get enough of feeling bad?

Their enthusiasm for the film notwithstanding, the critics had noticed this too and started to kick the issue around in the press. "*Open Hearts* . . . resembles a distillation of many of the recent year's biggest film successes," noted Kim Foss. Anders Rou Jensen of *Politiken* pointed out numerous similarities between the films and opined that quite possibly many people would get the feeling they had already seen this film. Ebbe Iversen wondered if "Dogme, and that which resembles Dogme, here in Denmark has led to a certain standardization of film art in the form of movies which are all low-budget, take place in present day Copenhagen and deal with similar subject matter."

While the term "creative crisis" seemed a bit strong, there did seem to be a troubling lack of bio-diversity, so to say, in recent Danish film. Was the Danish film industry now doing what they had always scorned

Hollywood for—playing it safe, recycling popular themes to death and giving the people what they wanted at the cost of movies that were bold or daring? Susanne Bier's film brought all these issues out into the open.

This homogenization that seemed to characterize the state of current Danish cinema had several root causes:

1. **Screenwriters.** It seemed that most recent Danish films were written by just two screenwriters—wonderboys Anders Thomas Jensen and Kim Fupz Aakeson. They both had a knack for snappy dialogue and were both good at plumbing everyday subject matter for material.

2. **Actors.** With *Open Hearts*, actors Mads Mikkelsen and Paprika Steen were accused of being overexposed, of hogging all the good roles and consequently blocking the way for new, unknown actors. Aalbæk Jensen, for his part, stated that they had intentionally sought out the pair for *Open Hearts*. "Mikkelsen, Steen, and Kaas are recognized outside Denmark for their earlier films. We have a humble hope of creating Danish stars who are also marketable outside Denmark."[43]

After all, when star Danish directors went on to make English-language films for the international market, very few Danish actors went with them! This was the way Danish actors could "travel," by staying right at home in Danish films. With so many of their directors fleeing the Danish-language ship like rats, Danish actors were left holding the social realist bag.

As for charges that this A-team of Danish actors seemed to appear in every single film, Steen spoke up in her own defense in the September 10th issue of *Jyllands-Posten*. "We are, after all, not in the U.S. where one can spread oneself over many different genres, from small dramas to big special-effects films. Due to budget limitations, Danish films are small fish, and with an action film you get maybe a single explosion—and so we make these 'everyday stories.'"[44] For all the recent success of Danish film, they still couldn't compete with the American studios when it came to producing certain types of films. Horror and science-fiction, for example. These kinds of pictures were almost never made in Denmark, and when they were, as in the cases of *Angel of the Night* (1998), *Possessed* (2000), and *Cat* (2001), they underwhelmed.

Some claimed there was nothing to be done about the purported overexposure of certain actors, that this was simply "the star system" in action and that it had always existed. It seemed like Poul Reichhardt and the great Dirch Passer had appeared in every single film back during the decades when the Danish folk comedy reigned supreme. And there were many other examples. As in every other country, audiences wanted known faces. Filmmaking, complained producers, was enough of a financial gamble without betting on unknown talent. In Hollywood, where the casting of big stars functioned for producers as a kind of collateral, the lesson had been learned long ago.

> **3. Economics.** The popularity of *The Celebration* back in 1998 had shown Danish producers that everyday subject matter could be hot stuff for audiences. Furthermore, these kinds of films were relatively cheap and quick to make. For a comparative pittance one could produce a film that knocked 'em dead at

Paprika Steen, star of several Dogme films and a top draw at the Danish box office.

international festivals, won awards and held up the banner of Danish cinema around the world. Domestic audiences connected with the homegrown stars and identified with the stories, while foreign audiences found the films engaging and extremely well acted. Success all around, so why not more?

Danish film had become a victim of its own success, admitted screenwriter, Kim Fupz Aakeson. ". . . in that a film can easily be made for 10 million Kroner (1.3 million USD). That's nothing. And what do you get for 10 million Kroner? You get the 'everyday.' You get Copenhagen. That is out-and-out the cheapest. . . . If one is a realist, one makes an everyday-drama set in Copenhagen."[45] The economic limitations of Dogme, noted Niels Bokkenheuser of *Easy Film*, meant directors could more or less only afford locations in Copenhagen, and that gave the films a homogenous look to them.

The producers, then, were just as responsible for this situation as the screenwriters and directors. Aalbæk Jensen even went so far as to blame the TV stations who co-financed much of what was being made. "The TV stations are pushing Danish film in a very mainstream direction . . . they only 'green-light' films that can produce the biggest ratings. These films must deal with the completely average lives and problems of completely average Danes. A little infidelity and a few laughs in between, eh? And always a hopeful ending. Those kind of films we can always get DR and TV2 to go in on." While there was truth to his charge, as TV2 program chief, Bo Damgaard, conceded, it was perhaps a bit ingenuous of Aalbæk Jensen to blame the TV executives since nobody was happier than he was to tote these little films about average people around to foreign festivals and bask in the glory when they became hailed as masterpieces.

It was not only the critics who complained about the situation. Several months before *Open Hearts* premiered, cinematographer Anthony Dod Mantle, weighed in on this recent trend in Danish film. As noted, Mantle had filmed *The Celebration*, *Mifune*, and *Julien: Donkey-Boy*, and had become known as "the cameraman of Dogme," but about these new pictures he was anything but positive.

> *Just now a lot of low-budget films are being made here in Denmark for as little money as possible and without an over-all philosophy behind them. They're made fast. The visual component is completely at the bottom, and that is dangerous. Here in little Denmark we have a good situation at the moment, but we should not forget how beautiful an art form film is. We should remind ourselves that there is still a great deal of new territory to explore rather than just mass-producing things which have been made a hundred times before.*[46]

While local pundits and critics were busy accusing Danish directors of churning out a crop of average, "everyday" films, outside Denmark Danish cinema was still perceived as bold and experimental, as being on the cutting edge.

In August 2002, for example, the acclaimed Swiss theater director, Stefan Bachmann, had been forced to cancel his experimental production of *Hamlet* at the Danish Royal Theater after three of the Danish actors quit in protest against his casting of a woman who suffered from Downs Syndrome in the role of Ophelia. They claimed Bachmann was manipulating and exploiting a person who had no understanding of how she was going to be presented. It caused a scandal that rocked the Danish theater world and prompted Bachmann to claim that Danish theater was not only backwards in relation to German theater but also in relation to Danish *film*. Film was the risk-taking art in Denmark, according to Bachmann. "How can so many exciting things be happening in Danish film?" he wondered. "It is as if the same actors behave completely different when they appear in a Danish film than when they appear in a theater production."[47]

Bachmann's assertion drew immediate response from, among others, writer and filmmaker, Christian Braad Thomsen. "Danish film does have a lot of momentum at the moment, but not because it is particularly progressive."[48] In his opinion it was quite the opposite, "mainstream," to use a word. And the reason for that, he ventured, was because funding was only granted to films that would sell tickets.[49] He could think of only one great Danish filmmaker who was original and inventive: Lars von Trier. "And he is also the *only* one. He can embrace both the avant-garde and the popular, and that is impressive."

As for von Trier, who had himself used mongoloids in previous films such as *Images of a Relief* and *The Kingdom*, he inserted himself into the *Hamlet* scandal with a letter-to-the-editor in *Politiken* on August 6, 2002 that read in full:

> *In connection with the shameful 'Ophelia case' at the Royal Theater, I hereby recommend that the theater stand in judgment of itself and subsequently shuts down. It is better to close the place before it is, quite justifiably, hit with an international human rights case or is cornered for genetic discrimination. To exclude someone from a job on the basis of a hereditary condition is, as far as I know, criminal, however much it is in step with other current abuses against humanitarian values in our country.*
>
> *If one should propose, in spite of this, to continue operation of the Royal Theater with this embarrassing blemish, one ought at least to continue to fire those who in their own opinion are genetically better-suited actors, who in their self-righteousness and intolerance have caused this situation. Reactionary behavior in an artistic as well as a human sense ought not to be the trademark of our National Theater.*

Von Trier's angry attack was felt deeply by one of the actors who had quit in protest, the 59-year-old Henning Jensen who considered von Trier a friend and had acted in three of his films. Von Trier's letter didn't cause him to regret his departure from the production, but it was clearly a blow as the filmmaker's utterances carried considerable weight.

The blockbuster success of *Open Hearts* had revealed a kind of gender gap within Dogme. Even though all the directors were making what could be categorized as relationship films that hinged on the interplay of couples and families, it was the gals—Scherfig and Bier—

who had made the two love stories that had turned out to be massive hits, while the guys were making the "daring works of art" that relatively speaking didn't draw flies. They were all domestic melodramas with a twist, but the lines seemed clearly drawn: the fellows made the raw, hard-edged films that were transgressive, ground-breaking, and experimental, while the women made, well . . . "women's pictures," that promulgated a more sentimental set of values and which tapped into a potentially much larger audience. And with three of the next four Dogme films to be made by women (Natasha Arthy, Annette K. Olesen, and Charlotte Sachs Bostrup), one had to wonder how that would effect the perception of Dogme as a totality, as an artistic concept.

#9—Old, New, Borrowed & Blue/The Dog's Called Fiat 128

As noted in the previous chapter, it seemed pretty obvious by now that Dogme pushed movies in certain directions, that it tended to produce certain kinds of stories told in a certain style. By the same token, Dogme seemed particularly unsuited to certain types of films, and its "no genre-films" prohibition aside, seemed to flat-out exclude certain genres like history and biography ("must take place in the here and now") and science-fiction ("no props," etc. etc.) Other forms, like musicals, fantasies, and horror all seemed to chart somewhere between hard to impossible to make under the yoke of Dogme.

All considered, then, Natasha Arthy was a strange pick to make a Dogme film; all of her previous television and film work had been strongly anchored in the children's fantasy genre.

Rejected twice by the Danish Film School, she ended up getting a film education by doing just what Søren Kragh-Jacobsen had done, getting her foot in the door of the Children and Youth Department of Danmarks Radio and making television for the younger set.

She eventually got a chance to make a short film, *Penny Penniless* (1997), which showed promise. Her feature-film debut in 2000, another youth film entitled *Miracle*, hit the jackpot, winning over 12 different awards at festivals in and outside Denmark, and her film career was launched. Both pictures were fantasies imbued with grotesque as well as magical elements—not surprising for a director who claimed Hans Christian Andersen as her favorite writer. But Dogme? She never imagined she would make one.

After agreeing to do so and after reading the rules a little closer she was filled with trepidation. Strange enough that this would be her first "adult" film, but how could she bear to leave so many of her favorite filmic devices behind? She was out in new territory, but she wasn't alone since her co-writer from *Miracle,* the ever-diligent Kim Fupz Aakeson, had signed on to write the script.

Even though this was the ninth Danish Dogme film, Aakeson, for his part, saw the concept as anything but obsolete. "Films cost a lot of money to make," he commented in issue 15 of *Film,* "so you're not allowed to play around. There's a great deal of caution associated with filmmaking, whereas there is still a certain sassiness or rawness about Dogme. 'Hey! We'll just damn well do it!'"

Together they worked out a story. This film would be a black-comedy for grown-ups that availed itself of some of the time-tested mechanisms of melodrama. "Serious and cruel in places and very funny in others," noted Aakeson.

The film was shot over May and June of 2000 in chronological order, so that it would be, in the words of the female lead, Sidse Babett Knudsen, "like a living organism." Unlike a lot of other Dogme films, this one used a lot of locations. And there would be no 'shaky camera,' but there would be lots of improvisation.

Arthy had always used a lot of music in her films and wasn't about to forego that. One character wears a Walkman (also like in *Open Hearts*) and that permitted the use of some music. Additionally, she cast a trio of real musicians who function as fantasy figures, suddenly appearing now and again to provide a kind of mood music that reflects the state of mind of various characters at given points. People suddenly breaking out into song (or music) was something she had freely used in *Miracle*. This was her style—the unexplained merging of fantasy and reality, the kind of thing children could accept perhaps better than adults.

It was difficult for her to get a sense on the set as to whether they were succeeding with this noble Dogme experiment, but the vibes were good. She would just have to wait until she got into the editing suite where it all came together, and where you couldn't bury mistakes and deficiencies under the sound of a hundred violins.

Editing progressed through the summer and fall, putting the film on target for its January 2003 domestic release.

From the very beginning, the film had adopted a curious working title: *And the Dog is Called Ford Mustang*. This was largely because a car played a big part in the picture, but they had to drop the "Ford Mustang" because no one involved in the film had such a car and the no-props rule forbade them from renting or otherwise acquiring one. The title was then shortened to *And the Dog is Called . . .* , leaving everyone even more in the dark. Eventually they found the right car, a beat-up Fiat 128, which ended up resulting in the two English titles.

The film sharply divided Danish critics.

A scene from Old, New, Borrowed & Blue.

"Finely balanced between the serious and the amusing, between the grotesque and the normalcy of the 'every day' . . . at once the most cuttingly vicious and most amusing Danish 'feel good' film I have seen to date," raved Julie Moestrup in *Jyllands-Posten*, while a more skeptical Ebbe Iversen found the film hard to get a handle on, dwelling as it did in a strange no man's land between comedy and psychological drama. (It had been billed as a "comedy/drama.")

In any case, once again a Dogme sister had failed to make "great art."

It also seems unlikely that this was the movie Arthy would have logically made after *Miracle*. It is more likely that this was the movie the screenwriter wanted to make. Giving the screenwriter such importance would run counter to von Trier's own philosophy that Dogme should get completely *away* from the script. Throw the damn thing out and forget it! Let the *actors* create the story. Did these two prominent Danish screenwriters, Aakeson and Jensen, have too much power? They pumped out the hits like shiny new cars and that was great, but was this the right way to go about making a *Dogme* film? Was this what Dogme, which had always presented itself as the antithesis of the pre-formed, the premeditated, and the commodified, should be all about? This raises the question of how a director, at this late stage in the game, came to make Dogme. Were they appointed? Chosen? Assigned? If so, that would seem like a violation of the original spirit of Dogme, even though this subject had never been addressed or anticipated in the original charter.

The main idea had always been that Dogme should be tied in to where a director was at a specific point in time, both career-wise and mentally. Was it time to go play? Timing was everything, and ideally the making of a Dogme film was contingent on internal rather than external factors. Apparently not so, now that Dogme was beginning to resemble a minor league farm team, a way to break new talent into the majors. But shouldn't a director have something pressing to say first and then arrive at the conclusion that Dogme was the only way to say it? Ideally that seems how it should work, but no, it had never worked that way from start. Filmmakers were picked and chosen and invited. It was the "cinema of the chosen ones."

Most directors paid lip service to the restorative powers of Dogme, claiming it had opened up new ways to tell the story, but weren't they really just talking up the finished product in the cause of good old PR? And what about these stories? *Old, New, Borrowed and Blue* had not laid to rest the debate over Dogme's homogenizing effect on Danish film. In her February 14, 2003 column in *Politiken*, Bettina Heltberg complained that this film wasn't really "about" anything, either, just more drivel. The same old. Wasn't there anything these screenwriters and directors were dying to say? Weren't there any problems to be debated, any positions to be taken on anything? Were Danish films incapable of dealing with anything at all outside the sphere of intimacy, she wondered? Dogme had always been about good stories and now people were complaining that it was just the same old story.

And was Dogme really the only way to make these films, or had the directors and screenwriters simply been paired off by producers to find a story that fit the concept? What about the manifesto's assertion

Sidse Babett Knudsen (left) and Björn Kjellmann in Old, New, Borrowed & Blue.

that the artist should reject the *auteur* concept, that they should tame their egos, go uncredited (Rule #10), and put the film first? Dogme had in this way purported to shift the importance from the director to the work itself, but in fact, for all practical purposes it had placed the focus more firmly on the director. It demanded that all their decisions and methods measure up to the highest standards of purity and left these nervous acolytes vulnerable to charges of heresy and sin by the high priests while giving every ticket-buyer on earth the right to endlessly second-guess them! Never had directors been *more* in the spotlight. Never had a specific filmmaking style managed to steal so much attention away from the movie itself.

Had Dogme come to violate its own natural laws? Karma was everything with Dogme, the purists would argue, and tampering with the unwritten rules, the *spirit* of Dogme, was as bad as breaking the written rules.

Such were the contradictions that were starting to come to the fore as Dogme entered its eighth year in existence.

#10—*In Your Hands*

Some critics were starting to wonder if Dogme was supposed to be funny. It seemed so. Most of the recent Danish Dogme films certainly had a tendency to fall back on humor when things got too bleak. You couldn't subject viewers to too much, apparently went the accepted wisdom, and the laughs always arrived like clockwork to raise the spirits of audiences in danger of being beaten down by so much emotional distress and dreariness. Danish film in general shared this tendency. This was partially due to the fact that the Danish audience was basically a mainstream audience. Specialty niches in the small Danish market hardly existed, and so for a film to succeed it was best if it was pitched to Mr. and Mrs. Jensen, and the TV companies that pumped money into feature film production also wanted films with broad appeal. Two other contributing factors were the previously noted and very busy screenwriters, Anders Thomas Jensen and Kim Fupz Aakeson, who were fond of this approach and had a knack for snappy dialogue that could lighten things up. Their movies offered a bit of everything, laughs included.

Not so with the Dogme films, *The King is Alive* and *Kira's Reason— A Love Story*. They had really separated themselves from the pack. And both had paid a price for it. Clearly the lack of mitigating humor in *The King is Alive* had contributed to its crash-and-burn at the Danish box office, and ticket sales to *Kira's Reason—A Love Story* were also hugely disappointing, particularly in light of all the critical praise it had received.

In Your Hands also departed with a vengeance from the comfortable formulas, and this was a relief to at least one participant, actor Nikolaj Kopernikus, who said that he looked forward to being in a Danish film that was un-funny all the way through.

The story, set in the woman's wing of a high security prison, was no barrel of laughs, and looked set to give *The King is Alive* competition in the "feel-bad film of the year" department. Inside these cold concrete walls two very different women meet; a newly ordained female priest who grieves over the fact she cannot have children, and a prisoner who has caused the death of her baby. Fatal and as yet un-divulged consequences follow.

Scheduled for release in August of 2003, this would be no "women's picture," but if it effected the audience as forcefully as it effected the director and much of the cast, tears would flow. It was a bleak and tragic story they were attempting to tell.

The director, Annette K. Olesen, Film School grad ('91) and wife of Åke Sandgren (director of Dogme film *Truly Human*), wrote the script together with the above-mentioned Kim Fupz Aakeson. He had also co-written the script to *Minor Mishaps*, Olesen's acclaimed family drama that had won the Blue Angel at the Berlin film festival in 2001, and had earned praise from *Variety* critic Derek Elley, who called it "effortlessly entertaining . . ."

Maybe it was too effortless. Maybe it was getting to be too easy to wring pathos and humor from such tried and tested "everyday" subject matter, and when talk turned to their next project, Aakeson told Olesen that he wanted to do something that took place in a prison. "I will not be funny anymore," he said to her.[50]

In Your Hands was certainly a women's film in the respect that all the lead characters were women. (None had been told that the film took place inside a prison until they had agreed to participate.) They were given ample opportunity to get "into character," and preparations included meetings with ex-addicts who had hung out in Copenhagen's notorious Halmtorvet area (frequented by addict-prostitutes), and discussions with medical-aid personnel who worked the streets.

The project was shrouded in a fair amount of secrecy as shooting approached in November of 2002, mainly because nobody really knew what was going to happen until the cameras started rolling. The actors knew their characters inside-and-out, but there was a lot of room for taking things in different directions. During the filming they had full input into the process, and there was lots of discussion, although at times Olesen was compelled to assert control and make decisions about where the characters were going. "Otherwise, it's too much consensus and we thereby end up with the lowest common denominator choice."[51]

Dogme would once again be reduced to pure story and pure acting. In the barren confines of the prison there was little to focus on other than the actors, and they would be left to carry the full weight of the story, to make it credible.

The shoot was an intense experience for all involved, with three of the six weeks spent filming inside Nyborg State Prison, in a wing temporarily vacated for renovation. Cast members were all given the chance to spend a night in a cell to get further into character, but there were no takers. "It's a bit of an unpleasant schism that we go around here and play at something that is a reality on the other side of the wall," noted Olesen in remarks made to *Berlingske* at the end of the shoot. "It's a great advantage to be able to shoot in a prison, however cynical that might sound, but it is also a lot to deal with emotionally. At times I cried at my monitor over some of the scenes in this film. It's a black story."

And it was also purported to be the *last* story, with the powers that be decreeing that this was finally and definitely and unequivocally the last Dogme film. . . . That is until January of 2003 when news broke that two more Dogme pictures were entering the first stages of pre-production.

VII

Individuals and Institutions Essential to Danish Dogme

The Danish Film School

Almost every single Danish Dogme director is a graduate of the Danish Film School—the institution's importance to the movement cannot be overestimated.

The idea of founding a film school in Denmark had been proposed way back in the '30s by Theodor Christensen, a central figure in Danish film through the pre-and-post-war periods. His book, *Film* (1936), was the first in-depth look at the aesthetic qualities of the motion picture. During the war he was the leader of the Danish Underground's film cell which produced works such as *Det Gælder Din Frihed* (*Your Freedom is at Stake*) which attacked the policy of passive cooperation with the Nazis. After the War, he worked for the United Nations and UNESCO and was employed for five years in the '60s as a teacher at the Cuban Film Institute. When the Danish Film School was founded in 1966, Christensen was the first teacher they employed. I.C. Lauritzen, the critic, producer, and author of such

One side of the compound which housed the Danish Film School in its original location.

books as *The Film* and *What is Film?* was its first headmaster. And there were 15 students.

The establishment of the Film School at this point was in response to the realization, also abroad in other countries, that film was not just a business or an entertainment medium, but an art form that could have cultural and social significance and be worthy of study. (The founding of the film department at Copenhagen University in 1967 was also a part of this trend.)

Originally housed in a 160-year-old brick building on the island of Amager in Copenhagen, the school was in a state of drift during its first years of existence and experienced a string of ups and downs. Christensen died in 1967 and Lauritzen resigned as headmaster in 1969, the same year the school was "occupied" by 35 radical, young, long-haired artists who were members of the aforementioned ABC Cinema group. Neither the President nor the students were particularly happy about being liberated. These were tumultuous times and traditional assumptions about film as well as society itself were being passionately questioned, but such actions only served to further dim the school's reputation.

It was not until 1975 when an ex-student, Henning Camre, was named headmaster that the school found its footing. (Camre had photographed some of the key works of '60s and '70s Danish cinema, including *The Perfect Human*.) It now became a more professionally oriented institution with an accent on the technical trades. The employment that same year of teachers like Mogens Rukov also contributed to this changing of the guard.

As Camre would later recall,[52] "We wanted to remake the world and educate a generation of people who would go out and renew things . . . create a new industry, because at that time there wasn't so much happening on the film front."

The school was now organized into "lines" which placed the focus on specific crafts such as producing, editing, directing, sound, and cinematography. Only five students on average were accepted every second year into each line, with the period of education lasting three years and later extended to four. It was a small school and the selection process was stringent.

"We couldn't afford to make a mistake when accepting students," recalls Camre, "but if we did, as everyone does, we coined the expression that then at least it should be an interesting mistake. . . . The minimum requirement was that a student should be qualified for a job when they graduated, but it was not just about being absorbed into the existing film milieu, it was more that you should have the guts to go out and do something new. The students were encouraged to stick together and go out and create new companies. We didn't want to educate a bunch of functionaries."[53]

Camre left the School in 1992[54] and was replaced by the quiet-spoken and diplomatic Poul Nesgaard who remains in that position to this day. Nesgaard came from Danmarks Radio where he had worked for 23 years in the youth programming department.

A sense of typically Danish solidarity characterized life and work at the school, or at least that was the intention if not always the result. The fact that the student body was small and that demands on their time and energy were great necessitated a spirit of cooperation. And language was no barrier since most of the students were Danish—a result of both the high cost of the education and the fact that classes, if not special guest lectures, were taught in the native language. This was no international film school, and they could hardly be bothered to spend the first year teaching the new students Danish, the way the main Polish film school takes the first year to teach foreign students Polish.

This spirit of solidarity often continued after students graduated, as ex-students frequently formed partnerships and assisted on each other's productions. And formed companies—Zentropa and Nimbus being just two of many examples.

While all film schools encourage this kind of thing to some degree, probably no other national film school is so intermingled with the industry as the Danish school. Suffice it to say, the School looms large in Danish film life.

Perhaps too large.

There is unavoidably something of a club mentality bound up in it. With the web of tight connections and alliances that revolve around it, the School is perceived by some as a kind of privileged preserve for the well-connected, giving nourishment in some quarters to at least the perception that "outsiders"—be they foreigners or simply Danes without connections —have a harder time getting into the program. (In fact, the relatively few number of graduates with ethnic backgrounds usually go on to careers *outside* of Denmark.) To many would-be directors it is all to easy to believe that the School is the only route to a career in film.

Not true. Successful directors like Søren Kragh-Jacobsen, Ole Bornedal, and Nicolas Winding Refn, just to name three, never attended. But a surprisingly high percentage of the country's directors, not to mention producers and technicians, are graduates. The list includes von Trier and Dogme mates Thomas Vinterberg and Kristian Levring, as well as second-wave Dogme directors, Lone Scherfig, Åke Sandgren, Ole Madsen, Susanne Bier, and Dogme Minister without portfolio, Jesper Jargil. (The "von Trier posse"—all of the above and more—constitutes a kind of club-within-a-club.) Bille August was a graduate.

Other graduates who are lesser-known internationally but important in Denmark include Per Fly, Søren Fauli, Linda Wendel, Anders Thomas Jensen, and Christoffer Boe, just to name a few.

Other entry-level portals into the industry do exist, most notably The European Film College. Founded in 1992 in the Jutland fishing village of Ebeltoft, it accepts approximately 110 students from 20-plus different countries for an eight-month course in production and theory, with English the teaching language. Many of the Danish EFC grads go on to attend the Film School while others go straight into the industry. Additionally, there is Zentropa's "smått" (Little Ones) system, a kind of internship arrangement, and The Danish Film Workshop, located in the Film House, which serves as a kind of hub for what could be called the Danish underground. And since 1999 there has been "Super 16," an auton-omous organization formed that summer by several people who had just been rejected by the Danish Film School. They set up their own film school without headmasters or administrators and it has since gained respect within the Danish film milieu and earned the cooperation of various bodies including the Danish Film School itself. Graduates of Super 16 have since gone on to produce a number of highly regarded feature films.

In 1997, the Film School relocated to newer if less cozy premises on Holmen, further out on the island of Amager.

Today, one hundred-plus students study in eight different lines, with two generations of approximately six students on each line (dir-ection, photography, sound, production, editing, animation, TV and manuscript—the latter being a two-year course). Half the education is classroom teaching and half production. Each semester, several con-cepts are introduced and then put into practice in the productions. All students are required to attend certain classes, such as dramaturgy and film history, for example, with special seminars presented by both Danish and foreign lecturers. This teaching aims to give students a common basis of film knowledge so they can communicate across their line specialties.

The Danish Film School in its current location on Holmen.

It costs 200,000 kroner (26,000 USD) per year for one student to attend the Film School, one of the country's most expensive educations. It was no surprise then when in March of 2001 the Culture Minister ordered an 11% cut in the school's budget. The move met with immediate and forceful protests throughout the film milieu. "Film Folk Furious at Funding Cuts" and "Don't Touch Danish Film's Dynamo" blared the headlines of full-page articles that scored the Culture Minister for her hypocrisy in basking in the international success of Danish film on the one hand while cutting the school's budget with the other. In fact the cuts had been part of a plan to reorganize and integrate all of the country's art academies, such as the schools of design, architecture and art, but little visible furor was raised over their cuts. The Film School, to many, had become a sacred cow.

The surprise election in November 2001 of a staunchly conservative government that won with a promise to cut taxes did not bode well for the school's budget, but surprisingly in October of 2002 they announced a four-year plan that would scrap previously proposed cuts and shoot 95 million kroner (12.6 million USD) into improving conditions in all the State art schools.

The Danish Film Institute

Despite the previously noted refusal of the Danish Film Institute to fund the launch of Dogme, neither Lars von Trier or Dogme would exist without this institution. Its charter is the bedrock upon which modern Danish film is based, a cinema which until only relatively recently was an unknown commodity to the rest of the world. And for good reason.

From the post-war period through the 1950s, the Danish commercial film market was dominated by popular comedies and light melodramas that preached the rewards of hard work and belief in family and God, virtually to the exclusion of all else. The comedies were cast with well-known and beloved actors like Ib Schønberg and Dirch Passer, while the numerous film adaptations of the works of the previously noted popular novelist, Morten Korch, sated the public's appetite for light drama.

Seemingly all was well.

And yet ticket sales started to slump in 1959 when television began to make serious inroads with the movie-going public. The fall-off continued through the 1960s as neighborhood theaters closed *en masse* and the industry continued to contract.

This crisis gave occasion for a new debate on Danish film and culture in general, and a belief took hold among politicians and opinion-makers that there should be more diversity in Danish cinema. This coincided with the new thinking that film was art, not just mindless entertainment, a realization that already existed on the more enlightened fringes of the filmmaking community where admiration for the works of the British Free Cinema and the French New Wave was widespread.

This desire for a different kind of film was given voice in 1964 by the Danish Cultural Minister, Julius Bomholt, who stated that "When film is art, we ought to ensure that citizens throughout the whole of the country get access to these cultural values, get admission to a diverse cultural orientation." And it was quite clear that without financial support, artistic but commercially marginal films would never be made.

That same year, on May 5th, a "film law" was passed in Denmark to encourage the production of films that had artistic or literary merit, and to this end a new film fund was established that via a ticket tax would generate money to support these films. The proceeds were funneled back to Danish producers, but in most cases they dumped the money into the making of popular entertainment films rather than

*The Danish Film House is today home to the
Danish Film Institute and the Film Museum.*

so-called art films. This, in combination with the continued fall-off in ticket sales, doomed the fund as any kind of real solution, and the crisis deepened. It was now obvious that without state support, the Danish film industry itself would cease to exist and that the production of *all* films would be imperiled.

In 1972, a new Film Law was passed and the Danish Film Institute was established to allocate funds for production directly from State coffers. The Institute moved into the same cozy compound of buildings on Amager that housed the Film School, and was soon joined by The Film Museum to create what was known as The Film House. Both The Film House and The Film Law—which Danes invariably boast is the best in the world—were based on the pre-existing Swedish model.

In 1973, the DFI put into effect "the consultant system," whereby professionals from various sectors of the film world were hired to select projects worthy of support. Filmmakers who sought funding applied directly to an individual consultant who evaluated their proposal and rejected or accepted it. The advantage was, according to the popular wisdom, that producers dealt with a single person and not with a committee or a faceless institution, and if rejected by one consultant, they could apply to another. If accepted, the consultant would then help guide the film through the various stages of production, advising on content, casting, etc., and just generally trying to keep up the filmmakers' spirits over the long haul from conception to release. They also helped filmmakers find additional sources of funding since DFI support was only a part of the budget.

The advantage of getting money from the DFI was that it came with almost no strings attached. In other words, the producer didn't have to trade off rights or make casting or creative concessions (apart from "recommendations" from the consultant) to get the money, as is so often the case in the commercial film world, particularly with American money. And while in theory the money had to be paid back if the film made a profit, very little money was (or is) ever paid back.

In return for this support, the film had to be "shot in Danish with the overwhelming bulk of the artistic and technical personnel being

Danish." In 1989, amendments to the Film Law liberalized this requirement to read that a film only need be "shot in Danish or exhibit a particular artistic or technical quality which contributes to the advancement of film art and film culture in Denmark."

But film laws and nuances of phrasing aside, the consultants had a great deal of autonomy right from the start, and the Board at the DFI usually rubber-stamped their decisions. That Lars von Trier's first feature film, *The Element of Crime* (1983)—in English and with a largely British cast—got funding even when the stricter interpretation applied, is evidence of that.

The consultant system has been plagued with controversy over the years, and was put to the test right from the get-go when Jens Jørgen Thorsen, a well-known artist with a penchant for provocation and pornography, took his proposal for a film about Jesus Christ to the two consultants then employed, a journalist and a director. The journalist said no but the director said yes and recommended 600,000 kroner (80,000 USD) in support, which the Board approved.

Shortly thereafter, Thorsen was photographed with a large sky-rocket between his legs, declaring that "Jesus will also have such a big one in my film." The case exploded in the western media. The Pope condemned the (would be) film while numerous countries—including France—declared it would never be shot on their soil. The Board repeatedly gave Thorsen postponements, but finally, when he refused to divulge the shooting schedule, ostensibly for the sake of security, they rescinded the grant.

In 1975, a new consultant approved 900,000 kroner (112,500 USD) in support so he could try again. This time the State prosecutor's office got involved and declared the film in violation of the Christian moral code and production was again halted, though the manuscript was published.

The Return, as it was eventually entitled, was finally made with a new manuscript in 1992, not under the consultant scheme but under the new so-called 50/50 arrangement. This was a matching-funds deal put into effect in 1989 and geared more towards films that had a fair possibility of attracting a sizable public. It turned out that through most of the '80s, very few big "popular" films were made because producers preferred the type of film that a consultant would agree to fund. Looking back, most of the '80s is widely considered to be a drought period for Danish cinema, what with the consultants approving so many strange little films that proved to have no public whatsoever (*The Element of Crime* and *Epidemic* are perfect examples).

Change was needed. With the 50/50 arrangement, half of the production cost of the budget would be paid by the DFI if a group of experts agreed that the film had a "fair chance to attract a large public."[55] This funding mechanism is credited for the comeback of popular entertainment films and a Danish film scene that, complaints about "new Danish realism" aside, is today heralded for its quality, diversity, and ability to sell far more tickets. Producers could still secure potentially much bigger amounts of money through the consultant arrangement, up to three times as much, but now popular mainstream films were easier to get made. Ironically, the Dogme films, many of which have been huge mainstream successes, are being funded by the consultant system, drawing complaints from those who say they should be funded by the 50/50 arrangement wherein they don't suck away so much of the public support monies that should be saved for more "special" or "difficult" films.

Profits never figured into the picture for *The Return*: Thorsen's long-awaited movie was slammed hard by most critics and viewers stayed away in droves with a mere 7,451 tickets sold.

Still that was a good 2,500 more tickets than Lars von Trier's second feature, *Epidemic,* sold in 1987. And both films were relative blockbusters compared to the many other flops the DFI has supported over the years, with 1990's *Perfect World* (directed by von Trier's former cameraman, Tom Elling, and produced by his partner-to-be, Peter Aalbæk Jensen) probably holding the record for least tickets sold at 69!

Depending on one's viewpoint, therein lies the central strength or weakness of the system—the fact that films that have virtually no public can get made if just one lonely consultant believes in them.

And despite the mass of rejections consultants are obliged to dole out, criticism remains minimal in the industry itself.

On the other hand, since all films are made with public money, every citizen has a right to complain and things can get noisy. Outraged film writers frequently accuse the DFI of throwing the public's money down the drain, and movie-goers regularly vent displeasure on the editorial pages. Even politicians have joined the fray. Most recently the pro-American right wing Danish People's Party (DF) complained about the use of public money in the making of von Trier's *Dogville*, which in some quarters was seen as anti-American, and which they complained was a piece of pure political propaganda.

Politics aside, the main issue is one of economy, and now and again a specific film can rattle the whole system. One such recent case involved the elderly veteran director, Gabriel Axel, who had been instrumental in launching the modern resurgence of Danish film with *Babette's Feast* in 1987. For his experimental feature film, *Laila, the Pure*, from 2001, a love story shot in Morocco with no dialogue, he got ten million crowns (1.3 million USD) in DFI support. The film opened in a lone second-run Copenhagen cinema and attracted a mere 812 viewers. In essence then, the DFI had subsidized each ticket sold to the tune of 10,000 kroner (1,300 USD). This raised debate as to whether the DFI could put pressure on theaters to give such films bigger openings, but it was decided to leave market forces in play. The DFI had in any case little leverage over the theaters, in spite of the fact that by funding all the big Danish hit films that filled their auditoriums, they were also indirectly supporting the exhibition sector.

In 2002, Zentropa had an even bigger flop with *Charlie Butterfly* which drew a total of only 284 people. Every sold ticket thereby cost tax-payers 25,000 kroner (3,125 USD) in film support.

While examples like this seem to highlight obvious flaws in the system, it is also true that DFI support throughout the years for experimental and non-commercial films has allowed some of the country's most successful directors to develop their craft and language. Von Trier is the most prominent though far from the only case in point. Without

DFI support he most certainly never would have made *The Element of Crime* or *Epidemic*, and probably never would have been heard from again after his Film School graduate project, *Images of a Relief*, in 1982.

Another issue at play is the objectivity of the consultants or lack thereof. For example, as noted, Claes Kastholm Hansen, the consultant who backed *Epidemic*, was a personal friend of von Trier's and the film was agreed to one night over dinner when von Trier bet him he could make a feature film for the cut-rate price of 1 million kroner (130,000 USD), or about an eighth of the cost of an average feature. Von Trier seemingly continues to enjoy the friendship and largess of consultants, perhaps not surprisingly since it was recently revealed that 90% of the support doled out to his studio since its foundation in 1992 had been granted by consultants who later went on to be employed by Zentropa.[56]

Postscript—The Danish Film Institute

For as long as anyone could remember, these kinds of conflicts-of-interest seemed to be just part-in-parcel of making films in Denmark, but in November of 2002 the whole issue exploded in the press in a series of articles that revealed a milieu rife with patronage and nepotism beyond what anybody had suspected.

The exposés, published in *Politiken* and *Berlingske* from November 17th onward, initially centered on Peter Aalbæk Jensen and his relationship with Mikael Olsen who had been employed in 1998 and 1999 as a DFI consultant. Both before and after that period he had been employed by Zentropa as a screenwriter and then a producer. During his employment as a consultant, most of Zentropa's funding applications ended up on his desk, producers being allowed to choose which consultant to whom they wanted to apply. He had granted substantial sums to the company and according to some had functioned as their "point man" inside the DFI. A closer look at some of his actions on Zentropa's behalf provides a revealing glimpse of why at least the perception of nepotism is so widespread in Danish film.

The DFI had agreed to grant *Dancer in the Dark* 10 million kroner (1.3 million USD) in public support, but Olsen wanted more— 12 million kroner (1.6 million USD)—and tried with various arguments to raise the extra 2 million. He argued in a written memo that the unseemly controversy over whether *Dancer in the Dark* was a "Danish film" (it was shot in Sweden in English with an international cast) should be laid to rest by granting it the full 12 million. When that didn't sway them, he later claimed that he had in fact given Vibeke Windeløv a "verbal promise" for 12 million. That worked and the grant for the film was raised from 10 to 12 million.

In the spring of 1999, Zentropa found itself in a liquidity crisis while attempting to finance the massively expensive *Dancer in the Dark*, prompting Aalbæk Jensen to request 5 million kroner (625,000 USD) in "emergency support" before shooting began. Olsen's superiors at the DFI said no. The project appeared to be on financially shaky ground and Zentropa had not provided them with the documentation they needed to assess the viability of the project. To disburse monies before Zentropa had given them guarantees on the overall financing of the picture could prove to be a violation of the Film Law.

Aalbæk Jensen started to panic. Just prior to Easter of 1999 he called his employees together in the cafeteria and told them there was hardly enough money to cover their next paychecks. On the morning of March 26th, he rang to Henning Camre's deputy, Thomas Stenderup, and demanded that 5 million kroner be transferred into Zentropa's account before 2 o'clock that same afternoon. Stenderup refused and the conversation reportedly ended in a shouting match.

Aalbæk Jensen then went into attack mode, savaging Camre, Stenderup, and the Danish Film Institute—or "The Evil Empire" as he called it—almost daily in the press. The general public, none the wiser to the root causes of this feud, was bewildered. This state of open warfare threatened to throw Danish film production into chaos. (Stenderup soon after quit his post in "the hot seat" at the DFI and took a position running a production company called Final Cut, and now the consultants found themselves in the position of receiving funding application requests from their former boss.)

While Aalbæk Jensen attacked from outside the gates with salvos of shrill invective, Olsen, according to the press reports, went to work from the inside in a much subtler fashion, pressing his colleagues to go along. He did some research and found it was actually possible to use public support to come to the aid of a private business and petitioned his superiors to that end. On March 30th, 5 million kroner (625,000 USD) was transferred into Zentropa's account, and the film and the company were saved. (In fact, the DFI had once before pulled Zentropa out of a liquidity crisis, when they were in the process of making *Breaking the Waves*.[57]) That same day, Zentropa put the necessary paperwork in order and sent it over to the DFI. Aalbæk Jensen, in an interview in the March 2000 issue of *Euroman* magazine, inferred that it had all just been a case of bureaucratic excess on the part of the DFI in demanding the paperwork, and that standing on such formalities in little old Denmark—where handshakes and letters of intent should be sufficient—was ridiculous.

Olsen dismissed all charges of nepotism as "grotesque" and maintained that all his efforts on the film's behalf were based on his belief in its artistic quality. It's true enough that consultants are often forced to go to bat within the system for the films they've backed, but it was hard for investigative reporters not to see something else at play here—not least in light of the fact that Olsen and Aalbæk Jensen had maintained a close personal friendship that stretched back many years.

They had even appeared together on the Danish TV contest program, *Friends for Life*, along with another ex-consultant who later got a job at Zentropa, Per Nielsen (whose old band, Buzzstop, had employed Aalbæk Jensen as a "roadie" in the early '80s). A photograph of the three "winners" in a jubilant group embrace—Aalbæk Jensen puffing on a cigar and clutching drink—now adorned two of the full-page exposés and seemed to sum up the hopelessly corrupt state of Danish film funding.

Of course, as everyone admitted, it was next to impossible to find two people with professional credentials in Denmark who didn't know each other. At different points in their careers, everybody seemed to wear different hats: Film School student, journalist, consultant, producer, Film School teacher, DFI functionary, etc., and they all interacted on various social and professional levels. Unavoidable, all that, but what bothered some was that the chumminess and nepotism seemed to be built into the system.

For example, consultants were picked from the pool of applicants after specific recommendations were made by the Film Council, which included the Board of Film Producers. Foreman of that Board? One Peter Aalbæk Jensen. When it was time to decide who to hire, he would put forward his three "recommendations."

The newly hired consultant was then in the awkward position of having to pass judgment on a film proposal submitted by a producer who had just pushed hard to get him or her employed. And after their period of employment (maximum five years), they would again need to find work in the film world, and that entailed submitting applications to the very same producers.

But however modest the pay, however plentiful the opportunities to make enemies with the many producers whose proposals were rejected, and however much stress and pressure had to be endured, the consultant was a *very* powerful person, the linchpin (or weak link, as some saw it) of the Danish film industry. Despite the fact that they had the full weight of the DFI's financial and legal expertise backing them up, it all came down to their call. Vast amounts of money were at play and careers and jobs hung in the balance. Friendships were put under strain, or rewarded as the dim view had it. There was hardly a cocktail party or a restaurant where a consultant could go and not find themselves cornered by an eager producer trying to push his case.

Sometimes they pushed too hard, as one consultant, Vinca Wiedemann, was well aware.

Like other consultants, she had been previously employed by Zentropa before being hired as one of the two new feature-film consultants in 1999. She had attended the Danish Film School in the same class as Aalbæk Jensen and Susanne Bier and her subsequent teaching stints at the school put her in contact with around 30 or 40 directors and producers. She pretty much knew everyone. Even her sister, Katrine Wiedemann, was in the business. Katrine had directed both film and theater productions, and they had even collaborated on Zentropa's *The Lady of Hamre*, with Vinca writing the script and Katrine directing.

Vinca claims that personal relationships don't affect her professional judgment, and that on at least one occasion she removed herself from a case that involved a personal friend, although that didn't stop her from considering and approving funding for good friend Susanne Bier's *Open Hearts*—monies granted purely on an evaluation of the film's quality, she maintained. And look at the results: critically praised to the skies and a blockbuster at the box office.

While *Berlingske* in its November 24, 2002 issue reports that she is accused by some of doing Zentropa's bidding in the same manner as Mikael Olsen before her, she apparently wasn't always quite as pliant as her old boss, Peter Aalbæk Jensen, would have liked.

Take one February evening during the 2001 Berlin Film Festival, for example. Most Danes in attendance had repaired to the Black Raven pub to celebrate that day's prize-winning success of Zentropa's *Italian for Beginners*. Vinca was there, and so was one Peter Aalbæk Jensen, who took the opportunity to lay a heavy press on her to approve the full 12 million kroner (1.6 million USD) in support of von Trier's next film, *Dogville*. Aalbæk Jensen thereafter asserted that she had given him a "verbal promise" for 12 million kroner which she flatly denied. She reiterated her denial in writing in a memo to her boss, Henning Camre, when it appeared that Zentropa was about to refer to this "promise" in official negotiations on the film. The studio, which had already received large sums from the DFI for manuscript development and shooting tests, ended up "only" getting 9 million kroner for *Dogville*, and Aalbæk Jensen to this day feels that he was cheated out of 3 million kroner on that picture.

In Camre's view, this showed that the system did work, that lonely consultants could withstand the pressure. It was tough work, and of course producers would try to press the system, he acceded, but the alternative, to return to "decision by committee," would be disastrous, he maintained. Others rose to the system's defense, including Jørgen Leth, who pointed out that the system was completely transparent, just like any true democracy. By clicking onto the DFI's website, anyone could see which consultant had approved which project. Nothing was hidden.

But Danish politicians were appalled by what they were reading in the papers, and were quick to attack the current system which seemed to be playing fast and loose with so much taxpayer money. Decision by committee was exactly what most of them wanted. Some even suggested employing foreign consultants. Pia Kjæsgaard's controversial Danish Peoples party (DF) was most critical. Said DF spokeswoman, Louise Frevert, in the November 18th issue of *Berlingske*:

> *There must be no doubts about the integrity of the film support system and therefore the consultant arrangement must be changed as soon as possible. It is very probable that the film industry will protest, but they are so spoiled that we can't be bothered to listen to their hypocritical nonsense any longer. They scream no matter what we do. We must have a board so that film support grant decisions are no longer made by a single person. This face-to-face decision making must come to an end.*

It was now open season on the DFI, and all the feature film consultants (there were just two of them, actually). Star director Ole Bornedal (*Night Watch*, 1994; *I Am Dina*, 2002) piled on in a sharply worded broadside that appeared in the November 19th issue of *Berlingske*. "It is no advantage that consultants are either people from the Industry who are on their way to retirement or people from the Industry who haven't had the competence to succeed there . . . we have consultants who have more or less never written a manuscript."

Bornedal had never managed to get support for his films through the consultant system, but had had to settle for lesser sums from the 50/50 arrangement, and *I Am Dina* had even been knocked down to the minimum support level of 3 million kroner (400,000 USD) because Vinca Wiedemann had declared that it wasn't a "Danish film."

"It's very normal that people who have not gotten support have that viewpoint," sniffed Camre in same article.

Through it all, Peter Aalbæk Jensen remained unapologetic. Of course he would fight and claw for his films—that was his job. And sure, the system was inbred, the system was incestuous. That was the Danish film milieu for the good and the bad. And no, he wouldn't remove himself from the consultant selection process, as Camre had suggested. Who would pick them? The Board of the DFI? They consisted of, among others, an ex-bank director, a school principal, and a minister. They clearly couldn't represent Industry thinking.

But Aalbæk Jensen and arch enemy Henning Camre were at least in agreement on one thing: How could the present system be so bad when it had resulted in so much success? When it had produced so many films that won so many awards and drew so many people into theaters? Of course there would be some disasters, but without taking chances there would be no successes either. There would be no Lars von Trier, for one.

The controversy continued to simmer unresolved through the summer of 2003 with some new wrinkles coming to the fore.

It had always been claimed that the "face-to-face" nature of negotiations between consultant and producer was an asset, but it appeared that the personal quality of this give-and-take could turn bad when things got, well . . . personal. And that they did in May of 2003 when a director alleged that his film was rejected after he refused to employ the consultant's actor friend in the lead role. The consultant denied it, but now the project was stranded with the producer standing to lose millions. A new consultant would be hired in the fall and they would resubmit it then, but in the meantime the entire system was once again being questioned.

The Dogme Studios—Zentropa and Nimbus

Two studios stand behind Dogme—Zentropa and Nimbus.

Zentropa was the first, and is today clearly the more prominent, of the two. It was the result of a relationship between Lars von Trier and Aalbæk Jensen that grew out of an encounter they had on the set of a commercial von Trier was shooting in February of 1988. Their paths had crossed once before, back when Aalbæk Jensen was a student at the Film School and von Trier had come by to introduce a screening of his favorite film, Dreyer's *Gertrud*, although at that point he made no particular impression on his future partner.

At that chance meeting in '88, von Trier asked Aalbæk Jensen if he would help him produce his next feature film, *Europa*, and Aalbæk Jensen said yes. They were both at rock bottom at that point and had little to lose. Aalbæk Jensen's production company, Fortuna Films, had just gone bankrupt after a disastrous involvement with the aforementioned *Perfect World*. And after the financial failures of *The Element of Crime* and particularly *Epidemic*, von Trier was himself, career-wise, bankrupt.[58] On top of it, nobody could stand him

*Originally a tobacco factory, pictured here is Zentropa's
first studio on Ryesgade in Copenhagen.*

because he was so hard to get along with. "So we clung to each other," recalled Aalbæk Jensen, "as if we were two shipwrecked castaways who held together in the belief that that would prevent us from drifting off into deeper waters."[59]

The Danish Film Institute would not grant funding to von Trier's little company, Element Film, to produce a relatively big film like *Europa*, so Nordisk Studio—where Aalbæk Jensen had coincidentally just been fired, allegedly for laziness[60]—produced it and Aalbæk Jensen was reinstalled in an office there in their old Valby complex (the oldest continually operating film studio in the world, actually).

Following the release of *Europa*, the two made plans to form their own film company together with Ib Tardini and Lene Børglum. It would be called Zentropa, after the train company in the film, and the main aim was to give von Trier total creative freedom with his next film, *Breaking the Waves*. Additionally, they hoped to be able to help other directors they admired make films in conditions more relaxed and humane than was usual in the dog-eat-dog film world.

On June 15, 1992, Zentropa officially took up residence in a building that had once been a tobacco factory on Ryesgade in the Copenhagen neighborhood of Østerbro. Von Trier now applied himself with diligence to the making of commercials, the profits from which they reinvested into film equipment.

In 1993, at Aalbæk Jensen's invitation, a film company called Nimbus joined them in the Ryesgade location. Nimbus' co-founders, Bo Ehrhardt and Birgitte Hald, were, like the Zentropa duo, both graduates of the Danish Film School, from the producer's line. Hald had gotten to know the two of them when she had worked on *Europa* as a student, and the move to the Ryesgade facility turned out to be a good one since it had more space than their first home, Empire studio (now a cinema) in the Nørrebro neighborhood. It was also fairly cheap and they could use Zentropa's equipment. A third company, Peter Bech Film, also had its offices in the building and they all shared certain facilities such as the cafeteria, etc.

Nimbus has maintained this equipment-sharing arrangement through the years, and by virtue of it Zentropa has secured co-producer status on all their films and owns a minority share of the company. There is a general misconception that Zentropa owns Nimbus, like they own for all intents and purposes, a lot of other independent companies, and in fact they did want to buy Nimbus at one point but Ehrhardt and Hald wanted to maintain their independence and refused to sell.

When Zentropa relocated to a vacant military barracks in Avedøre, dubbed "Film Town," in 1999, Nimbus went with them, and the two companies have maintained their symbiotic relationship ever since, with Nimbus typecast as the little brother studio. They have developed in more or less the same direction and generally share the same philosophy and approach to filmmaking, both occupying territory somewhere between art-house and mainstream. The arrangement has worked out well for Nimbus. They never had any desire to own their own equipment, and Zentropa doesn't meddle in their creative decisions the way most co-investors do. In return, Ehrhardt and Hald give their own directors total creative freedom.

Most of the directors working with Nimbus are local talent, graduates of the Danish Film School, with whom they tend to maintain loyal and long-lasting relationships. For example, they produced Thomas Vinterberg's 1994 short film, *The Boy Who Walked Backwards*, and his first feature, *The Greatest Heroes*, so it was only natural they should be in on Dogme from the beginning and share in the success of his Dogme breakthrough, *The Celebration*. Another director with whom they've worked closely from the start is Natasha Arthy of *Old, New, Borrowed and Blue*. They produced her short film, *Penny Penniless*, as well as her first feature, *Miracle*. With their willingness to produce shorts as well as features, they are in a position to help promising filmmakers get started. Ole Christian Madsen is another director they've worked closely with in this fashion, and the list goes on.

In this way Nimbus has, over the years, followed a somewhat more conservative path than big brother Zentropa, who regularly over-extend themselves with big international productions, who gamble more recklessly on untested talent, and who have more balls in the air at once. For example, over the course of Winter 2001–2002, Zentropa was shooting three films—von Trier's *Dogville*, Peter Fly's *The Inheritance*, and Lone Scherfig's *Wilbur Wants to Kill Himself*—a situation which gave Aalbæk Jensen, in his own words, nosebleeds due to his anxiety over how to pay all the bills the next day and keep it all running.[61]

While Nimbus recently produced two international English-language productions (Vinterberg's *It's All About Love* and Søren Kragh-Jacobsen's *Skagerrak*), they intend to stick to shorts and feature films for the Danish market and to feel their way forward with more care, to pick and choose their spots. Zentropa on the other hand is more scattershot. "Zentropa has a completely different structure, says Ehrhardt.[62]

> They have co-produced a lot, invested in equipment and worked from a studio concept. They have contributed their equipment to as many co-productions as possible and in that manner have accumulated rights to quite a few films. Peter and co. have obtained a 50/50 partnership in all possible companies. Aalbæk Jensen is extremely good at building up networks and contacts. He is charming and as naughty as a butcher's dog, and being the charismatic person that he is, he can plunge into anything.
>
> Our goal on the other hand is to have the lowest possible operating costs and thus to have the freedom to gamble our money on the films we believe in. Zentropa, to the contrary, has expanded outward, created some physical frames and afterwards has said to people, 'come and work with us!'. We have two different ways to go forward that work well together.

Today, the Zentropa octopus is attached to approximate 40 companies all across Europe and in the States. Their modular, decentralized structure gives an unusual amount of independence to producers and directors, and in the event that a big production goes belly up, it protects these independent units from getting dragged down in the wake. This cell structure has given Aalbæk Jensen occasion to quip that Zentropa is like some kind of underground terrorist group governed by a fractured command structure with everybody on a "need to know" basis.

His rhetorical excesses aside, Zentropa has become so accepted and respected in Denmark—even winning an honorary Bodil award—that no one dares to oppose them. Much to their own chagrin, everybody is showing them too *much* respect, leaving Aalbæk Jensen clearly nostalgic for the good old days when it was them against the world.

In the beginning we just wanted to be against. That suited us, and the tragic thing is that now people ought to be against us. One starts as a rebel and ends up as the person who ought to be hung upside-down like Mussolini. We think that today Zentropa gets too little opposition in the professional arena, and so we have been forced to create the opposition ourselves, and we have done that by easing off on our own power. We have created a mass of separate units, firms and production entities that in principal are autonomous inside the frame of Zentropa. We don't interfere with what they make, and at the

Since 1999, Zentropa and Nimbus Studios have been located here, in a former military staging ground in a suburban area south of Copenhagen known as Film Town.

moment the whole milieu is flourishing. It has shown to be the case that after Lars and I have stopped meddling so much, we get more quality in our films and make more money into the bargain.[63]

Zentropa is today the largest studio in Scandinavia in terms of output and has almost single-handedly created a kind of hot-house atmosphere in Danish film. Its product line is diverse: everything from Dogme to mainstream comedies to children's films to borderline underground pictures and "difficult" art-house films like *Portland* (1996). Yet the *quality* of their product varies widely. They have produced big hits like *Italian for Beginners* and *Open Hearts,* but also staggering flops like *Charlie Butterfly* (2002) which, as noted, drew only 284 customers. One might perhaps wonder if they aren't sometimes a bit too "hands off."

Specifically regarding Dogme, it was Nimbus that produced the first two big hits, *The Celebration* and *Mifune,* while Zentropa stood behind von Trier's polarizing *The Idiots* and Kristian Levring's praised but commercially marginal *The King is Alive.* Zentropa would go on to score the next two big hits, *Italian for Beginners* and *Open Hearts,* but with Dogme investment partner, Danmarks Radio, taking a third of all proceeds, the profit from Dogme is not as big as one might assume from all the hype. And Danish studios have very little clout outside Denmark, so in most cases they have to settle for very unfavorable distribution deals. *The Celebration,* for example cost 7.5 million kroner (1 million USD) to make and earned a whopping 90 million kroner (12 million USD) internationally, but when expenses and cuts to foreign distributors were made there was approximately only 9 million kroner (1.2 million USD) left.[64] Nimbus shot that back into the company and also made Vinterberg (who Zentropa once tried to steal away[65]) a co-owner of the firm. Zentropa claims they had the same kind of disappointing returns on *Dancer in the Dark.* Then again, one never hears a company boasting about making huge profits since the DFI would immediately want to see some payback.

As for day-to-day conditions at the two studios, the smaller and quieter confines of Nimbus actually feel like film company offices, while the spiritual vibes over at Zentropa give it the flavor of something more akin to a cult religion. Maybe a kind of happier version of Jonestown. Aalbæk Jensen leads Friday morning sing-alongs in the cafeteria, and with his own patented mix of inspirational oratory and bitingly ironic humor, cultivates (or attempts to) a spirit of discipline, loyalty, and solidarity, which has prompted some in the industry to label it "Zentropologi" (e.g. "Scientology").

Postscript—Zentropa

In November of 2002, Zentropa found itself once again in the eye of a media storm as two separate controversies competed for column space in the Danish press. As usual, it was Peter Aalbæk Jensen doing all the talking while von Trier remained silent.

One of the imbroglios dealt with allegations of unethically close personal ties between Aalbæk Jensen and a number of DFI employees and consultants (see "Danish Film Institute—postscript" chapter), while the other stemmed from charges raised back in May by the Danish Actor's Union that Zentropa was not paying actors residuals. The Union specifically claimed that Zentropa had failed to pay actors from *The Idiots* residuals from the normally lucrative French and Italian markets, and instead had "parked" or hidden the money in one of their foreign companies.

It wasn't the first time that doubts had been cast on their bookkeeping practices: Back in 1998, allegations had surfaced that Zentropa had "sheltered" profits from *Breaking the Waves* with its foreign companies to avoid paying back public grant support to the DFI. Aalbæk Jensen had in fact once remarked that Zentropa's international web of over 40 foreign subsidiaries could appear to be a bit "Cayman Islands-like," but countered that many of these companies were merely inactive holding rights entities. Now the Cayman Islands comparison was starting to look more credible to some. Was Zentropa just playing a shell game as politicians and DFI officials looked on like rubes about to be taken?

By agreement between the actor's and producer's unions, 10% of all profits of a film earned in foreign markets was to be disbursed as residuals among the actors. Films by Lars von Trier usually played particularly well in the French and Italian markets, and yet five years after the release of *The Idiots*, the actors hadn't received a penny from those territories. The idiots were starting to feel like chumps. Hadn't a couple of them chuckled out loud when during the shooting of the film von Trier had wisecracked that they had to keep in mind that "There is a goal greater than ourselves—Zentropa's income."[66] Now it looked like the joke was on them.

It was a bitter pill for at least some of the actors to swallow since Zentropa had convinced them to accept lower-than-average pay in lieu of a healthy residual check down the road. After all, this was a "Lars von Trier film" they were told, and his pictures always played strong in foreign markets. They went along with it, just as actors in all the first Dogme films went along with low pay, all in the spirit of being part of this exciting new (low budget) movement.

Peter Aalbæk Jensen loved to talk about his past as a communist and old hippie, and frequently pointed out how modestly he and von Trier lived, but allegations about the firm's financial dealings painted a decidedly different picture, the picture of a company acting in the worst traditions of corporate arrogance and secretiveness. Was Zentropa the Che Guevara of the Danish film world—or the Microsoft?

The studio could play hardball when it wanted. As noted, they had done so when negotiating with the actors from *Italian for Beginners*, who were expected to also play in *Wilbur Wants to Kill Himself* and got the shaft instead. And now these allegations about the residuals from *The Idiots* had been submitted for arbitration. The whole situation poisoned at least temporarily the relationship between Zentropa and Danish actors at large, some of whom were now even hiring agents to represent them in contract negotiations—to this point a far from common practice in the Danish film world.

Specifically regarding the case of *The Idiots*, Zentropa had transferred the rights for the French, Italian, and Swiss markets to a company called Liberator Productions, which had invested in the film. What the actors didn't know was that Zentropa owned 50% of the company and Vibeke Windeløv owned 25%, in essence giving Zentropa a 75% share of the company.[67] Zentropa used this model to finance all of von Trier's films and plenty of others.

Commenting in the November 10, 2002 issue of *Berlingske*, Windeløv rejected the assertion that Liberator had any obligation to pay actors residuals, stating that Liberator's function was to accumulate money in France that would go to von Trier's next film.

Aalbæk Jensen, defiant as usual, countered that if anyone got paid more, it should be the directors, and that if arbitration went against them, Danish actors could kiss goodbye any hopes of landing parts in Zentropa's big international feature films. Furthermore, he fumed, this 10% royalty rate was absurd. "There is no place in the world where film producers pay such a big percentage of profits of a film to actors as in Denmark. No foreign partner will agree to that."[68]

The rate was high, agreed the foreman for the Danish Actor's Union, Henrik Petersen, "but there is also no place in the world where a film actor's daily wage is so low."

A mere three days after the story hit the press, Aalbæk Jensen and von Trier were threatening to leave Denmark, as bold headlines in the November 13th issue of *Berlingske* trumpeted. Or in any case they'd move their international productions out of the country. "Danish actors are too expensive," claimed Aalbæk Jensen, taking the opportunity to also blow off steam about the unfavorable Danish tax codes and the unfairness of being expected to pay back state support if a film turned a profit. They would go to Scotland, or Sweden, or . . . somewhere. "We'll pack a little sack, put it on a stick, throw it over the shoulder and head off down that country road."

It was hardly the first time they had threatened to leave Denmark and likely wouldn't be the last, but rarely had they expressed it so poetically.

For their part, few actors wanted to be quoted in the exposés, understandable since it could damage future job prospects in a field in which Zentropa occupied such a central position. However, Mads Mikkelsen, who was so popular he need not fear retribution, did offer his thoughts on the subject to the daily *Information.* "When we negotiate with producers we always hear the same old song that there is no money in the production, and thus far Danish actors have not seen much money from the great Dogme film successes. It is as if it was the 11th Dogme rule that actors must be under paid."[69]

Peter Aalbæk Jensen—Dogme Mother

While Lars von Trier's business partner, Peter Aalbæk Jensen, is virtually unknown to the international public, he is certainly already well known to readers of this book as well as to virtually every man, woman, and child in Denmark whoever happened to pick up a newspaper. Every inch of his cluttered office has been photographed over the years as eager shutter-bugs from the press stood in line to snap his picture while he posed in every conceivable position. In the space of ten years

Peter Aalbæk Jensen on the prowl at Cannes 1998.

he has gone from being a complete unknown to being a highly visible and controversial figure with a battle-tested ability to provoke, irritate, and intrigue—and not least to make movies.

Soon after he founded Zentropa film studio with von Trier in 1992 as a 50/50 partnership, he began to adopt the exaggerated persona of the hard-ass, cigar chomping studio boss, a crass "uncultured idiot," to use his own phrase, who delighted in toying with journalists and attacking the powers that be, regardless of whether it was to his own advantage. It was a role partly forced on him by his press-shy partner's refusal to be any kind of spokesman, and partly the result of his own belief that any press was good press.

Ten years and 1,001 publicity stunts later, he has reached the same dizzying heights of celebrity as that other legendary eccentric of the Danish business world, Simon Spies, the late high-stakes gambler who pioneered the low-cost, package vacation industry in Denmark, and who, in a state of advanced age, was invariably surrounded by a bevy of busty blondes who were usually nude on top it, if the press photos were anything to go on.

Aalbæk Jensen's conquests in the film world, if not the sexual sphere, are equally as impressive. While von Trier largely attended to his own creative concerns, Aalbæk Jensen attended to business and turned little Zentropa into the most diversified and productive studio in Scandinavia. He kept the firm in the black even as the near collapse of big films like *Breaking the Waves* and *Dancer in the Dark* threatened to drag it under, and he never lost his taste for taking a risk. For a man who claims he is so bad at accounting that customers have to help him add up the numbers so he doesn't cheat himself, this is not bad.

In the autumn of 2001, an oral biography, entitled *Without Cigar*, was published about him by journalist Kirsten Jacobsen, and finally Danes had access to a somewhat more nuanced picture of a man whom it seemed was never quite what he appeared to be.

Jacobsen queries Aalbæk Jensen about all possible subjects in a diversity of settings. She follows along as he gives a speech to an association of entrepreneurs, as he roams the studio, as he cooks dinner, and as he lays on a couch in his office and talks to the ceiling. She balances out the material by interviewing all manner of participants in his private and professional life and succeeds in presenting a well-rounded portrait.

For one thing, he's not nearly as bad at numbers-crunching as he pretends, although the actual nature of his true talent is the subject of much speculation. A general consensus emerges that he is skilled at getting people to see things his way, to read moods, to put folks at ease, and to tailor his message to the recipient, whether he's dealing with film buyers from Japan, America, or Armenia. Behind the ironic and self-depreciating facade lurks a skilled, relentless and sometimes mer-

Without Cigar, *Kirsten Jacobsen's oral biography of Peter Aalbæk Jensen.*

ciless negotiator who apparently hasn't been nicknamed "The Eel" by his Danish colleagues for nothing.

There are interviews with his wife, brother, childhood friend, parents-in-law, friends of the family, competitors, business partners, and von Trier himself as well as arch enemy, Henning Camre, whose leadership of the Danish Film Institute he savagely attacked in the press for years. It is no surprise to discover that he is more complex than the cardboard image he himself likes to project.

His relationship with von Trier also comes into focus, and it appears to be more a marriage of convenience than a "meeting of the minds," if no less fruitful for it. When they first joined forces in 1988, Aalbæk Jensen was no great fan of von Trier's work, unable to even sit through his first film, *The Element of Crime*, or to much appreciate his second, *Epidemic*. Yet Zentropa was first and foremost created to give von Trier total artistic control over his films and Aalbæk Jensen has proven loyal to the cause, duteously backing and producing pictures like *The Idiots* which he never understood or liked, as well as the risky, experimental work, *Dogville,* which he termed "insane" when he first heard about it,[70] finding it too minimalist for words. For his part, Aalbæk Jensen is grateful von Trier never jumped ship and signed on with a foreign producer who could offer him bigger budgets. Exactly how much input he has on the creative formation of von Trier's films remains uncertain. Despite his cavalier claims that he never reads scripts, he obviously wields some influence, but the book gives precious little insight into the actual working process between the two.

Jacobsen's questions are on occasion tough and pointed, but the bulk of what we get from the other interviewees is unqualified praise, and even Henning Camre bends over backwards to be charitable to his persistent nemesis.

Ironically, it is Zentropa producer Vibeke Windeløv who comes the closest to being brutally frank about the cigar-puffing subject of the book. Aalbæk Jensen put the brakes on her plans to form a sister company called "Internationale." The idea was that Internationale would make the international films and she would own 50% of the company. "All possible charlatans who come along can easily get a 50-50 arrangement with Peter, while we who work ourselves to the bone 24 hours a day for Zentropa never can," she complains, further stung by the fact that he questioned her loyalty in the bargain. Windeløv also finds it galling that he is given all the credit for everything Zentropa accomplishes when in fact producers like she and Ib Tardini do a great deal of the work.

The resentment of co-workers is perhaps to be expected, but more surprising is the fact that animosity for Aalbæk Jensen and Zentropa does exist in the Danish film world, yet the reader never gets insight into this.

For example, Jacobsen tells Camre at one point that, "I have had contact with many young people in the film milieu who unfortunately don't openly dare to criticize Zentropa and Peter Aalbæk Jensen because, with or without justification, they are afraid that it might damage their future career prospects." Unfortunately, we get little follow up on this type of thing and perhaps too much on his upbringing, his family life, and his marital relationship. Some of the focus on his youth no doubt owes to the fact that his father, the priest Erik Aalbæk Jensen, was one of the most popular Danish authors of the post-war period (and, as we discover, a tyrant and a philanderer), but how many readers could really care to hear about all his teenage crushes? This extensive investigation into even the most obscure corners of his personal life is testimony to the degree of celebrity he has achieved. He has become a kind of tabloid figure who transcends the world of film and is well known even to Danes who never go to the movies.

The book seemed to lay to rest his long feud with the DFI and as of 2003 Aalbæk Jensen appears to be a bit more grounded if as unpredictable and outspoken as ever. He is, when all is said and done, a classic Danish personality. He wages a daily and very public battle to defy "Jante Law" Denmark,[71] and while his contentious and willfully egocentric act would flop in Hollywood, it plays well at home. At the same time, his success in bringing Danish film culture to foreign markets has made his countrymen proud, and his stock assortment of jibes—such as his boast that America will soon have to impose a quota on the importation of Danish films to protect Hollywood—play well in the press. He is a bit like the short kid at school who has to shout louder to get the same respect, an analogy that can be applied to him personally as well as to his position as an ambassador for Danish film and Danish culture out in the wider world. He's got the respect now but he keeps shouting because it's the only form of communication he knows.

He has become a revered figure and his studio has become an institution in the film world, and both of these facts cause him endless agitation. He must try all the harder to remain prickly, irreverent, and sacrilegious, but today too many people are laughing along at his jokes even before he gets to the punchline.

Vibeke Windeløv and Ib Tardini—Zentropa's Dynamic Duo

In a day-to-day operational sense, no one is more valuable to Lars von Trier than favorite producer and kindred spirit, Vibeke Windeløv, who together with three staffers runs her own department inside Zentropa. She does much more than simply find money for his films. She reads his scripts, gives encouragement and advice, and receives trophies and awards on behalf of the notoriously travel-shy director, as well as deal with the press when he's mad at them or just can't be bothered. It's not just a professional relationship but also a personal one: After his wife gave birth five years ago, she was the first person allowed in to see the little family.

Windeløv got her first film production experience back in 1976 on the set of a film being shot by her boyfriend and later husband, the artist, Per Kirkeby. (Kirkeby had previously made a number of short films as a member of ABC Cinema group, and he created the artificial-light landscapes used in *Breaking the Waves*.) The film was *The Norsemen* and Windeløv proved her mettle by supplying him on short notice with 600 gratis walk-ons. After that experience, she was sold on the business.

Almost ten years later she was asked to produce *Epidemic*. As she recalls:

> *I was asked if I would produce* Epidemic, *but I was working on another film at that point and didn't have time. I only knew Lars second-hand back then and he seemed to be spoiled rotten and was always scolding people . . . much has happened with him since and he has become much more mature. But in the beginning it was insanely difficult. I experienced a Lars who was unpleasant, sophomoric and sarcastic. The whole time. One could never relax with him.*[72]

Years later, after the formation of Zentropa, she came on board at the last minute to produce Susanne Bier's *Family Matters* (1993) and stayed. She went on to become von Trier's resident producer and produced *Breaking the Waves*, *The Idiots*, *Dancer in the Dark*, and *Dogville*. Aalbæk Jensen gave von Trier the security he needed, and she gave him the support he needed. And equally as important to their working relationship, she knew how to deal with his outbursts and sometimes lacerating sense of humor. She apparently never challenges his creative decisions too directly while still—according to her—being forward enough to disagree on occasion and give him constructive criticism. Aalbæk Jensen on the other hand, from all evidence, almost never raises creative questions about von Trier's films-in-progress. How much tough advice von Trier gets or wants on his films in their formative stages from *anybody* is very much an open question. He's always been extremely confident in his own creative decisions, and it's unlikely he's softened much there.

As Zentropa grew, Windeløv became the company's increasingly not so secret weapon, however fated she was to labor in the shadow of the controversial and attention-grabbing Aalbæk Jensen. Yet many of those in-the-know in the film world tend to credit her talent and efforts, rather than his smoke blowing shenanigans, for the company's success.[73]

She hasn't had it easy. Von Trier, for one, was never known as Mr. Predictable, but over the years she's become better at dealing with complicated personalities (maybe because she is surrounded by them). Her ability to put out fires would stand her in good sted on several occasions. She was there at ground-zero during the great filterization scandal when, following the release of *The Idiots,* von Trier went ballistic after discovering that she and Aalbæk Jensen had ordered the lightening of release prints—a breech of Dogme rule #5.

And then there was the traumatic production process of *Dancer in the Dark* when she was forced to deal with their unpredictable star, Björk. Von Trier and Aalbæk Jensen were, for their part, both badly rattled by the behavior of the Icelandic pop singer. Lars was continually on the point of a nervous breakdown and Aalbæk Jensen (who later boasted that he never exchanged a single word with her) went around in a tizzy declaring that he was going to shoot her.[74] Thus it fell to Windeløv to spend countless hours and days trying to coax, cajole, and convince her to get with the program. Ultimately for Windeløv too, the go-rounds with Björk left lasting scars, and despite winning the Palme d'Or, she looks back at the whole experience as hugely unpleasant. But everyone survived, if just.

Zentropa seems to have continuing use for Windeløv's brand of diplomacy. A recent example was the "firing" of Nicole Kidman in the international press on July 24, 2001. Aalbæk Jensen, still haunted by their dealings with Björk and infuriated by what he saw as Kidman's delaying tactics, confided thusly to the Danish press about his decision:

> *Lars has begged me to make sure that he doesn't come into the same situation he had with Björk, because he cannot show sufficient firmness and consistency with his female cast members. I thereby feel myself obliged to throw the brakes. We are of course sorry not to get her in the film, but when contract negotiations play out like that,[75] I simply dare go no further. Björk was close to shutting down our company. Apparently von Trier does not function well with women, but we can hope that we are just as lucky as with* Breaking the Waves *where Helena Bonham Carter left the production at the last*

minute and we had the enormous luck with her replacement, Emily Watson.[76]

Windeløv, on vacation in Northern Italy at the time, had in fact received Kidman's signed contract some days prior, and Aalbæk Jensen was forced into an embarrassing climb-down and obliged to "re-hire" her the next day.

"What can I say . . . !?", Windeløv responded when queried about the incident,[77] "Peter is, after all, an excellent PR man, gradually even better than Simon Spies. But I would have rather used my vacation on something other than to talk on the mobile telephone until four in the morning in order to explain to the American agents who the hell Peter Aalbæk Jensen is. . . ."

In regards to Dogme, Windeløv's credentials are in order. She has produced about half of the Dogme films that Zentropa has made (#2, #4, and #8).

The other half (#5, #6, and #10) were produced by Ib Tardini.

Tardini is another one of Zentropa's unsung heroes. As a public figure he happily surrenders center stage to the flamboyant Aalbæk Jensen and the stylish and very visible Windeløv, but purely in terms of producing movies his recent success is hard to match. He's produced hits like *Minor Mishaps*, *The Bench*, and *The Inheritance*, while his Dogme production credits include *Truly Human*, *Italian for Beginners* and the upcoming picture by Annette K. Olesen, *In Your Hands*.

The son of Denmark's first television cook (his mom), Tardini was as a youth an exceptionally unmotivated student, thrown out in the 7th grade to continue his schooling in a series of alternative environments, including a school ship. Following this period, he worked various blue-collar jobs and became acquainted with different social environments. This gave him a class consciousness which he has to this day.

In an effort to have some impact on the world, he became a teacher, but he soon came to the conclusion that the mass media had usurped the roles of parents and educators alike and he began to make films instead, eventually becoming a producer.

Through the late '70s and '80s he produced political films and folk comedies as well as serious pictures for directors like Søren Kragh-Jacobsen and Bille August. But after producing *The Pain of Love* for Niels Malmros in 1992, his company went out of business. He was ready to throw in the towel; he had produced over 60 films at that point and on top of it was facing what he thought was a potentially terminal illness.

But then he ran into one Peter Aalbæk Jensen who convinced him to participate in the foundation of a new studio, and the two of them and Lars and a woman named Lene Børglum founded Zentropa. The most important thing for him was to get back his enthusiasm for the medium. And he got it back—in spades. Everybody had a whole new attitude at this company. His second career was launched and the bearded, quiet-spoken Tardini found a renewed sense of purpose in doing what he does best, quietly and effectively producing films and leaving the partying and grandstanding to others.

He is a "hands-on" producer who goes into the creative process with the director, but his main aim is to give them peace-of-mind, to set the frames in place without trying to make the project his. "I consult with a lot of directors 'on the way,'" he elaborates, "but at a given point I pull myself out of the process for a stretch of time in order to be able to see the project from the outside, with fresh eyes. And then I go back into it again very actively. The important thing is to be able to feel when it is okay to disturb a director and when not to . . . And then I go into the editing suite with the director for the last three weeks of the process. It's in the editing suite when the film becomes magic."[78]

Together, Tardini and Windeløv deserve a lion's share of the credit not just for the Dogme films Zentropa has produced, but for the company's success in general.

Mogens Rukov—The Mad Professor of Dogme

The sixty year old Mogens Rukov, mentioned repeatedly in these pages, is central not only to the Dogme story but also to Danish cinema in general via his position as the manuscript teacher at the Film School where he has had a weighty influence on many of the established and emerging talents. He has been called "the chief ideologue behind the Dogme concept,"[79] and even though that mantle more rightly belongs to Lars von Trier, Rukov's contributions loom large. He co-wrote and/or advised on the first three Dogme films, in addition to #7, and prior to that had a close collaborative relationship with the movement's two founders, having co-written Vinterberg's *The Greatest Heroes* as well as his current *It's All About Love,* and consulted on scripts to von Trier's *The Element of Crime* and *Breaking the Waves,* among other films. He will no doubt continue to work closely with his two former students, as well as to lecture and write about Dogme in and outside of Denmark.

With his bushy beard, often unkempt mane of hair, and an intense gaze that at first glance can be perceived as hostile, the otherwise short, slender Rukov can come across as gruff and menacing, "a fright in human form"[80] as one writer phrased it, "the possessor of a slumbering temper but also a man who at the same time can express enjoyment and sensitivity."[81] He is one of the more colorful personalities of the Danish cultural scene and his opinions, occasionally conveyed in the form of editorials, often have nothing to do with film. He is, for example, outspoken on Jewish issues and doesn't shy away from accusing his countrymen of being anti-semitic, and he was 100% in favor of the war in Iraq.

Rukov was born in the provincial Jutland town of Holstebro in 1943 and the next day delivered to an orphanage. He never knew his real parents. Eight months later he was adopted and given a proper upbringing. He was well-behaved, diligent, and good at school, much to his parent's obvious satisfaction. His mother, as he recalls,[82] was over-attentive, over-protective. It was a happy enough childhood, but later in life, as his mother grew older, she became senile and it was tough. "When I would go to visit her at the Home," he remembers, "she would always say to me, 'Mogens, you know the girls really like you.' And that was my signal to reply, 'Mom, the boys also really like you.' . . . she had been very beautiful in her youth."

As a teenager he grew long hair and became a Marxist—"a lame rebellion," he says.

He entered University and studied Scandinavian philology and film. He got married and had a child. For periods he drank heavily. He was a troubled young man who experienced bouts of restlessness and thought (and thinks) mostly about women. He was no "super achiever" type at this point and also no writer, claiming to have suffered a writer's block since the fifth grade.

Then one day at University he had to start writing a thesis. He pulled down the curtains and started to write, on a rigid schedule, five pages a day. He never re-read what he wrote lest he discover how awful it was and end up with an inferiority complex when he didn't measure up to the literary greats. He didn't refer to any books, he just wrote what he knew and remembered. He got a friend to re-write it and shape it up. Out of this came a 90-page thesis, but more importantly he worked his way out of his writing block and over to writing fiction where he found his voice.

Rukov's writing style today—judging from his editorials, not his scripts—is an impressionistic, staccato style characterized by swarms of short declarative sentences that seem to spring from pure impulse, pure instinct. He is, as Jesper Jargil commented, in possession of an "intuitive recklessness,"[83] and this has kept Dogme honest and vital, at least so far as his influence extends. This intuitive recklessness is his gift and lesson to Dogme. One can perhaps to a certain degree say that it also works its way into his verbal style. As Jargil recalled after a long interview with him for *The Purified*, "He's capable of talking pure nonsense for half an hour at a stretch, but when he hits the spot he is divine."[84]

He graduated University with a Masters degree in Scandinavian literature. Following this he worked for a number of years as a teacher and head-master of a language school for refugees. It was there he met a student, a nice looking Jewish girl from Poland, who became his second wife. This marriage lasted 27 years.

Rukov's employment by the Film School in 1975 as a manuscript teacher ironically had little to do with his previous involvement with writing, and as he himself admits, he didn't know particularly much about film,[85] and knew nothing at all about how a film was made in a practical sense. He got the job, rather, on the strength of his teaching and leadership experience at the language school. He did find, however, that what he had learned at University about structural analysis came in useful here.

Despite his lack of film knowledge he was a good fit. He came on board the same year the new headmaster, Henning Camre, was hired and things began to turn around at the School. In 1985, Rukov founded the manuscript department and gradually became something of a cult figure at the School and in broader cultural circles. And his own writing got better and better. "Today," he philosophized to reporter Nils Thorsen in a November 2000 interview, "I write rather well. And I believe that is a result of all the many attempts. I can remember others at University who wrote insanely beautifully but whose writing I think quickly became very, very thin. Writing must evidently not come too easily. . . . one must have a feeling of all the holes in the language and all that is illogical about it in order to become really good. For example, it is almost impossible to discern the difference in writing style from one journalist to the next. I believe that owes to the fact that they all too quickly develop an ability to write in an easy and carefree way. Consequently you can say just about anything at all to them and they just sit themselves down and . . . churn it out."

"After 28 years, has it become routine?" asked Thorsen.

"Not at all!" replied Rukov. "For one thing I'm very bad about saving notes. I *have* no notes. I *can* not repeat myself. For I have nothing to repeat . . . the thing is, when I have prepared myself, I have already narrowed the possibilities. When I haven't prepared myself, I draw on the whole of the experience list."

Rukov's teaching philosophy—to "liberate" himself from preparation in order to facilitate improvisation—is of course echoed in Dogme, and, taken a step further, this philosophy constitutes an unwritten tenant of the movement which maintains that the director should liberate himself from the script in order to take advantage of the opportunities that chance encounters present.

The essential thing to remember is that Dogme is no game of chance. To allow oneself to be "ambushed by the moment" actually requires a great amount of talent and all the instinct and experience a director can possibly accumulate. One's instincts have to be honed to a sharp edge and one has to disconnect from one's own ego—to avoid the trap of thinking that "this is the greatest script in the world and I will be the greatest director in the world." This kind of filmmaking requires a willingness to depart from the script in the event that something else better comes along. It requires the patience to wait for it, the vision to see it and the wisdom not to force it. It is not a path for cowards or glory seekers or directors primarily interested in making a great career for themselves.

This is the approach constantly articulated and promoted by Rukov, and yet ironic and certainly self-defeating it would seem to be for a manuscript teacher to tell a director that he should "free" himself from the script!

One could say that Rukov has departed from the script in his personal life. And all for the better, since he seems to be today, for all his wildness of appearance and mannerism, a more grounded individual. He agrees with that.

"When I was young I thought the chaos was inside me and that the world was in harmony. Now I think that I function perfectly and that it is the world that's going to hell."

In November 2002, Rukov published a collection of his essays and articles entitled, *The Celebration and Other Scandals*, and gave Danish critics the opportunity to pay tribute to his peculiar mastery of intellectual issues. *The Genius Lunatic* ran the headline of *Berlingske's* November 13th review, penned by Ebbe Iversen.

"Has any person ever completely straight-out understood what Mogens Rukov means? Hardly, but in a way that doesn't matter. As a mentor, guru, and source of inspiration, Rukov has had a colossal and constructive influence on Danish film art over the course of the last years. . . . To read a massive book of articles and essays by Mogens Rukov is, in the mean time, another and more difficult case. Those who have heard him give lectures know that he can talk for hours without pause, and that is more or less the way he also writes. His style is intense, flighty, philosophical, unbridled, illusive, penetrating and manic. In other words, thought-provoking and, to no less a degree, exhausting."

Jørgen Leth—The Obstructed Man

The 66-year-old journalist, poet, and filmmaker, Jørgen Leth, is a popular and respected figure in Danish cultural circles. He has published collections of essays and volumes of poetry, written for radio and television and has for years been a guest lecturer at the Danish Film School. A member of the previously noted ABC Cinema group, he started making films in the early '60s and has had a significant influence on Denmark's current generation of filmmakers both because of what he has done and what he is doing.

After graduation from the Danish equivalent of high school, Leth wrote for a number of dailies, primarily about jazz and later about film. He interviewed directors such as Godard and Antonioni and became intrigued by the possibilities of film as a visual medium. He had by now already published his first collection of poems, and he carried over his feel for storytelling honed in the poetic style to his first short films.

In an August 15, 2002, interview in *Jyllands-Posten*, he ruminated about how poetry had influenced his film language, and it is not difficult to see the parallels to Dogme.

> There is a great overlap between my poems and my films. Poetry is the purest form of expression because one can write directly without having to employ any form of defense. Poetry is a spontaneous expression, and I have attempted to bring the same spontaneity to film. I have always sought a film poetry where the end product was just as direct as a poem. I will not permit technology to block what I am trying to express, and

*I have always worked best when the inspiration came directly
from the heart to the hand.*

Leth has never figured as a part of the commercial filmmaking
world. He is best known for his short experimental films and for his
later-period documentaries that span a range of subjects from investi-
gations into the mythology of sport and eroticism to films that deal
with the creation of art to explorations into foreign cultures and value
systems. *66 Scenes from America* (1981), is a kind of fiercely subjective
travelogue that belongs to the latter category. It's a mix of events,
things, people, thoughts, and feelings, a stream-of-consciousness
investigation of the mythology of America in its many guises. In one
notable scene, Andy Warhol eats a hamburger.

With the assistance of his long-time cameraman, Dan Holmberg,
Leth recently completed a re-make of the film, entitled *New Scenes
from America* (which premiered in conjunction with a Jørgen Leth retrospective held September 12–18 (2002) at the Museum of Modern
Art in New York and was also selected for Sundance 2003). Leth is well

Andy Warhol eats a hamburger in Jørgen Leth's documentary, 66 Scenes from America.

regarded in foreign avant-garde circles and he was able to shoot scenes with cult figures such as Dennis Hopper, the filmmaker Robert Frank, the poet, John Ashbury, and John Cale who supplied music for the film. America is a source of great curiosity and a rich lode of mythology for most Danes, and in a way Leth lives out their dreams: Who wouldn't want to go over and travel around America and capture one's adventure on film—and meet all the coolest people in the bargain? Leth can, thanks in part to a life-long grant he received in 1995 from the Danish Arts Foundation.

Among his early experimental pieces, he is best known for the 13-minute film from 1967, *The Perfect Human.* In it an attractive young couple act out the rituals of daily life with all the premeditated stiffness of display objects or life-size puppets. These are the "perfect humans," the sum of their generation's preconditioned desires and expectations. They play their parts as the flesh-and-blood mechanisms of a consumer society on cruise control: They wear nice clothes, they eat, they talk, they drink wine, they show affection—all of it in a cold and spartanly furnished studio setting where the glare of direct lighting emphasizes the almost scientific nature of the investigation. The measured and dispassionate narration contributes to the sense that this is some kind of lab exercise. It's a biting sociological satire on the shallowness of life among the Danish middle-class of 1967, as well as an ironic comment on the tendency of documentary filmmakers to blindly worship the gospel of objectivity. Von Trier, for his part, has seen the film many times over and has told Leth that he considers *The Perfect Human* to be a nearly perfect film.

Leth's work always challenged the accepted wisdoms and status quo of the day in terms of art, politics, and the film form itself. He was something of the same kind of rebel von Trier would become, but a generation earlier. The two had much in common and they would become good friends, a friendship based on mutual admiration.

While Leth was not officially in on the formulation of Dogme, he was in every sense a "fellow traveler." His experiments in film structure and the language of cinema and his refusal to rely on the technical wizardry of the medium clearly had an influence on von Trier. Leth challenged himself every time he made a movie, challenged all his own preconceptions and assumptions and always came up with something different. His influence is felt on von Trier's more experimental work, from Dogme 95 to *Dogville*.

When on May 6, 2002, von Trier launched his Dogumentary movement, transposing the merciless discipline of Dogme to the documentary genre, Leth was there, along with von Trier's uncle, Børge Høst, and *Politiken* editor, Tøger Seidenfaden. All four contributed a manifesto (see appendix) to the launch of the movement, everything laid out in that day's edition of *Berlingske*. Leth's manifesto, an abstract rumination on the illusive nature of reality, penned April 11, 2000, in Paris (and translated by author) reads in full:

The Moment is Found

What I like most in a film is when one can feel time flow through a single scene. There should always be room for time. A film should breathe naturally. When we go out, it is to set a trap for reality, to lure it into the frame we have constructed. We are calm, attentive and expectant. Things happen when they will happen. We are just as wise and just as stupid as fishermen. We can go out in any defined direction and once in a while we will stumble upon that magic moment. That is what we are after but we must not be too eager or too certain about it. It will not come when we strain for it, or when we have use for it.

Experience tells us it exists. In our own work we are armed with instinct, with our eyes and our ears. We involve ourselves with the empty spaces as well as spaces that are full. We listen to the silence and the noise. We trust in the limitless gifts that chance presents us with, and yet the spot that we have positioned ourselves in is not completely accidental. The moment comes suddenly but we are not surprised by its arrival. We are there. We are ready to capture it. To corral it. We don't know where it will lead us.

> *We follow along, we'll see where it takes us, what it will show us. We see it take form and come together but we must contain it while it is still flowing and not too defined. We would willingly have it sing, have it explain itself. It is as if we are in love. A feeling has hit us, we try to grasp its meaning as it moves elusively by us, and yet we are afraid of losing it again by understanding it too well.*

Leth's involvement in von Trier's Dogumentary movement was born out of his belief that exciting things were happening with the genre.

> *The documentary film is in a fruitful and changing period. Experiments are now taking place and there is hope for renewal. That's where it is all happening at the moment, in the documentary genre. . . . Some of the best American directors are now using reality directly in their films. Film directors over most of the world have entered into this exciting territory where fiction is mixed with documentary, where borders are crossed.*[86]

The first direct collaboration between Leth and von Trier to spring out of all this was the experimental film entitled *The Five Obstructions*. In it Leth would re-shoot *The Perfect Human* five times in different versions that would take place in different locations around the world, each time with a new set of severe preconditions (technical, moral, or other type) supplied by a teasingly sadistic von Trier.

For the first version, von Trier had Leth shoot in Cuba, reportedly because he knew he didn't like Cuba, and the hindrances for this 2-day shoot were of a technical nature. The second version was shot in Bombay, India in August of 2002 and the preconditions this time were of a moral nature. Here Leth himself would consume the famous meal of fish and wine, clad in suit and bow-tie and seated at a table in the middle of a teaming Bombay street. After each version Leth and von Trier would discuss the results, their give-and-take recorded on video and edited into the film. These hindrances were an attempt to force Leth to think on his feet, to economize and improvise in the same way that the Vow of Chastity attempted to force filmmakers to use limitations as creative fuel, to make the most of serendipitous encounters and to incorporate these moments into their films.

The whole thing was an entertaining and challenging play, as Leth described it in interviews over the course of the summer of 2002.

> *I have always liked to be able to play in my work. When I start a film it makes me very happy if I do not know where it will end up. . . . One is forced to be inventive and creative if one is to slide or dribble around von Trier's tackles. But the most satisfying thing about it is that it becomes a reinvention of the film language, of film grammar. That is something that has always interested me, reinvention of the language. In this respect I greatly admire von Trier for daring to make a film as radical as* Dogville.[87]

Leth re-drew the playing rules for his own life in 1991 when, in the midst of one depression and with three marriages (that had produced four children) behind him, he suddenly moved to Haiti to get away, be alone and rebuild himself. Today he lives seven months out of the year there, but when back in Denmark he can often be seen on the streets of Copenhagen's "homiest" neighborhood, Vesterbro, giving readings in boho performance spaces or attending a punk film festival in the beat confines of the basement Terra Nova club. He retains a kind of "street credibility" that the thoroughly suburbanized von Trier lacks in spades, and has remained extremely active and productive.

Tómas Gislason—Beyond Dogme

Although he hasn't made a Dogme film, Lars von Trier's long-time creative partner, Tómas Gislason, has contributed to the formation of the Dogme aesthetic as well as to stylistic developments in Danish cinema in a broader sense.

Accepted into the editing line of the Danish Film School as a mere 17 year old, he found himself in the same class (1979–1982) as the notoriously difficult von Trier, but the two worked well together. Gislason edited von Trier's graduate project, *Images of a Relief,* as well as *The Element of Crime* for which he won a Robert award. Barely out of his teens, his career was launched, and his subsequent work on TV and feature films soon won him the reputation of an editor who could save a film.

But he was still young, and spending all his time in the cloistered darkness of an endless string of editing suites started to take a toll on him. At the start of the '90s he quit editing and began to direct documentaries. As he recalled, "If I was to continue in this business, I had to get out into the open air and personally engage myself with the things I made, and in that way let the work form my life."[88]

In the meantime, his sense for film had extended beyond the craft of editing, and von Trier, for one, would continue to find use for his ideas and talents. He co-wrote the shooting scripts to *Europa* and *The Kingdom* and contributed to the visual expression of several of von Trier's films, such as *Dancer in the Dark,* for example, for which he helped to develop the "100 Eyes" camera concept.[89]

He went on to direct three of the more noteworthy Danish documentaries of the '90s: *Heart and Soul* (1994), about Jørgen Leth; *The Patriots* (1997), about the American white supremacist movement; and *Maximum Penalty* (2000), an investigation into the disappearances of two prominent Danish communists in the Soviet Union at the end of the '30s.

At the start of the '90s, Gislason's personal life was plunged into turmoil due to, among other things, a divorce, and he entered a period of depression. At about that same point in time he was contacted by Leth who wanted him to edit his film, *Kærligheds Kataloget* (*The Catalog of Love*). Leth was himself also battling through depression. "A friend of mine met him in a supermarket," Gislason recalls[90] "where it was taking him half an hour to choose between two frozen pizzas." This led to an exchange of letters between the two, with each arguing that the other one should edit the film since neither of them could bear to leave the house (Gislason ended up with the job).

In the meantime, Leth pulled up stakes and moved to Haiti where he worked his way out of his depression. Gislason was intrigued by Leth's unorthodox creative and working processes and hence decided to make a documentary about him. In this way documentary film-making became a more relevant and organic part of his life, rather than just the simple continuation of his chosen profession. He had already had plenty of success at that, and probably at too young an age.

In 2000, Gislason made his first fiction film, *P.O.V.*, short for the trade term "point of view shot" which indicates a subjective or personal perspective.

The film, a road movie shot in chronological sequence across some of the more spectacular landscapes of the American west, would take this subjective approach to extremes. It would embrace some of the principles of Dogme (hand-held camera, liberation from the script, and shooting done on location), but with his no-holds-barred

Gareth Williams and Trine Dyrholm, as Rock and Kamilla, motor through the American West in Tómas Gislason's P.O.V.

commitment to improvisation and his determination to incorporate "real life" into the film, Gislason would go beyond Dogme.

The story starts with a young Danish couple who have decided to get married in Las Vegas, but when the big day arrives the bride, Kamilla—played by Danish *ingenue* (and veteran of *The Celebration*), Trine Dyrholm—gets cold feet and dashes out of the chapel still clad in her wedding gown. She jumps on the back of a passing motorcycle, driven by a character named Rock, and demands to be taken "anywhere."

This sets in motion an impulsive journey that leads across the desert to Big Sur in California and up the Pacific coast to Washington, giving Gislason ample opportunity to employ the scenery as a central presence in the film and to pay homage to a distinctly American sense of wanderlust. *P.O.V.* is, in fact, a very specific tribute to the '50s beat generation and the feeling of rootlessness and adventure it recalls: Kamilla reads a copy of Jack Kerouac's *On the Road*, while both Kerouac and William Burroughs can be heard on the soundtrack along with the jazz of John Coltrane. Joyce Johnson, Kerouac's widow, even has a cameo.

P.O.V. was improvised to a far greater degree than any Dogme film. (Much has been said about improvisation in this book, and while it was never mentioned specifically in the Vow of Chastity it is a recurrent theme in Dogme and could be considered one of the unwritten rules.) The male lead, a grizzled, emotionally wounded loner who finds himself under the sway of violent right-wing philosophies, is played by American actor Gareth Williams. Williams got the part when he arrived at what he thought was a meeting to discuss the role and instead was requested to act out a scene and improvise the dialogue. He was offered a chance to prepare himself but waived it off and plunged in—and got the job. It was precisely this kind of fearlessness Gislason wanted since there was no manuscript for the film. The idea was that the actors would use a part of their own lives to form the characters.

As Gislason explained the process, "the actors received ten pages outlining their characters and background. And every morning they got a 'frame' for that day's action. But they had the freedom to leave in the middle of a scene and take a plane back to Denmark if they wanted. The intrusion of reality influenced the film in many ways."[91] For example, Gislason proposed to his girlfriend in Big Sur where a decisive change in the relationship also occurred between the two main characters. There was a real closeness between the small cast and crew which traveled together under the same conditions over the course of the 2 ½ month shoot. No "star treatment" here. It was a real-life experience, perhaps even an adventure, if not a completely unplanned one, but certainly no vacation. As a working process it was both extremely taxing and fascinating—a bridge beyond what Dogme had ever attempted.

By keeping "real life" interactive with the creative process of the film in this fashion, Gislason reckoned *P.O.V.* was more a refinement of what he had done before in his documentary work than a big step out into fiction filmmaking. And it was a process ideally suited to allowing the participants to incorporate real emotions and genuine happenings into the film as Dogme had always attempted to do. Gislason had certainty now gone further in this respect.

An interesting experiment, but was it a good movie?

P.O.V. won a top prize at the 2000 Mannheim Film Festival, the same festival that had given *The Celebration* its first international exposure, and it had caught the attention of audiences and critics at the San Sebastian festival (2000). Danish critics for their part deemed it an intriguing if not totally successful experiment, but it was largely ignored by the Danish film-going public.

Jesper Jargil—The Fifth Beatle

Back in November of 2000 the four original Dogme brothers got together for a kind of reunion. During a lull in the conversation, von Trier raised a frivolous question: Which of the four Beatles did they each correspond to? Among much jovial give-and-take the issue was debated but no final conclusions were reached. *Politiken* scribes Erik Jensen and Hans Jørgen Møller, however, took this light-hearted slab of speculation a bit further and in the paper's August 3, 2002 edition came up with the following conclusions:

Von Trier was the eccentric and creative John Lennon. Thomas Vinterberg would be the melody-maker, Paul McCartney, good-natured and maybe a little bit too willing to please. Søren Kragh-Jacobsen would be the laid-back, modest, but experienced George Harrison, while Kristian Levring would be Ringo Starr, just happy to be along for the ride.

Taking this line of inquiry even further, one might venture to say that father-figure and whip-cracker, Mogens Rukov, is a good fit as the group's producer/manager, George Martin. Or maybe he's Ravi Shankar, since he's frequently described as being a "guru" and setting the ideological line.

And who would the shadowy "5th Beatle" be?

That would certainly have to be Jesper Jargil. A close personal pal of von Trier's, he is an experienced filmmaker in his own right, having directed scores of short films and over 500 commercials. And he always seems to be hovering on the edges whenever the four Dogme brothers get together. He was in fact present at the above-mentioned reunion, filming it.

Jargil began making films in the mid-'90s as a way to explore the mechanisms of the artistic process that so intrigued him. How did artists behave, think, and act when enmeshed in the creative process? And this led him to the documentary form where he was able to seek answers, or rather, to seek the right questions.

He chose the Danish artist Per Kirkeby as his first subject. Through the Fall, Winter and Spring of 1994–95 he filmed from a fixed camera position while Kirkeby went to work on his largest oil painting yet. He accumulated over 100 hours of film of Kirkeby painting, thinking, scraping, sketching, sleeping, reading, and talking to, among others, himself. This footage was fashioned into a film entitled *Winter's Tale* (1996). It won much critical praise and stands as a unique contribution to the art-documentary genre.

In 1996, Jargil also filmed a work by Lars von Trier, a "living art exhibition" which he had been commissioned by the city of Copenhagen to create in conjunction with their host status as Europe's Culture Capital of the Year. It was called *Psykomobile #1: The World Clock.*

The installation took place in the Art Association's cavernous old building on Gammel Strand. There, 19 rooms were transformed into living environments (a bedroom, a living room, a hospital room, etc.) and inhabited by 53 actors who were given characters created by von Trier and long-time writing partner, Niels Vørsel. The actors would improvise various loose scenarios alone and in groups, their moods— and by extension their course of action—cued by the illumination of one of four colored lights installed in all the rooms. Which light was lit depended on the behavior of ants in an anthill in New Mexico, USA, which was being monitored by video. The images were transmitted to a computer in Copenhagen that coded them into signals that represented modes of behavior, such as aggression or passivity, for example, and activated the corresponding light bulb. Hence ants in New Mexico would be controlling the behavior of a human community-in-miniature half-way around the globe. This "performance" played throughout the fall of 1996 to full houses and was a huge hit.

Jargil came out of the experience with a documentary entitled *The Exhibited,* (which wasn't released until 2000).

In 1998, he was back with von Trier on the set of *The Idiots.* He had von Trier's permission to film anything he wanted, and proceeded to shoot with the same sense of fluidity and mobility that von Trier was using on the film itself, resulting in footage that was largely interchangeable. The result of this was *The Humiliated,* a documentary about the making of *The Idiots* that places a special focus on von Trier's emotional transformations over the course of the production.

On the surface it seemed odd that a perfectionist like Jargil, who specialized in taking a whole day to shoot the perfect picture of a glass of milk, would be so intrigued by the raw, grainy, unpredictable world of Lars von Trier, but that was exactly what attracted him to von Trier's films and to documentary in general—the challenge of the unpredictable.

On New Year's eve, 1999, Jargil was again "armed and anonymous," as he shot behind the scenes while the Brothers went about making *Project D-Day.*

In November of 2000 he filmed the above-mentioned Dogme reunion which took place over a day and a night in von Trier's home. It was time to look back and appraise the achievements, or lack thereof, of Dogme and to assess its future prospects. But Jargil wanted something closer to the bone than just the nostalgia of "Dogme revisited," and while keeping himself out of the picture he prodded and challenged the four to confront themselves. Had they been faithful to the rules? Had they emerged with their artistic integrity intact? And how close had they come to making a "pure" Dogme film?

Seated on sofas, the Brothers watch clips on a monitor, scenes from their own Dogme films selected to raise questions about their adherence to the Dogme rules. We also see "behind the scenes" footage of the directors at work. And at various points Mogens Rukov appears on the monitor to sternly hold forth on various aspects of Dogme, these being excerpts of a long interview Jargil had previously filmed.

The four joke, laugh, and chide each other, but there is also an undercurrent of competition and things also get serious and occasionally prickly. Interesting personal dynamics emerge as the four interact.

Von Trier tends to be the most puritanical, almost fascistic, about adherence to the rules, although he has broken a few himself. He is the most contentious of the lot and is sensitive to criticism in an almost childish way. His trademark ironic wit is on display, but it is only in evidence when he is in control of the conversation, and he seems to be genetically devoid of any sense of easy-goingness.

He and Søren Kragh-Jacobsen are the dominant personalities of the group. The other three grew up listening to the songs and watching the movies of Kragh-Jacobsen; he has a secure and respected position in the Danish film world and in this little group as well, even though his film, *Mifune,* is the most critically scrutinized here. He staunchly defends it, but is the most relaxed and easy-going about it all. When the others start harping about the rules like Dogme police, he reminds them that the main impetus behind Dogme was to rediscover the joy of filmmaking. He constantly refers to the fact that he was "invited" to join Dogme as if to distance himself, not from Dogme *per se*, which he is happy to be a part of, but from any interpretation of Dogme as a religious, absolutist phenomenon of the type to which von Trier seems to subscribe. He doesn't want to be a member of a Lars von Trier cult. To Kragh-Jacobsen, Dogme is a matter of degree, not purity, and fixating on the rules is a sure way to ruin the joy.

Thomas Vinterberg is perhaps the most verbal of the four, launching into sustained explanations and accounts. He seems totally self-confident, but on the other hand tends to navigate between positions staked out by the others and doesn't break much new ice. He points out rule breaks, but shows more enthusiasm for supporting and contributing to arguments raised by the others, particular von Trier. As a personality he seems to be von Trier's diametric opposite and perhaps that is why they work so well together. Kristian Levring is unto himself, making his good points and not being shy about it but never challenging the others too directly. He seems to take more pride in identifying himself as a Dogme brother than Kragh-Jacobsen, and this is the perfect opportunity to profile himself as such.

The various rule breaks are illustrated up on the monitor.

In *Mifune*, Søren Kragh-Jacobsen used music in a questionable way, used the headlights of a car to light a scene, and, utilizing sketches, had directed Sofie Gråbøl step by step in her legendary orgasm scene. As Vinterberg points out, "You wanted to make a very aesthetic scene here . . . you have clearly arranged what takes place here and exercised full control over it. The camera positioning and everything is arranged here." Von Trier is upset that Kragh-Jacobsen employed standard filmic storytelling techniques with such clear premeditation. He considers that to be a cynical manipulation of the audience.

This has long been a point of debate in Dogme circles. Are we, the audience, being manipulated, one might ask, or haven't we in fact entered into an unwritten contract with the filmmaker agreeing to the use of such techniques? Techniques that work, that tell stories. That are synonymous with the craft of filmmaking. Techniques which in fact the audience craves. Does the fact that we are actually addicted to these techniques make us weak and spineless? Does Dogme make us strong again? Is Dogme saving us from ourselves, with Saint Lars von Trier leading the way, dragging a heavy cross? In any case, von Trier comes across as the most "religious."

For *The Idiots*, von Trier admitted to his sin of using professional porno actors in the group sex scene, and Vinterberg pleaded guilty to light adjustment and, separately, to the placement of a tea towel over a window to mute the light in one scene. Levring got off easy since no one could point to obvious rule breaks in *The King is Alive*.

Von Trier's use of professional porn models has been much criticized through the years. Rukov asserts that the scene rings false, that while some people are actually having sex, the characters we know from the film are faking it and that's probably why it seems dishonest and off-key. By this, von Trier is not being "true to the moment," as Rukov puts it, and is constructing or manipulating events rather than going where the spirit of truth and reality takes him.

But does everything that happens to a character have to be "real?" Levring counters that in his film a man hangs himself, but that in reality, of course, he didn't die. Should he really have died in the cause of being true to "the moment?" How much of a slave must one be to this sacred concept of "the moment?" Total adherence to being true to the moment would seem to inhibit (though not totally prevent) anyone from ever trying to tell a story. Dogme was all about fiction filmmaking, not documentary, and yet even the most sober-minded documentaries have to tell a kind of story. Stories make life interesting. But was all this theorizing about the rules sucking the life out of Dogme and turning it into some kind of sterile, theoretical debate?

Later on, Rukov gets personal.

"One of the rules," he declares, "speaks volumes about who has drawn them up. There sat two egocentric people who attempted to convey one thing or another while rapping themselves over the knuckles with prohibitions against the whole of the technical repertoire and forms of expression. And on top of it they must not use their names! But they *love* to use their names—to see their names in lights! They themselves are the most important people in their lives. I would therefore almost assert that this prohibition against being credited reveals the true nature of what the rules really are: a self-imposed act of humility designed to put the brakes on their natural tendency to think that it is so fantastic to be Lars von Trier and Thomas Vinterberg!"[92]

At another point in the evening, von Trier becomes thoughtful and reflective. "I feel to a high degree that one lives off predecessors. That what we get are after all copies of copies. But with these here rules, which are intended to give the filmmakers obstructions and challenges, one can at the last moment get a hold of something or other that is essential . . . that is consequently more valuable than that. In a despairing moment one can mistakenly get a grip on something or other. Something that suddenly has value. Something besides that of a technical or informational nature, something besides what others have done before."

The footage Jargil shot at this Dogme reunion would be fashioned into a film that would go on to constitute the third installment in his documentary trilogy—*The Kingdom of Credibility*—dedicated to exploring von Trier's creative *modus operandi*. It would be entitled *The Purified* (*The Exhibited* and *The Humiliated* counting as the first two installments), and it would eventually premiere at the Odense Film Festival on August 12, 2002. The next day it was broadcast on DR2 TV has part of a much-hyped "Dogme Week," shown together with the first four films and related documentaries and specials.

"The interesting thing about von Trier," Jargil would comment[93], is that he makes public commitments. He draws up manifestos and sets of rules, thus involving everyone else. He gives us the chance to learn about the creative act which is usually kept secret and shrouded in mystery. Von Trier opens the doors into art's secret chamber, and it's fascinating. Just what governs the process of artistic creation? Some think we destroy art if we reveal the mechanisms behind it. I don't feel that way at all. I think it just reveals even more layers. We enter new layers of magic that are even more fascinating."

Out of all the talk and discussion at von Trier's house, the Brothers managed to come up with at least one common declaration, that a pure Dogme film had yet to be made.

"I can well imagine," commented Jargil[94] at the film's premiere, "that the four Dogme brothers in a couple of years will each make a real Dogme film. I believe they'll show they can do it. They'll feel themselves forced to."

Anthony Dod Mantle—Leaving Dogme

"I don't like being called 'Mr. Dogme,'" protested the English-born cameraman, Anthony Dod Mantle in May of 2000,[95] but that was the tag he was unavoidably stuck with after lensing three of the most attention-getting of the early Dogme films: *The Celebration, Mifune*, and Harmony Korine's American Dogme film, *Julien Donkey-Boy*. Rarely had a "mere" cameraman reaped so much attention. Then again this was not surprising since Dogme placed such importance and responsibility on the cinematographer. The cameraman was not just a technician, but now an intrinsic part of the action, a catalyst and generator, a presence on the set no less crucial to developments than the actors themselves.

Born in 1955, raised in Oxford, Mantle became interested in still photography at a young age. Finishing the UK equivalent of high school, he took a trip to India to hone his photo-journalistic skills, and following that enrolled at the Royal College of Art in London where he studied for three years.

He first traveled to Denmark in 1979 after meeting a Danish girl in a London hospital where he worked the night shift. He knew nothing about this tiny Scandinavian country and had never expected to end up here. As it happened, the relationship fell apart soon after, but it was here he would find his life's calling when, much to his own surprise, he was accepted into the Danish Film School in 1984.

"And when I finished four years later," he recalled,[96] "I found myself in the midst of a new and developing film generation."

These were exciting times in the Danish film milieu as the inertia that had gripped the industry throughout most of the '80s was giving way to new energy and new visions. This new surge of momentum owed in large part, as noted earlier, to a breakdown of the old hierarchies on the set where the director had always reigned supreme. Now actors, writers, directors, and cameramen worked together in a more collaborative manner. The fact that the film milieu in Denmark is so small had something to do with this new synergy since it often seemed cast and crew members had all gone to the Film School or worked together previously.

Following Mantle's graduation from the Film School, he went on to shoot documentaries. *Deadly Nightshade*, about the AIDS epidemic in Africa, was one of them. The film was representative of his search for a balance between, as he phrased it, "politics and poetry." He didn't look upon film as a mere profession. This was personal stuff.

He was also supposed to shoot *The Kingdom* for Lars von Trier, whom he'd first met back when von Trier was writing the script to *The Element of Crime*, but he had previous commitments and Eric Kress got the assignment instead. Of the first six feature films Mantle photographed, one (*The Birthday Trip*) was for Lone Scherfig and one (*Operation Cobra*) was for Lasse Spang Olsen. Both directors would go on to have huge success some years down the road. He shot another film, too, called *The Greatest Heroes,* for a boyish looking Film School grad by the name of Thomas Vinterberg. The young director had already signed on to something called Dogme, but this here was a straightforward road movie (set in Sweden) about the adventures of an escaped convict and his young daughter.

They worked well together and Vinterberg wanted him to shoot his Dogme film, *The Celebration,* warning him in advance that "It's not a normal film . . . it means a strange status for the camera."[97] He didn't care so much about that. It was the story that intrigued him.

They both wanted to shoot *The Celebration* on film and started making tests on 35mm, but had to economize and were bumped down to 16mm, a decision with which Mantle was dissatisfied. At one point he planned to shoot the interiors on video and the exteriors on Super-8, but finally word came down that it was all to be shot on video. He chose to use the tiny Sony PC7-E camera, a first generation consumer camera that afforded total mobility. This choice of camera would have a big influence on the fluid, subjective look of the movie, and by manipulating grain and exposure he was able to capture the bleak, pitiful, and yet absurdly comic atmosphere of the family reunion in a suitable style. Disintegrating images to tell the story of a disintegrating family.

While *The Celebration* was Mantle's big breakthrough and would remain the film with which he would be most closely identified, his very next picture was the extremely un-Dogme like *Voice of Bornholm,* a classically photographed drama of human struggle and determination set on the Danish island of the same name.

Following that, he lensed Søren Kragh-Jacobsen's *Mifune* and was back in Dogme country. And yet he shot *Mifune* in a very different style since it had very different rhythms to capture. He shot it in 16mm and then it was blown up to 35mm to bring out a more grainy texture and highlight the harsh contrasts. "It was pastoral, you had this broken-down farm, you had landscapes, the flat fields of the south of Denmark. It was very much social realism and that's the tradition Søren comes out of. He's a humorist, he likes it gentle, with just a few characters."[98]

His next assignment was the American Dogme film, *Julien: Donkey-Boy*, a tale of schizophrenia and psychic mayhem directed by the very un-gentle Harmony Korine. "We did each scene without reference to the previous scenes, instinctively and spontaneously. There are pros and cons to this approach, but it is hugely stimulating."[99] For his work on the picture, Mantle won a Spirit Award nomination.

As noted, he had now been typecast as the "cameraman of Dogme," and yet each of his Dogme films had been completely different!

In a broader sense, his reputation as a skilled and inventive cameraman was now assured both in and outside of Denmark, but he was no mere technician. He was and is deeply involved in all the films he makes, working closely with the directors to find the best style by which to tell that specific story, a kind of "co-director," intensely and personally engaged in each new project. "The red-headed Anthony Dod Mantle looks like a zealot prepared to sacrifice himself for any project that arouses his passion," was the way journalist Liselotte Michelsen phrased it.

"Anthony is very spontaneous and has a gift for finding ways to express feeling," elaborates Vinterberg. "He is, after all, first and foremost a talented cinematographer who is very experienced. He constantly reevaluates the language of film and always tries to do things in new ways. He is in that way unusual—an anomaly in what is otherwise a very conservative profession. He constantly seeks change."[100]

And change he did after *Julien: Donkey-Boy*, leaving Dogme altogether and going on to shoot a series of high-profile Danish films that were all very different from each other and all very different from Dogme. Today he is one of the most in-demand cameramen in Denmark, respected (and outspoken) in the milieu. And his reputation internationally is likewise secured with directors like Wayne Wang, Gus van Sant and Steven Soderbergh sending him scripts to read. But he has no great desire to work in America, choosing to stay closer to home and family. He works for the most part in Denmark or Great Britain. His latest film, at time of publication, is Danny "Trainspotting" Boyle's *28 Days Later.*

Dogme should at this point be a footnote in his career, but despite an impressive and growing resumé, he is still, to his mild irritation, constantly queried about it.

Jyllands-Posten reporter Anders Hjort caught up with him at the Danish Film School on April 18, 2002, interviewing him just after he had finished lecturing a class of cinematography students.

And of course the first topic of conversation. . . .

"Today it's been five years since Thomas Vinterberg's *The Celebration* opened," said Mantle, "and nonetheless the students here are still taught about Dogme film. Dogme came about for many reasons, but first and foremost the principles were created to remind people who were trapped in a routine that film could be made differently and in a new way. That students should be taught about Dogme here at the Film School—that smells like they are urging them to make Dogme films and that I believe is wrong. All considered, I'm shocked that Dogme still exists as a phenomenon here in Denmark. It was an important wave and a kind of reaction to how things looked then, but that it is still going on and has become an industry, that I'm a little depressed over."

Mantle had always viewed Dogme in more of a local context, as a rebellion against all the technically flawless, nice-looking Danish films of the '80s which lacked good stories and performances. And as he confided to another Danish paper, he wasn't particularly thrilled about what Dogme had wrought. "In the wake of Dogme there have followed a lot of cheap films whose only apparent quality is that they are cheap. A dirty wave of mediocre films which incessantly win Bodil and Robert awards. Good enough—but I'm not impressed. They ought to be more daring."[101]

VIII

Foreign Dogme Films

Introduction

There has always existed a kind of a schism between the Danish Dogme films and the foreign (e.g. non-Danish) Dogme films. In Denmark, the foreign films suffer from a kind of class prejudice. They're seen as second-class citizens, as somehow illegitimate. How good could the foreign films be, the pundits wonder aloud, if not a single one has yet played a commercial run in a Danish theater?

Some critics go even further, complaining that the foreign Dogme films have dirtied the reputation of Danish film in general, Dogme having become a kind of trademark for their nation's cinema. What Dogme lacks thus far, say many in Denmark, is a successful *foreign* Dogme film.

Zentropa producer, Ib Tardini, who stands behind three Danish Dogme films, weighed in on the issue while he was down in Berlin in February of 2001 celebrating the triumph of *Italian for Beginners* at the film festival there.

"At the moment it appears that only we Danes can make Dogme films. But that's because our best directors are doing it, and because we all abide by the playing rules. It cannot be to anyone's advantage that young directors out in the world believe that Dogme is the route to international success. Dogme is a playground for professionals . . . But every time we win a prize, it enhances the good reputation of Dogme. It would be cool if a director, like, for example, Milos Forman, made a Dogme film. There seems to be a tendency to look down on Dogme films, and that's because they make them so badly outside Denmark. But as it happens, the Dogme brothers have decided that there won't be any 'Dogme police,' so we cannot make demands."

If the "Dogme police" had disbanded, it appeared that the "Dogme jury"—every Dane with an opinion—was still in session and in a hangin' mood. No prisoners taken with these "foreign films!"

But weren't Tardini's conclusions perhaps a bit harsh? Not to say possibly elitist and simplistic? In any case, there seemed to be two separate schools of thought emerging on the hows and whys of Dogme.

Tardini was correct in his assertion that foreign directors were not professionals looking for playgrounds, seeking escape from the Apparatus. But hadn't the biggest Dogme hit up to that point, *The Celebration*, been made by a young Thomas Vinterberg who was anything but a seasoned professional? It would seem that if everybody had to be a seasoned professional then a lot of things were being excluded from the start, and this would run against the grain of at least the perception that Dogme was inclusive rather than exclusive. And as we have seen, a number of *Danish* Dogme films have been made by relative newcomers. Was Dogme, then, just for Lars von Trier's chosen circle, his cozy little in-crowd of old friends and collaborators and directors who happened to be "in" with Zentropa at the moment?

Outside of Denmark Dogme had largely been embraced as a kind of underground movement. *Julien Donkey-Boy* was a prime example of that. But Danish Dogme filmmakers saw it as something completely different, as a process of purification, not a process of putrefaction. They had no desire to give birth to monsters, to create the kind of transgressive, subversive "underground" films that so many young film freaks and film students the world over were thirsting to see. The kind of films a young von Trier had championed. Films "the color of blood" as the American rebels had put it back in 1961.

Instead, the Danes were making family costume dramas, romantic comedies, and calculated "women's pictures." And Dogme's founder himself was making some of the most sentimental melodramas around. Subversive? Only in a very few cases. And whatever the considerable respective merits of the Danish Dogme films, *they* were the ones who had turned it all into business-as-usual, being the great businessmen that they were. "Dogme has become a trademark, like Coca Cola," said Aalbæk Jensen as far back as 1999, and many others had also since come to that conclusion. The greatest danger was not that Dogme would swamp the world in bad films, but that Dogme had become a commodity, and if anyone was to blame for that, it was the Danes.

But no, "Dogme is not for amateurs," they sniffed, looking on in vague discomfort at what they had created, refusing to take responsibility for their flock of feral children, for this rabble of dirty-faced peasants who had gathered at the castle gates at their behest, armed with pots and pans and sticks and ready to make war. Denmark was not big enough to make a wave by itself, so they had invited the world to join, the great unwashed.

American Dogme Films

(Note: Unless otherwise credited, all quotations in the remainder of this chapter are drawn either from interviews the author conducted with the filmmakers or from their own published press materials.)

Dogme's relationship to America is particularly paradoxical.

American cinema is synonymous with Hollywood and Hollywood is what Dogme is most against, and yet nowhere is Dogme more enthusiastically embraced than in America, where 12 out of the 22 foreign Dogme films are American. More Dogme films have been made in America than any other country, including Denmark, and the sense of "Dogme fatigue" so acute in some quarters in Denmark is nowhere in evidence on the other side of the Atlantic. (Dogme *hostility*, perhaps, but not fatigue.)

For one thing, Americans tend to be much less burdened by all this "wave baggage" that seems to preoccupy the Europeans, not least the Danes (not least the four Dogme brothers), who spend perhaps far too much energy wondering when it will or should end. To these pessimists there is nothing worse than a wave that has outlived its purpose. These European romantics are predisposed to judge Dogme in terms of its life span and to evaluate the films through a prism of purity, while in America, Dogme-haters aside, no one seems particularly worked up over the fact that Dogme might outlive its usefulness. "Dogme will survive as long as they sell DV cameras," predicts the American director of Dogme #10, Rick Schmidt, with the kind of easy-going optimism that he seems to share with so many of his countrymen. To Dogme purists, however, this sounds like a prophecy of doom.

Americans are largely intrigued by and attracted to the politico-revolutionary rhetoric of Dogme, but they don't really buy it since this mix of ersatz socialism and avant-garde nostalgia out of which Dogme attitudinizing was born is foreign to their experience. But it *sounds* great! (It is ironic to note that while the Brothers laid claim to wanting to do away with all the romanticism and egotism bound up in the *auteur* concept, they ended up replacing it—intentionally or not—with the equally dense romanticism of revolutions and revolutionaries, ensuring that their films would remain trapped in precisely the same kind of box from which they were proposing to free them: Film in the service of revolutions instead of film in the service of egotistical old men.)

Another difference between European and American Dogme directors is their relationship to money . . . hard, cold, dirty *cash*. To the Danes it is an undignified issue better left to the men in boring suits, while to Americans it is *the* essential issue, never more than a sentence away when the subject turns to Dogme. Truth is, the vast majority of American filmmakers and would-be filmmakers have no access to the various forms of funding that nourish independent filmmaking in Europe, and America has nothing resembling their network of film

workshops that provide entry-level access to the equipment and materials. To 99% of Americans, filmmaking is a hideously expensive—not
to say masochistic—undertaking. Dogme has given many of them hope
that it is not as impossible as it seems. Is it bad to give people hope?

Many of the Danish Dogme directors have gone to great lengths
to make it clear that Dogme has really nothing to do with money.
"Dogme is an artistic concept, not an economic concept," declared
von Trier back in 1996 when Dogme was being mentioned in the
same breath as "low-budget films." Almost eight years later, at a panel
discussion at Sundance 2003, Susanne Bier elaborated on this line of
thought. "One makes a mistake if one believes that Dogme is only a
question of making cheap films. More or less all the directors of
Danish Dogme films could have gotten much more expensive films
financed without any problem, so for them Dogme is also a choice
they make."

Bier might have added that Danish directors also had the lux-
ury of casting the very best actors and could shoot on any format
they chose.

The options look considerably different for, say, a young would-be
filmmaker from Salt Lake City sitting in the audience. Outside of a
few filmmaking organizations in a handful of cities, such as the FAF
in San Francisco, the BFVF in Boston or the Millennium in New
York, there is no way "in" to such a money-driven medium. It's a geographical thing. Said would-be theoretical filmmaker could spend
four years and many tens of thousands of dollars attending a big-name
film school, if he were lucky enough to get accepted, or he could just
beg/borrow/steal a DV camera and start shooting and in one fell
swoop subvert the whole process of exclusivity, not to mention paying
lots of money to big corporations like Kodak to process his film, etc.

Was Dogme not for this kid, as Tardini had implied?

The whole entry process into the medium is so different in
America and Europe that it calls into question the very premise of
Dogme as an exportable commodity. And the distasteful subject of
money is at the heart of it, as witnessed by the inventiveness the

Americans must bring to the process of funding their films. Rick Schmidt (#10), as we'll see, did it by working within the context of a film workshop, and Matthew Biancaniello (#29) raised money by appearing as "The Human Garbage Can" on late night talk-shows like *David Letterman*, eating the most disgusting things imaginable (more on that later). And this doesn't just apply to the funding of Dogme films. A very fat book could be written on the various amazing schemes to which American filmmakers have resorted in order to raise money for their movies.

As for the issue of inexperience, if a few first-time filmmakers make a few bad films, what's the disaster in that? Many Danes seem to view with alarm the possibility that young, underfunded filmmakers might make some bad films, while Americans seem less troubled by the prospect. The good films will find a way to reach their public, while the bad films will fade away. Americans, to generalize, seem to take a more relaxed and democratic approach as to who can make films. "Nowadays anyone can make a film," says American Dogme director Rich Martini (#15). "Start with a short, put it up on one of the short-film websites like ifilm.com. Tell a good story, about your life, about the people around you. Sell it on Amazon.com if you want to make your money back, or to your friends, and make enough money to do it again. Filmmaking has become like painting: pick up a brush and let your heart dictate where it should go."

There are also some fundamental collective differences between the Danish and American films as far as content and approach are concerned, differences that have more to do with mentality than finance or technology.

Some of this can be ascribed to the different ways in which Danes and Americans view themselves in relationship to wider society. Americans, their famous sense of patriotism aside, tend to have a more "localized" sense of identity and to view themselves as members of a distinct social subset, while Danes tend to see themselves as part of the more unified Danish "family," which abides by long established traditions and norms, for the good and the bad. As noted, most Danish Dogme films, with the possible exception of *The King is Alive*, have an engagement to varying degrees with this wider sense of Danish culture. Hence, they have a recognizable (if far from cohesive) feel of "Danishness" about them. This has in turn imbued them with a specific character that the American (and other foreign) films lack. This "Danishness" is part of the reason why they have been successful, because they convey an identifiable sense of place and mentality and are grounded in a specific culture, while the non-Danish films don't seem to resonate beyond the individual stories they are trying to tell.

The Danish films offer foreign viewers a chance to experience a specific emotional topography, to discover "hidden Denmark" as it were, a land of arcane and Byzantine social norms and traditions, a place that is at once absurd, comical, and mortifying. Von Trier's *The Kingdom* series was part of all this too. To foreign viewers this is new territory, something to discover, and in a strange way they find it exotic. Denmark doesn't have palm trees, but it does have its share of dark secrets, bizarre social rituals, and the kind of general psychological mindset with which ethnologists could have a field day.

And Western audiences can access it all, thanks to the fact that Danish culture is still a Western culture and that Dogme is inevitably imbued with a realist perspective which invites engagement. It's not an impenetrable experience, like watching a movie from India and knowing that real people simply don't act like that. Additionally, the films play as a kind of series of very loose sequels, even with some of the same actors. "Okay, here we are back in Denmark." Giving audiences "follow-ups" is never a bad idea.

By contrast, American society, via its exportability as a popular culture, is a known commodity. There aren't any dark little corners left that haven't already been revealed by the hyper-intrusive film and TV medium. Or in any case that's the perception. The worldwide viewing audience is already over-saturated with penetrating and skewered takes on the Great American Freak Show, and while there will always be more stories to tell and different ways to tell them, American culture is anything but exotic. Stories set in America can accomplish many things, but they can't arouse the kind of curiosity and sense of discovery that have given the Danish films, at least for a while, an edge to them.

And what is "American-ness" anyway, if one discards all the clichés and stereotypes? In fact, it is probably just a complete disinterest in the whole subject. *The Celebration*, it has been said, could have been set in plenty of other countries, but it is hard to imagine an American version that would have tapped into American-ness with the same intensity that Vinterberg's film tapped into Danish-ness.

It is erroneous to say the American Dogme films don't examine social issues. A few do, but they tend to do so in a more overtly political way that is more "issue oriented." That is a much more American than Danish approach, and perhaps also explains why American filmmakers seem to find the political/documentary aspect of Dogme to be its most interesting quality.

Chetzemoka's Curse

For a lot of younger American filmmakers who ventured into theaters in the early months of 1999 to see *The Celebration,* it was a revelation, almost a shock, something completely new. But more experienced members of the off-Hollywood filmmaking community were not so startled by what Vinterberg had managed to capture. They understood the mojo. For decades, veterans of the American underground, people such as Mike and George Kuchar, Larry Jordan, Tom Palazzolo, and others had been teaching students to boil the process down to its basics, and it's no stretch to say that the trends and ways of thinking that Dogme encouraged had long been embraced by a hardcore within the American independent film community.

Rick Schmidt, who stood behind Dogme #10, *Chetzemoka's Curse,* was one of them. For many years, decades in fact, he had been working on a parallel track to Dogme. "Have your eyes open," he counseled back in 1991, "and pick up on the gifts that occur." He'd been operating on that basis over the course of many films, and had even taken tenets of this general philosophy further than the Danes.

Moving to the Bay Area in 1966 to study sculpture, he happened to take a video class along the way and ended up going in that direction. One fine day in 1970, as a 26 year old, he took a camera (Sony portapack with 1/2-inch video tape) to his ex-wife's house, set it up on a tripod, aimed it at her face and asked "What went wrong with our marriage?" For the next twenty minutes the camera recorded their heated exchange without tilts, pans, or cutaways, just one static unedited take. Very simple stuff. "And yet," Schmidt recalls today, "my friend's faces turned white as they watched it—this train wreck of a relationship."

He was now hooked on the ability of film to capture this kind of raw emotion, but he still needed to develop his craft, to make a real movie, and he began searching for a script to shoot. Wandering a flea market, he found an old copy of *True Confessions* magazine and decided to shoot one of its stories, *What Flirting Cost Me*, straight off the page. That broke the filmmaking ice for him.

Following this, he launched into a feature film, *A Man, a Woman and a Killer*, with his roommate at the time, a fellow who would go on to considerably greater fame in the film world—Wayne Wang.

Many other projects followed in 16mm and video formats, and he even got a few grants along the way, although none of this led to anything that could be called a commercial breakthrough. He did, however, obtain a fair amount of exposure on the film museum and festival circuit, and over the years his films played at such prestigious festivals as Rotterdam, London, and Sundance, and at museums like The Whitney and the Museum of Modern Art. His second feature, *The Remake*, from 1988, was bought by the U.K.'s Channel 4 and aired to an audience of millions.

That same year, Schmidt founded Feature Films Workshop, a kind of traveling bare-bones filmmaking studio based on his book, *Feature Filmmaking at Used Car Prices* (published in 1988 and reprinted in 1995 and 2000). A typical Workshop production would involve up to

10 collaborators, "people off the street," who would all contribute on as many levels as possible to the making of a feature-length film on a crash schedule. The film would start without a script or sometimes even a basic idea. The non-actors (usually) were then placed in situations and locations they could relate to, and, supplying their own lines, the story would form itself. Sometimes they wouldn't know what the movie was about until the last day of editing.

Schmidt was excited when friends raved to him about a new movie they'd seen, *The Celebration,* made by some Danish guy.

"I've spent half my life trying to get down to the brass tacks of reality using the movie camera as a tool to root out those kinds of unvarnished, personal moments, and along comes a group of Danish filmmakers who hit it big by delivering those kind of intense relationships captured with the dynamic of fluid, grainy, 'indie style' camera work. This I had to see!"

It was the intensity of the drama as much as the DV camera-play that struck him. "We all wish we could just shout out the truth, especially about our families, and there was someone doing it, standing up against all the undercurrents and niceties. What a pleasure."

Schmidt decided that he would make his next Feature Workshop film—his eighth—a Dogme film. It would end up being called *Chetzemoka's Curse* and it would be made in accord with his usual production process that fit everything—script, casting on the fly, shooting and editing to a master Betacam SP tape—into a ten-day schedule. There would be no rehearsals. To tell the story he would go after connections between real people and rely on instinct, while at the same time making sure to get the building-block pieces he would later need in the editing suite. It was "free-fall moviemaking," designed to utilize the talents and ideas of everyone involved and to be agile enough to take advantage of anything unexpected that came along.

Dogme complimented Schmidt's approach nicely. With no light set-ups he could move quicker and take advantage of new ideas that emerged mid-stride. No sets, costumes or props—fine. Schmidt liked to place his non-actors in their own environments anyway since their

clothing, their rooms, and the kind of things they surrounded themselves with were valuable clues as to who they were in real life. And it
took money to rent that stuff, and time to arrange it; two commodities
in short supply.

The way in which a woman named Maya Berthoud got the leading
role in *Chetzemoka's Curse* was typical of Schmidt's *modus operandi.*

The 23-year-old waitress from Port Townsend, a small harbor
village on Washington's Puget Sound where the film was being shot,
had come to his attention just two weeks before shooting was to
start, having left him a phone message to the effect that she heard he
was making a movie and wanted to be involved. Schmidt sent her
the standard one-page form via which would-be participants supplied info on possible college degrees, film/video experience, and "life
experience/school of hard knocks." They were also asked to describe
"a great real-life story that I want to share" which doubled as a
required writing sample.

They met at a cafe for breakfast to discuss it and he found himself
immediately struck by her strong presence and decided to cast her in the

Maya Berthoud and Rick Schmidt converse during the shooting of Chetzemoka's Curse.

lead. The story would now form itself around her. There were seven writer/directors who worked on the picture, and she was one of them. In fact, she was technically the first female Dogme director and *The New York Times*, no less, was forced to print a retraction (on January 27, 2002) when they erroneously credited Lone Scherfig with that honor.

Reviewer Julie Schachter was particularly impressed with the acting in *Chetzemoka's Curse,* crediting the performers for their ability to quickly improvise without even knowing the direction a scene would take. She also praised what she saw as Schmidt's "uncanny sense of what to say to prompt the actors to reach deeper, and knowing when it was appropriate to take that step."

While the original Danish Dogme brothers have all moved on and left Dogme behind them, Rick Schmidt continues, just as he has for the last 30 years, to preach the gospel of "reality" filmmaking and to put its tenets into practice.

The Bread Basket

Dogme's influence on acting has been stressed over and over again until it has almost become a slogan. "Dogme liberates actors," goes the popular wisdom, and in movie after movie actors have lined up to praise Dogme. The paradox is that Rick Schmidt, like a lot of his fellow foreign Dogme directors, rarely even *uses* actors, preferring instead non-actors, real people so to speak, and for his part Lars von Trier wanted his actors to get away from "acting." Thomas Vinterberg used the best actors Danish cinema had to offer, and they acted. Still others who subscribe to the wisdom that Dogme liberates actors are appalled when they start acting—"they're *acting!*" Indeed, the whole concept of a "reality" film would seem to go against the notion of acting. Where to draw the lines here? The rhetoric can get confusing. Should Dogme liberate actors to be non-actors? Or does it liberate non-actors to act . . . or to "be?" There are various schools of thought on this.

In any case, actors seem to love Dogme and several who have participated in Dogme films, including Jean-Marc Barr, Udo Kier, and

Jennifer Jason Leigh, have directed their own Dogme or Dogme-like films. In American Dogme, the actor's viewpoint is articulated most forcefully by Matthew Biancaniello, the 34-year-old director of the very last American Dogme film, #29, *The Bread Basket*. An actor himself since the age of 20, Biancaniello sees Dogme almost exclusively through the prism of acting.

After taking classes with Stella Adler, he went on to appear in over 22 films and in various theater projects in New York and around the country, all the while supporting himself with a string of day jobs that included selling erotic art and magazine ads, working as an animal trainer, etc.

In the mid-'90s, while living in Santa Barbara, he formed his own production company and became more personally involved in the nuts and bolts of filmmaking, putting together a 5-minute short out of footage he shot as an underwater videographer, and directing, producing, and acting in John Patrick Stanley's *Danny and the Deep Blue Sea*. These experiences motivated him to get his own work together and put it on film.

He briefly returned to New York and there he created his own one-man show, *Purge*, where the original monologue for *The Bread Basket* was conceived.

Relocating to Los Angeles, he began working on the film with his girlfriend, Sara Berkowitz, who would co-star with him and co-produce. It was loosely "and sometimes not so loosely" based on their relationship and how food got in the way of it (see the Plot Synopsis section in the Appendix). Some of the emotional give-and-take between them is pretty close to the bone and at points it doesn't seem like you are watching a movie anymore. (A phrase that often pops up in connection with Dogme.)

To help fund the project, Biancaniello enlisted the aid of his alter-ego, "The Human Garbage Can." He appeared on *The Tonight Show*, *David Letterman* and *Ripley's Believe it or Not*, eating the most repulsive things imaginable and in the process raising 10,000 USD for the film.

He chose to shoot it on DV and to do it as a Dogme film. Like so many other filmmakers he was profoundly inspired by *The*

Director and male lead of The Bread Basket, *Matthew Biancaniello, confronts his inner demons.*

Celebration, and his eyes were opened to Dogme. He was mostly impressed by the fearless way the film had treated such deeply serious and personal subject matter, the way it had created such an intimate and private world. That was the direction in which he himself wanted to go. And he found the acting to be exceptional, not only in *The Celebration* but also in the other Danish films he would later see. He wasn't alone here. Many foreign observers are likewise smitten with the acting in Danish Dogme, but one has to wonder if this was the effect Dogme had on actors or if this was because Danish Dogme had privileged access to the country's very best thespians?

Biancaniello has his own theories that tend to support the former. "That kind of great acting is very hard to find in most modern films because of the limitations filmmaking puts on the acting process. Actors who especially come from the stage are used to the scenes building up and moments happening spontaneously, and film is often a roadblock to that experience due to the multiple camera and lighting set ups."

He also draws attention to the fact that actors remain more involved in a Dogme film. "In most films, shot on film, you're acting maybe 45 minutes a day. In my Dogme film you're acting 50 to 75% of the time. . . . As an actor you're so involved most of the time that you are forced to stay connected to your character. You are holding onto the emotion, the actions and the relationships to the other characters. And no one talks about this enough in relation to Dogme, but you can decrease your days to 8–10 hours. You get more out of your cast and crew. I noticed the morale was higher because we didn't have to get up super early or go to bed very late." (Lars von Trier appears to have taken this approach to its furthest possible extreme in his latest film, *Dogville*, where he insisted that all the actors remain in-character and on stage regardless of whether or not one of their own scenes was coming up.)

Biancaniello also shot his film true to the chronology of the plot, something other, though not all, Dogme directors have done. "This became an important part of the filming process. Again, being the lead actor, it was very important to have the emotional build-up of the character happening naturally. When one shoots in order, you, as an actor, are very clear in what you are feeling from scene to scene because you have created a natural history. It's in your body, mind, and soul. You know and remember everything up to that point and it becomes very exciting because of the clarity you feel."

Biancaniello's views on filmmaking today are marked by the same sense of optimism that most of his fellow American directors also display. And that's a bit odd since they are the last people one would expect to be upbeat, considering all the trials and tribulations bound up in making and releasing a movie in America.

But he is optimistic, as well as dead certain that actors have to become more involved in the process: "I think film is moving in the right direction, and the only revolution that should exist is the revolution for the highest truth and creativity we can achieve. To keep making highly personal films that can be achieved beautifully by more and more actors writing and directing their own material. I feel most actors have a lot to say and doing their own work will be the best, most unique, and ultimately the only way to express it."

Camera

"Dogme is a playground for *professionals*. . . ."

Ib Tardini's words continue to echo. And yet very few experienced filmmakers working in the commercial arena outside Denmark have thrown their hats into the ring. Of the Americans, Rich Martini, director of Dogme #15, *Camera,* is about as close as one comes to such a director.

Born and raised in Chicago, Martini went on to graduate from Boston University and later earned a film degree from the University of Southern California. Daryl Hannah appeared in his student short, *Lost Angels.* He then went on to work in various capacities on a host of Hollywood pictures. He was an assistant director on Robert Towne's *Personal Best* (1982) and wrote scripts for, among other films, the Charlie Sheen comedy, *Three for the Road* (1987). He finally directed his own feature in 1988, *You Can't Hurry Love,* a quintessential '80s romantic comedy that featured the debut of Bridget Fonda.

At some point in the late '90s on his film-related travels he ended up at the Cannes film festival where he heard talk going around about this Dogme thing. He was intrigued by the idea, but had no plans to make one himself. Still, it got his juices flowing and at some point thereafter he scribbled down a plot outline on a yellow legal pad:

"A video camera is stolen from a photo shop, it goes around the world on this adventure, stalking wives and girlfriends and spying on people . . . shooting weddings, videos, whatever cams do in society. Then I get my hands on the camera and try to make a 'no budget film' and everyone tells me no, since the people I ask to be in it have already appeared in the camera's film. At the end when someone suggests that I make a film about a camera, the last shot of the film is the first shot of the film—setting up the shot in the photo shop."

And he made the picture, just like he'd jotted it down.

Although Martini was inspired by Dogme, *Camera* was not, as noted, intended to be a Dogme film. It was only after he'd completed it that he realized it adhered to most of the Dogme dictates and he applied for a certificate.

And he got it, becoming Dogme director #15. He admits however that it is probably the least "pure" of all the Dogme films, the one with the most rule breaks. "Maybe they were just sending out certificates that day and ignoring the films," he ventures.

All these rules. . . .

"I think people might have taken what was originally a funny, irreverent way to look at film and put it into another straitjacket of rules and regulations. . . . In light of the fact that this is a set of rules laid out by filmmakers who are breaking the rules, and they line up a set of rules to insure that the rules are being broken—well that sounds like some kind of existential Danish conundrum to me. . . ."

He admits his film might deserve a good spanking, but is unrepentant: "It's hard to chastise someone for breaking the rules when the concept is based on breaking the rules."

Martini won't be governed by the Danish rules, but he agrees with many that in general the Danish Dogme films are of another class. He points out several specific reasons for this, one of which bears on a technical issue that the film critics never mention: the close relationship between the two Danish studios and the Copenhagen film lab, Hogus Bogus, which oversees the transfer from DV to 35mm. If done improperly, the results can be horrendous, and the Dogme rules further complicate the procedure by prohibiting post-production filtering processes. The fit that von Trier threw when certain scenes in *The Idiots* were lightened illustrates the way that Dogme has handcuffed even the technicians. In addition to that, the content of the films is stronger in his opinion, and finally he credits the amazing networking and sales abilities of Zentropa and their marketing arm, Trust Film, for giving Danish Dogme films a leg up.

Like most of his American Dogme brethren, Martini is optimistic about the direction in which film is going, and talks glowingly about the democratizing effects that DV has had on the medium. And he's untroubled by the possibility that somewhere out there somebody might be making a bad film. "People should be allowed to make as many good or bad Dogme films as they want. It's up to the public to see them or pass."

Julien Donkey-Boy

Clearly the highest profile American Dogme film was the first one, *Julien Donkey-Boy*, directed by the controversial Harmony Korine, son of documentary filmmaker Sol Korine.

The film hit while the iron was hot and Dogme hype was at its apex. And it featured the participation of some very eye-catching names. Hero of New German Cinema, Werner Herzog, who knew Korine personally and acted as a kind of mentor to the young American, had a part, and so did Korine's gal pal, Chlöe Sevigny, the sassy young starlet of *Kids*. The lead was played by none other than Ewen Bremner of *Trainspotting* fame, while veteran cinematographer Anthony Dod Mantle signed on to shoot the picture, intrigued by the challenge of filming such an unorthodox piece.

And then there was the wiry, long-haired Korine himself, an ex-skateboarder, all energy and defiance, a fount of offbeat ideas and surreal quotes. He was seen at the time as one of the best bets to inject some youthful integrity into moviemaking and was as much a star of the film as any of the on-screen personnel.

His rise to fame was made-to-order for writers looking for a hook. He had reportedly been discovered by photographer Larry Clark while hanging out in Manhattan's Washington Square park, and this meeting led to their collaboration on the provocative 1995 feature, *Kids*, with Korine penning the script in a mere three weeks. He followed that up with his own feature debut in 1997, *Gummo,* one of the most polarizing films in recent memory. It was savaged by mainstream critics with a fury not seen since *Pink Flamingos*. Janet Maslin called it the worst film of the year in *The New York Times,* and others attacked it as pointless, exploitative and insulting, while advocates praised its inventive use of mixed formats (Super 8, hand-held video and even Polaroids), and lauded what they saw as its compelling evocation of the midwestern heavy-metal mindset.

As the '90s came to a close, Korine was hot stuff, embraced by trendy style magazines as the epitome of post-grunge punk attitude and hailed by some in the underground as the filmmaker least likely to sell-out. His 15 minutes had arrived.

In the midst of all this he caught the attention of the Dogme brothers and was asked by Thomas Vinterberg to make a Dogme film. He accepted. It wouldn't be much of a stretch anyway, being basically how he normally worked. And it threw a new plot twist into stories on indie-cinema as the millennium came to a close: Harmony Korine meets Lars von Trier—the *enfant terribles* of American and European cinema join forces and spit in the face of the powers that be.

Author Richard Kelly, in his *The Name of this Book is Dogme95* from 2000, gave voice to the excitement that surrounded Korine's collision with Dogme. ". . . Korine and the Brotherhood recognized kindred spirits in each other, and so, symbolically, joined hands across the ocean, making a small but significant avant-garde. Doesn't this at least offer the prospect of an international solidarity among young filmmakers, demanding the impossible, eager to assault the mainstream, rushing onto the streets to tell their stories from down there?"

Whatever else *Julien Donkey-Boy* managed to do, it definitely "assaulted the mainstream." Like *Gummo,* the film had no discernible story, no plot. Korine disliked plots and felt that like life itself, things should just evolve, should just begin and end. He supplied detailed scene descriptions, but they weren't really in any order and the "script" was more like one long poem. Actors improvised madly. (Korine's ability to direct improvisation is a point of some dispute.)

The film was beyond bleak, attempting as it did to depict the inner life of a deeply schizophrenic and troubled young man called Julien, a forlorn character with an unkempt mass of curly hair and a vacant stare who tramps around the streets of Brooklyn talking gibberish to himself. Korine conceived this character as a young early-20's version of his real life uncle Eddie, at the time in his mid-40s and confined to a psychiatric hospital in Queens. Korine claimed he wanted Eddie himself to play the role, but that proved impossible and it went to Bremner, a Scot, whose toughest challenge was not playing a psychotic but playing an American (that new accent and all). But he was game, and prepared for the part by volunteering at a psychiatric hospital for six weeks.

Julien leads a barren existence. When not wandering the streets or holed up in a school for blind children where he spends time washing their feet, he's at home being abused by a sadistic father, played by Herzog with heavy German accent intact. He seeks refuge in his room and in imaginary conversations with the likes of Adolph Hitler. His pregnant sister, Pearl, is played with dreamy detachment by Chlöe Sevigny. She refuses to reveal to a doctor who the father of her unborn child is, and with few clues to go on, save for the enchanting effect she has on Julien, the viewer is left to fear the worst.

But tragedy strikes: Pearl falls while ice skating and has a miscarriage. At the hospital Julien manages to get his hands on the small corpse and flees, taking it home . . . on the bus(!)

This scene left a lasting impression on everyone involved, not least the bus passengers who had no idea that the sicko cradling a dead

Harmony Korine and Werner Herzog on the set of Julien Donkey-Boy.

baby (a doll) wrapped in a dirty towel was really part of a film shoot. Their reactions, secretly recorded by several fellow passengers (Mantle & Co.) rigged up with a host of different types of spy cameras, ran the range from disbelief, confusion, disgust, and anger to outright sorrow. It was a very chancy situation that could have turned violent, a painful ordeal for everyone including Korine who couldn't bear to be witness to it and remained safely ensconced in a van, paging through a magazine. When the bus stopped and the passengers got off, production assistants packed into a trailing van got out and caught up with them to explain they'd been in a film and to try to get them to sign releases.

Whatever its respective merits or lack thereof, *Julien Donkey-Boy* was completely different than any of the other Dogme films made before or since. Its subject matter, its non-linear structure, and its overall style—a potpourri of degraded and diffuse images shot with between 20 to 30 different types of cameras—resulted in a strictly underground type of film of the kind that rarely surfaced in commercial theaters. In this way it differentiated itself dramatically from the art-film conventions of European Dogme or the primitivist diarist narratives that typified many of the American pictures.

In relation to Dogme it was something new, but in relation to underground cinema it was anything but.

In its refusal to offer the audience any of the sweetmeats that filmmakers normally dole out, like *plots*, or characters the viewer can identify with, etc., *Julien Donkey-Boy* harkened back to the formalist experimental works of any number of 1960's underground *auteurs*. And Korine's presentation of an outsider's world of abject misery and amoral excess taken to an almost absurd degree was clearly grounded in the works of John Waters (*Female Trouble* and *Desperate Living*) and David Lynch (*Eraserhead*), not to mention *Even Dwarves Started Small* by his hero, Werner Herzog. And even the kind of cut-n-paste technical primitivism that Korine favored on both *Gummo* and *Julien Donkey-Boy* had its antecedents, most notably in the 1980's 16mm work of Hawaiian-born, Brown-educated Jon Moritsugu. His 1989 feature debut, *My Degeneration,* about a female rock group that sells out to the meat industry, was more challenging. Made on an almost 1:1 shooting ratio, it employed every mode of filmic expression under the sun, from negative frames, emulsion scratching, and model shots, to crude animation and original footage. Aside from getting your ankle chewed by a rat, it's the most low-tech experience one can have in a movie theater and remains a hallmark of punk cinema.

But Korine had been embraced in much broader circles. Mainstream film critics were being asked to take him seriously, and his film seemed all the more radical and outrageous when seen in the context of mainstream film culture. In any case, he was at this point everyone's favorite "bad boy"; he had gate-crashed Hollywood's well-catered party where even the rebels were supposed to have table manners and play by the rules. But he had proven he could clearly compete with von Trier on at least one level: his films were equally as polarizing.

Upon its release, *Julien Donkey-Boy* was the talk of the international festival circuit, hailed at festivals like Venice, Rotterdam, and New York even as the brickbats from mainstream critics rained down on Korine. Yet even some voices from the fringe found it to be maddeningly fractured and incoherent and reprimanded indie cinema's dark prince for his failure to seize the opportunity and get to the heart of these strange characters of his. So much promise, but . . . .

One thing was certain, though: Harmony Korine had not sold out. He'd given the film establishment something that stuck in their throats, something that they could not digest or assimilate, the way they seemingly assimilated all the good ideas and good directors who had risen up out of the primal indie muck.

Purely in regard to his effect on Dogme, Korine's influence looms large, particularly with the current generation of young indie/underground American filmmakers.

Amerikana

While there are no overwhelming plot or theme similarities in the remaining American films, they all, in their own way, even more than the previous four movies just discussed, deal with themes, approaches, and concerns that are quintessentially American.

Amerikana (#13) by James Meredino is, for example, a true-blown road movie. In basic essentials it's an update of *Easy Rider* with the chopped hogs replaced by a Vespa motor scooter. The Vespa needs to be transported from South Dakota to Los Angeles, and two pals take on the job, piloting the vehicle through the kind of classic wide-open western scenery that is integral to the genre ("no genre movies" alert!). Their journey sets in motion deeper ruminations on what America—and life—is really all about, with the two main characters taking wildly divergent views. One of them buys into the classic romantic myths on America while the other takes a darker view, and sees the country as a wasteland and its people lost and adrift.

Amerikana's director, James Merendino, had been born and raised in Utah and when his formal schooling was finished he traveled to Italy to study film. He eventually settled in Los Angeles, and like Dogme brother Rich Martini (#15), he made something of a career for himself in Hollywood, having, prior to his Dogme film, directed half a dozen 16mm and 35mm features. Probably the best known to date is his film, *SLC Punk,* about the Salt Lake City punk scene, which was a hit at the 1999 edition of the Sundance Film Festival.

Amerikana was co-financed by Zentropa, a German company called Gemini Films/Appollo Media, and by Straight Edge Filmed Entertainments, an American outfit. Through the 1999–2001 period, Zentropa was bullish on Dogme and seemed to be constantly in the press announcing new production package deals that involved X number of new international Dogme films. On May 20, 1999, for example, it was announced in the Danish press that Zentropa had made co-production deals for no fewer than 16 Dogme films, 8 of which would be from Scandinavia. But aside from their Danish films, *Amerikana* was, according to their final list, the only foreign picture they co-produced, leading one to conclude that foreign Dogme suffered from a sky high infant mortality rate.

Bad Acting

Unlike Merendino, actor Shaun Monson, who helmed Dogme #16, *Bad Acting,* was still trying to get his foot in Hollywood's door when Dogme came knocking. Despite appearances in several films, he had not yet managed to get his SAG card (which requires a speaking part). He had had a role that contained a line of spoken dialogue, but when the movie came out he was mortified to discover that he had been dubbed-over with a blubbering idiot's voice. Classic Hollywood story.

His only previous directing experience had been the troubled and little-seen feature, *Rough Draft,* which contained no dialogue.

He found out about Dogme and wanted to make a film, but was at a loss for the right material. Then he ran into an old acting acquaintance. The fellow came on all pretentious and self-absorbed. As Monson recalls, "He would say things like, 'I am an actor. I will always BE an actor, and I will never be anything BUT an actor,' which was so melodramatic. . . . Actors often speak very dramatically about what art and performance and emotion really is, and they tend to believe this makes them exceptional among people because they see themselves as artists. The truth of the matter is they're just earning a living like everyone else, and they're no more or less important than a plumber, a weatherman or a grocery store clerk. However you don't hear plumbers saying, 'I am a plumber! I will always BE a plumber and I'll never be anything BUT a plumber!' But there is just something about that word 'Artist', which is usually self-given, that makes people think they're better than anyone else."

Monson filled a classroom with 10 of the superior beings (actors) and re-created an acting class situation/environment. He had not written a proper screenplay but just a script outline, which in any case he kept to himself. He told the troop of actors to come to class just as they normally would and to behave very "actorly," to find their "inner ham."

Five cameras were used to shoot in the classroom. Each cameraperson was fitted with an earpiece under their headphones so that they could hear both the actor's dialogue and Shaun's camera direction, transmitted via a walkie-talkie from an adjacent room where he sat in front of a small bank of monitors. These classroom scenes were shot in a single day. Driving sequences took another day and the film was in the can. The actors improvised everything and all of them used their real names (a new Dogme rule?).

Reunion

An acting class . . . that was a good premise for a Dogme film. Dogme film #20, the Belgian picture, *Strass*, had also taken place in an acting class. It was a natural when one casted about for a realistic setting to which actors could relate. And yet far more frequently used by Dogme directors as a setting was the reunion or celebration. Six of the 33 Dogme films took place in such set-ups which easily lent themselves to the kind of improvisation and ensemble acting for which Dogme was best suited. And these kind of situations had universal appeal. The drama was familiar to viewers from all cultures, and a large number of characters could be shifted into the mix without all sorts of plot mechanizations.

Reunion (#17) was one such film. Set and filmed in Ojai, California, it told the story of a group of former school chums who all meet up again at their 20th high school reunion. The production-writing team of Kimberly O'Hara and Eric Klein created the film's premise and scripted the characters—and started casting—even before bringing in first-time director Leif Tilden to helm it.

A vague perception exists among some in Europe that the American Dogme directors are a bunch of inexperienced provincials who have jumped on the Dogme bandwagon out of purely financial or technical necessity, and yet Tilden, like many of the other American directors (Merendino, Sorenson, etc.) was well-traveled and had previously lived and pursued his craft in Europe, in his case having acted in theater productions in "the old country" after finishing up four years at NYU.

He took a very open and collaborative approach to the task of directing *Reunion*, seeing himself more as a "guide" than as a director.

Unlike in most Dogme films, the actors in *Reunion* were experienced Hollywood players, they had all been in other films before and were used to a certain way of doing things. Dogme was new to them, but they began to see the light after a few early bumps. "At first I found it annoying," notes actress Rainer Judd. "I'd think, 'I don't have time to deal with shopping for my character, doing my own make-up.' And then I thought about the times that I'd spent getting into character, and I'd have this flurry of activity around me with the hair and the make-up, and two hours later I'd think, 'my character wouldn't look this way!' . . . on this film I was going deeper into the character inside and out."

Judd's comments hit on something that was central to Dogme, that an actor had to supply their own character as well as their own wardrobe. The actors were thus involved more as collaborators than as just employees.

"Dogme is quite voyeuristic," adds another member of the cast, Marlene Forte. "There's a shift toward watching the action unravel, rather than planning its unraveling, that is much more engaging. It's less predictable and people love that. That's why we watch car accidents: it's a tendency human beings have to 'peek' at life."

Pizza, beer, and memories are the order of the day in Reunion.

For their part, O'Hara and Klein found the stripped-down Dogme approach to be ideally suited to the making of a next-to-no-budget indie film, since it freed them from having to deal with lighting, costumes, make-up, etc., all the nitty-gritty that producers of low-budget films get sucked into dealing with. Instead, they had more space and energy to deal with the essentials of the film itself.

Resin

Of all the 33 Dogme films, none are more politically charged than *Resin* (#23), a "harsh polemic" on aspects of the California criminal justice system, as *The Chicago Tribune* termed it. The film was born out of a sense of anger and came about via a series of serendipitous encounters between people and ideas.

In 1996, filmmaker Steve Sobel started working on the script. It would be his second feature film. He was living in the Haight Ashbury neighborhood at the time, getting up at 3:00 A.M. to deliver natural foods, and working on the script when he got home in the afternoon. It was here in San Francisco that he became aware of the anti-Marijuana prohibition movement, and the issues surrounding the then-upcoming vote on Proposition 215 which would have permitted the private consumption of Marijuana for medicinal purposes. At one point, a friend who was suffering from AIDS took him down to the Cannabis Buyers Club on Market Street (which was raided by DEA agents just three months later). His mother being a civil lawyer and his dad a criminal defense attorney, Sobel had always been politically engaged and these experiences had a strong impact on him—and the script.

By the Fall of 1998, he had moved to Hollywood to make the film. The script already contained references to California's notorious "Three Strikes Law," which stipulated a mandatory life-in-prison sentence for anyone convicted of a third felony, but after viewing Michael J. Moore's documentary about the law and its repercussions, entitled *The Legacy*, it became a central focus of the film. He was determined to expose the outrageous injustice of the law, and this further motivated him to get the picture made.

But meetings with potential investors were discouraging. They found the script, about a drug dealer who gets busted and faces life in prison, to be too "down" to gamble their money on. The drug dealer, Zeke, was not a particularly likable character, not a character with which one could readily identify. By refusing to make the main character "sympathetic," Sobel was bucking the unwritten laws of commercial dramaturgy and going for realism.

At about that point in time he heard about the Dogme 95 movement, and soon thereafter got a chance to see *The Celebration*. He was bowled over. The next night he brought his cinematographer back to see it and they both agreed that this was how they would shoot *Resin*. By going with this mobile, lightweight shooting approach they could do a more intuitive, gut-level take on the story and give it a much more realistic feel, thereby avoiding crime-story clichés. And shooting on DV would be cost-effective.

Sobel's chance encounter in Santa Barbara with the Russian filmmaker, Vladimir Gyorski, who was then on one of his extremely infrequent speaking tours, provided him with his director. Gyorski enjoyed considerable cult repute in Russia, but was little known outside the country despite his prodigious output. A few of his better-known films included *Sunlight* from 1958, *Alla* from 1962, and *Tomorrow*, which was shot in the midst of uprisings that took place in 1968. He was renown for his abstract, often quirky style, and highly regarded for his political commitment which had several times landed him in jail.

Coincidentally, Gyorski had also embraced Dogme and its "documentary, non-commercial and overtly political approach to filmmaking" (as *Resin* press materials expressed it), and in 1998 he had formed "The New Russian Dogme" with a group of Moscow student filmmakers. He intended to make a Dogme film himself, but had not yet done so. When Sobel told him about the "Three Strikes Law" and its use as a tool in the "war on drugs," he found Gyorski agreed with his positions. And Gyorski was intrigued when Sobel told him about the film he was trying to get made. Having lived so long under a politically repressive government, he could understand the mechanisms at play. This war on drugs was, in his opinion, nothing more than "America's crazy war against its own people."

He agreed to direct the film, and Sobel would write and produce.

Gyorski brought an outsider's perspective to the subject matter and took a very instinctive approach to the directing. His first move was to toss the script. Instead he used lengthy conversations with each individual actor to flesh out their characters and the environments in which they moved. Consequently, the actors knew *who* they were but not what the story was. In this fashion, scenes were "prepared for" but not rehearsed. The actors would be set in motion and some basic things would occur to which they would react, and the story would form itself out of this.

"As shooting progressed," notes press material, "the Dogme manifesto created a range of situations no one could ever have imagined. For example, during the fight scene between Zeke and some drunken frat boys, Zeke was filmed throughout the course of the night selling pot at various real parties around town and had no idea that anything was about to happen to him. Yet, when more cameramen appeared, something foreboding suddenly hung in the air and created for Zeke very real tension. The people on the street believed a real fight was occurring despite the presence of the cameras, so much so that in outtakes one good Samaritan can be seen trying to break up the fight, even ordering the camera people to stop instigating a violent situation."

In this way, fiction and reality merged throughout the film.

The second half of the picture largely bears on Zeke's interactions with various lawyers and court officials and has an exceedingly realistic feel to it, reportedly due to Gyorski's use of real-life prosecutors, D.A.s and judges. In these sequences, "You forget you're watching a movie," as Joe Baltake of the *Sacramento Bee* described it in December 2001.

"While the ambiance of the film is often reminiscent of Steven Soderbergh's *Traffic* (2000)," he went on to add, "Gyorski's work is actually the polar opposite of Soderbergh's movie, eschewing that film's tendency to work as a public service message about America's 'war on drugs.' Still, one can imagine *Resin* as a vignette that was left out of *Traffic*."

Purely in the afterthought department, it is interesting to reflect on how Dogme can be seen as a fiercely political movement, when in fact it is not political at all. Yet that is exactly Dogme's greatest strength, the fact that it can serve as a source of inspiration for political filmmakers from totally different cultures—Sobel and Gyorski in this case—and that it can unite them with its vague prescriptions for revolution. The fuzziness surrounding Dogme allows filmmakers to see in it what they want to see and to fetch inspiration from it as they will. That they see Dogme for what it is not is essentially irrelevant and in no way devalues what they have created.

It's also striking to note how different all the American Dogme directors are from each other. They're an extremely disparate mix of people and come from backgrounds that are far more diverse than the Danish directors. A bunch so dissimilar that they're not even all Americans (Vladimir Gyorski, a Russian; Leif Tilden, born in Sweden; etc.) . . . a group whose only common trait is the fact that none of

A scene from Resin *featuring Zeke at his trial.*

them are esteemed *auteurs* of the type that Dogme has always dreamed of attracting. Paul Morrisey, Warhol's old assistant and himself director of classics like *Flesh for Frankenstein* and *Blood for Dracula*, would have been in their number, but his planned Dogme film, *The House of Klang*, a comedy about the fashion industry which was slated to be #5, the first foreign Dogme film, disappeared somewhere along the way. And Steven Spielberg, director of *E.T.* and other dreadnoughts of the silver screen, at various points declared his intention to do Dogme yet never found the time. Other notable American directors also said good things about Dogme but it never went further than that.

Security, Colorado

The very next Dogme film, *Security, Colorado* (#24), was directed by Montana born-and-raised Andrew Gillis, who had made several films previous to this and had worked as second unit director and additional music composer on the 1999 independent hit, *George Washington*.

The issues that Gillis was dealing with were very different than the ones that Sobel and Gyorski had addressed with *Resin*, concerned as they were with exposing the bleak realities of "the American gulag," so to speak. The reality that Gillis was seeking to capture was, by contrast, more bound up in the spiritual aspects of human relationships.

His philosophical take on the picture was laid out in a director's statement that reads as a meditation on the subjective nature of human memory. Considerably more pensive in tone than the dramatic manifestos issued by a young attack-minded Lars von Trier, it's more of an abstract reflection on what the movie meant to him than any kind of declaration of principal, and is here reprinted in whole:

> *We would like to believe in the judgment we practice on our own actions. We would like to think that we can learn from our mistakes. We would like to think that we can recognize our mistakes, that hindsight is 20/20. But our memories are never as clear as we think. They are clouded by perception*

A Polaroid of Andrew Gillis, director of Security, Colorado.

and emotion and everything that takes place between that which is remembered and the time it is being called upon. Events stack up like cardboard boxes, bending and sinking into each other, and soon lose their own importance in the numbers. There are few among us who can file through these images of the past bit by bit to pull fact from the impression. We cannot clear the corruption of our own influence from our thoughts in order to see reality in our memory. We can only use the personal truth of the effect, felt along with the images of the past, to guide us to a cause. However, for those who observe without bias, each event can be seen for what it is and many causes may be found for the effect they generate, each equally valid and truthful within the mind of the viewer.

Security, Colorado is an impression of the events which took place between a young woman's graduation and the subsequent re-evaluation of her priorities. And though this film was shot without temporal displacement and it all took place within the moment it was captured, it is now part of the past and the events present themselves like memories. It is the flash that fills its protagonist's eyes when asked why she has ended up the way she has. The answer to "why?" comes from the experience in total, not from one single distinguishable trauma, but from the gathering weight of the tiny decisions that slowly helped her to crush her own desire.

The film was made in accordance with the rules and ideas set forth in the DOGME 95 Manifesto and The Vow of Chastity without regard for any other conventional "rules." It was created, set in motion, and captured.

Andrew Gillis
10/21/01

Converging with Angels

For some American filmmakers, Dogme 95 was the push, the cover, the excuse they needed to get their films made. They used it to get people interested in working on their low-budget and in some cases very unorthodox film projects. Being Dogme helped, if only to infuse participants with a sense of solidarity and ensure some level of visibility at film festivals.

But it didn't help Michael Sorenson.

The director of Dogme #25, *Converging with Angels,* had quite a different experience. "What I found attractive about making a Dogme film drove a number of potential collaborators right out the door. You would not believe how hard it is to actually assemble a crew of professionals who have the maturity to look at the Dogme 95 manifesto and the Vow of Chastity as a rigorous creative challenge and not as an excuse for sloppy filmmaking."

Sloppy filmmaking was the last thing the 30-something-year-old Sorenson wanted. The New York native was at that point in the game a filmmaker with a very well-honed sense of professionalism and craft, having produced, written and/or directed an array of documentaries, public service shorts, music videos, and a couple of features, in the process relocating to Chicago.

His *Converging with Angels* was as different from *Security, Colorado* as *Security, Colorado* had been from *Resin,* being, at least on the surface, concerned with matters of a carnal rather than a spiritual nature. Several scenes were in fact physically explicit, and some of the dialogue was quite explicit as well. Not for children was this story of a high-class bi-sexual call boy and the woman he falls for after literally scraping her up (intoxicated) off the sidewalk and taking her home.

The script had undergone several re-writes and was at the time of Sorenson's conversion to Dogme—after seeing *The Celebration*—on ice in his filing cabinet. At that point it seemed to be headed in a very commercial direction and he was not particular enthused about it, but after giving it another look he realized that running it through the Dogme strainer would actually solve a number of the film's creative problems. For one, Dogme would rid it of the clichés and genre conventions that so often worked their way into stories about prostitutes and sex workers.

As he himself put it, "What drew me to making this as a Dogme film were the specific limitations placed on how the story could be told, preventing me from artificially manufacturing audience response. . . . For instance, as opposed to this being another 'hooker with a heart of gold' story, the audience is forced early on to disassociate from those genre conventions and really make a commitment to tracking the story through the eyes of a specific character. Any narrative action that occurs emanates honestly from character interaction. So as opposed to something that is driven largely by plot, it's really driven by the decisions that the main characters make over the course of the picture. Which could be completely random. I mean there are a number of scenes on the cutting-room floor that would have taken the film in a completely different direction, but this is the way I wanted to tell the story."

Sorenson encouraged improvisation, but only after exhaustive preparation and rehearsal.

The fact that he was making a Dogme film didn't carry much weight with the various film board functionaries and city officials they had to deal with as they went into production. Sorenson encountered from the community-at-large a general sense of indifference.

And the struggles didn't stop once the film got made. Lots of work was needed to give it a proper release in the bruisingly competitive U.S. market where independent films had to fight harder and harder for screen space and attention from the press. The whole process from concept to completion stood in sharp contrast to the Danish-made Dogme films. Those directors didn't have to raise funds by appearing on late night talk-shows as "The Human Garbage Can"; the Danish films were automatically guaranteed distribution, press, attention, and festival play. They were not considered by their respective public to be fringe art-house offerings, but rather were considered to be solidly mainstream. Back in the U.S. the playing rules were different. Even having celebrities in your picture was no longer a guarantee that it wouldn't just go directly to video or cable.

In any case, *Converging with Angels* did receive a limited theatrical release in February of 2003 and met with lukewarm critical response. According to Sorenson, this was due to the film's length (2 hours, 39 minutes), and, as he puts it, "the uninformed assumption that the entire Dogme 95 movement was just a marketing ploy and excuse for lazy filmmaking created by filmmakers seeking an entry into North America." The backlash against Dogme was well underway in America, at least among the professional set, and yet Sorenson found it ironic that he was being accused of using Dogme as a gimmick to get the film released in America, ". . . given the picture's praise in Europe, Asia and Canada as an emotionally uncompromising work that no one can imagine having been made in the United States!"

The Sparkle Room

Seven of the 33 Dogme films had at least one main character who was mentally disturbed (or pretended to be). Here was a trend in

Dogme that was a far reach from all the crowded parties and celebrations, one which took the viewer down into the tormented inner recesses and crevices of the human mind. For some reason, Dogme seemed to have an affinity for damaged or dysfunctional characters.

Dogme film #26, *The Sparkle Room,* was one of these films, but Alex McAulay's movie also immediately separates itself from all the others by virtue of the fact that it was made in North Carolina—the first rural, southern Dogme film.

Not that the 27-year-old McAulay was any backwoodsman. He'd been born and raised in Seattle and had gone on to study semiotics at Brown University (The Brown Semiotics department having earlier produced two other filmmakers of note in the underground: Todd Haynes and Jon Moritsugu). While at Brown, McAulay studied film under the tutelage of noted avant-gardist Leslie Thornton. And McAulay is also a musician, recording under the pseudonym of Charles Douglas and having worked with members of both The Pixies and The Velvet Underground.

No hillbilly, he . . .

Out in the backwoods with the first rural American Dogme film, The Sparkle Room.

The Sparkle Room was made under the auspices of Voltage USA, a company McAulay had founded with two colleagues in Chapel Hill, North Carolina, to produce and release independent films.

His and just about every other American director's problem with Dogme was the requirement that they transfer the DV material to 35mm to satisfy rule #9, which stipulated that the film format (screening format) must be in 35mm. It was a viciously expensive and tricky process, and seemed to at least one of the American directors, Rick Schmidt (#10), to be the rule that most directly contradicted the spirit of Dogme.

"This rule flies in the face of all the other 'truth-seeking rules'. . . . to produce a movie for under 4,000 USD, the cost of going 35mm will almost double the budget (and that's not counting the full 45,000 USD expenditure for 35mm blow-up which is common). The real moviemaker, though impoverished, aims his (borrowed) camera at reality-based subjects, then is expected to get some sponsor/investor to front almost 50,000 bucks."

Like *Resin, The Sparkle Room* had a political edge to it, and this was rare in Dogme despite the pseudo-political rhetoric of the manifesto. The film explored issues of class and wealth in American society through the prism of homelessness, and raised moral questions about the nature of power and control. One of the actors had in fact been homeless in reality at one point in his life and he brings an authenticity to the role.

But it wasn't purely a political film. As McAulay states, "I want to show the strange beauty that comes from the rot and grime of the world."

Dogme's Impact on America

Beyond the obvious effect that Dogme has had on the 12 directors making the American films, what has Dogme's wider impact been on America?

The directors themselves have mixed feelings. "The Dogme 95 movement in the States," comments Michael Sorenson (#25), "is (short-sightedly) thought of as a European intellectual curiosity at best, as evidenced by the fact that only two of the Dogme films produced in North America have received significant exposure." . . . "People in the U.S. don't know what Dogme 95 is," opines Rich Martini (#15). "Sure, there are spots of people here and there, but I'd say 95% of the viewing public thinks Dogme is the film made by Kevin Smith (*Dogma*, 1999)."

Thanks to the power of Hollywood muscle when it comes to saturation advertising, Martini's probably right on target with that last assertion, and it is also no doubt true that Dogme is little known to the broad spectrum of the American moviegoing public. And yet Dogme *has* had impact in America, and it has been felt in three specific areas.

(1) Dogme has had an impact on the art-house segment of the viewing public, those brave souls who can bear to read subtitles. While to this writer's knowledge no American Dogme film has yet had a full-fledged theatrical premiere followed by a legit run in a commercial theater, all the Danish Dogme films have. *Mifune* sold 100,000 tickets in America while *The Celebration* sold 200,000. And though the final numbers are still coming in for *Italian for Beginners,* it is clear that it will easily top them all. This is not even counting festival screenings. It's reasonable to assume then that at the very least upwards of 500,000 Americans and possibly many more have had bodily contact with Dogme. And the American film press has been more than attentive to it. With that said, all the Danish Dogme films and even the "big" English-language von Trier pictures have been confined to the urban art-house circuit where a film rarely plays on more than 30 screens simultaneously. These films do not, in trade parlance, "cross over" to mainstream theaters which house approximately 5,000 screens and where a subtitled film never shows its face. As Thomas Vinterberg once remarked while promoting *The Celebration,* it's a shame that Americans are so afraid to *read.*

(2) Dogme has had an impact on America's filmmaking community in a purely theoretical capacity. Nobody who travels in

these circles and has any engagement with the issues can today be unaware of Dogme. As illustrated in these pages, Dogme has given many hope and inspiration.

(3) Dogme has had an impact on mainstream American filmmaking, on its style and its language if not its message. Hollywood has adopted the grainy, handheld low-tech approach, and a growing number of Hollywood films exude an obvious Dogme aesthetic, if only in parts. The list of films by established directors, Hollywood and foreign, that are said to be inspired by Dogme includes pictures as disparate as *Bamboozled* by Spike Lee, *Time Code* by Mike Figgis, *Monsoon Wedding* by Mira Nair, and *Traffic* and *Full Frontal* by Steven Soderbergh. Other titles frequently linked to Dogme include *Chuck and Buck*, *Roger Dodger*, *The Insider*, *The Anniversary Party*, and even *Jackass*. Issues of creative inspiration aside, few of theses pictures would have been considered releasable in North America had Dogme not shown that this type of film could sell tickets.

Nonetheless, when all is said and done, no American director of the type that hip Danes really respect—auteurs like Martin Scorsese, Milos Forman, or Jonathan Demme—ever made a Dogme film, and due to this the expectations that Dogme gave rise to early on have never been fully met. To have just one of these directors turn their talents to Dogme would have confirmed the movement in the eyes of many and, with all due respect to Lars von Trier, given it the mark of legitimacy that only such a director can bestow.

Other Foreign Dogme Films

As unfair as it might be to group the remaining Dogme films under such a humble heading, they *are* an unclassifiable lot, and except for the Spanish films they constitute single entries from a host of widely scattered countries (Argentina, Norway, France, Sweden, Korea, Italy, and Switzerland). These films obviously cannot be placed in any broader national context and cannot even provide much evidence of how Dogme has taken root internationally, only that it *has*, to some degree, been embraced in other countries. (This is a new phenomenon; the French New Wave and The New German Cinema, for example, were never "exported" in such a way. Influential all over the world, yes, but not exported intact, as it were.) And yet the following films, however isolated they may appear, are all for various reasons important to the history of Dogme—important for what is indefinable as well as definable about it, and further mention of these pictures, beyond plot synopsis, is merited.

The Lovers (#5) was directed by actor Jean-Marc Barr, a Frenchman who had lived for years in America and who had appeared in several von Trier films including *Europa* and *Breaking the Waves*. There was considerable curiosity at the start of Dogme as to which film would be the first "foreign" Dogme picture, and after some amount of false starts and confusion, Barr's film became the first foreign Dogme film at #5.

This was back when Dogme was being taken very seriously and the assumption was that a foreign director would fly to Denmark with film in hand and submit it to the Dogme brothers to be judged. This was a far cry from Dogme at the end when you were just lucky if you could manage to shake up an e-mail reply from whoever happened to be manning the Dogme secretariat that day, let alone get any support or guidance.

It's unknown as to whether Barr actually traveled to Denmark, but judge his film the Brothers did and they even ordered him to make a few changes. This was the age of "high" Dogme to be sure, and soon after the Brothers abandoned such ceremoniousness.

Interview (#7) was made by the South Korean director, Daniel H. Byun. It was shot on DV and 35mm in Paris where he once studied at the FEMIS film school, and had a reported budget of two million USD. It made the rounds of film festivals eager at this early stage to show anything Dogme, and it drew a fair amount of criticism for rule breaks. The inability of the Brothers to enforce Dogme orthodoxy was already becoming clear. Filmmakers who were in violation of the rules had the option of absolving their sins by making a public, written confession, and many availed themselves of this opportunity. Some would break certain rules on purpose and then come forward and confess. Others were more or less indifferent and viewed the rules as guidelines rather than as binding dictates. And by confessing, one was spared from going to hell, whatever hell was in Dogme terms (probably being forced to spend eternity in a multiplex located in an American shopping mall). Confessing was yet another way to be heard and to put one's opinion forth in a roundabout way. And confessions generated more paper to be filed in the dusty Dogme library.

Fuckland (#8) by Jose Luis Marques, was from Argentina, and with a title like that the film was guaranteed a certain amount of attention. The world was holding its breath for a foreign Dogme film that was really great, and it would have to keep waiting. An audacious concept that didn't pan out and lost viewers along the way was the general consensus on Marques' film. Another one of those movies where reality and fantasy interweave. Dogme seemed to be prone to this kind of thing, which was strange since it was supposed to be all about telling a solid, simple, straightforward story. But films like *Fuckland* ran counter to this, although it did have its advocates.

Meanwhile, the Swedish *Babylon* (#9), the Italian *Diapason* (#11), the Swiss *Joyride* (#14), the Norwegian *Cabin Fever* (#19), and the Belgian *Strass* (#20) came out and received a modicum of attention on the festival circuit if only because they were the first Dogme films from their respective countries. Films were reported to be on the way in England and Germany, but like so many in-the-works Dogme films, they faded from sight somewhere along the line. Although some of the above-mentioned films are quite good, none of them managed to become international hits in any sense the way the Danish films had. In fact, several quickly disappeared into oblivion. An unmistakable weariness was settling in. What was the point, many wondered? Obeying the Dogme rules in and of itself seemed to guarantee absolutely nothing. The lack of any standards was glaring and the general public was starting to lose patience.

Unique among Foreign Dogme were the Spanish films: *Once Upon Another Time* (#22), *Wedding Days* (#30), which starred Spanish horror film veteran, Paul Naschy, and *The Ending* (#31). All three were made by the same director, he of the distinctive handlebar mustache, Juan Pinzás, and produced by the same studio, Atlantico, which Pinzás had co-founded in 1985. And they used a lot of the same actors. While many of the foreign Dogme companies were one-shot operations, founded by directors to make their Dogme films and then folded up and packed away like tents, Atlantico is a professional outfit which puts out some of the slickest publicity this side of Hollywood. And they've managed to generate considerable press inside Spain around their pictures. Those folks who claim there is no reason to make more than one Dogme film might question the need to make *three*, and it's a fair question that can only be answered by watching the movies.

Although it was probably not the intention, what the closing of the Dogme secretariat in June of 2002 accomplished was to shut down the foreign arm of Dogme film production while Danish Dogme continues apace. It's perhaps absurd to read "conspiracy" into this, but it

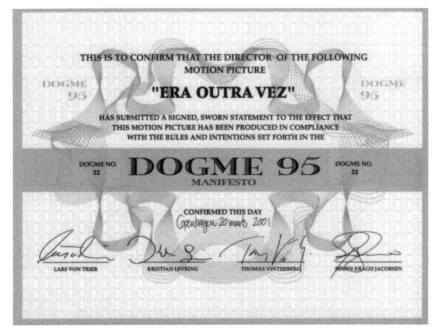

The official Dogme certificate for the Spanish film, Once Upon Another Time.

turned out to be a convenient solution to a bothersome situation for the Danish true-believers who were powerless to stop what Dogme had set in motion outside their borders, and powerless to control it.

IX

The End of Dogme?

At the end of old 1950's B-horror movies, a quivering question mark used to appear under the words "The End" as the theremin whined. The same question mark goes here.

Is this the end of Dogme . . . or just the beginning?

Dogme is in many ways indisputably dead. It was talked to death from the start by its creators in the holy cause of promotion, and last rites were read over its body by those very same founders even before it got a chance to have a mid-life crisis. Declaring something to be dead is a very dramatic thing to do and they indulged in the drama repeatedly, even if maybe it wasn't dead, whatever "dead" is.

As the dim view would have it, Dogme suffered a fate worse than death: it became popular, hip, trendy—the "now flavor"—and fell victim to its own hype. It's hard to be a rebel when you're the subject of all those panel discussions, when the academics have embraced you, when large auditoriums full of people are hanging on your every word. In a more solitary art-form maybe such a revolution as Dogme could have survived to reach maturity. Perhaps better that they had all subscribed to von Trier's vow of silence in Paris and never uttered a single explanation, but that's not the way the press-hungry film world works. The gears must be oiled. And then the term itself was exploited by every shyster and short-order cook who could chalk up a sign board, giving rise to Dogme furniture, Dogme used-cars, Dogme take-away and even Dogme ice-cream.

It became familiar with a vengeance and somehow people felt betrayed by that. Dogme fatigue indeed.

The vagueness and ambiguity that was part and parcel of Dogme's birth has functioned, intentionally or not, as a kind of built-in control mechanism to keep it going, to keep it revolving. The problem is that Dogme was born in drama and it hasn't been able to find a suitably dramatic way to die. Fassbinder: dead, bang, definitely the end of New German Cinema, time to move on. Dogme, instead, ages gracelessly, once the star of the show now hanging around in the wings being ignored, guilty of the worst crime of all—not being new anymore. And whatever it is today, it's not that. Seeing grainy DV images up on the big screen is no longer inventive, brave, or novel. It has become the standard. The audience is no longer even notified that a film originated on DV. And it's also true that the DV film that really shook up Hollywood, *The Blair Witch Project*, had no Dogme seal, even though it was Dogme in all its essentials.

Meanwhile, back in Denmark, as revealed in these pages, the feeling took hold that Dogme was pushing Danish cinema in a mainstream direction, with the full complicity of two studios named Nimbus and Zentropa. And that was never the intention of "the great experimenter," Lars von Trier.

No need to worry, counseled the sages, help was on the way in the form of a whole new crop of films by none other than the four original Dogme brothers—all archly un-Dogme and all set to open in the first half of 2003. It was left to them to save Danish cinema from their own monstrous creation, to give Danish viewers a shot of something new and fresh and different. And ironically, all these movies that were going to save Danish cinema were all English-language films, bigger productions aimed at the international market.

And one by one the new movies came out, and almost all of them were met by barely repressed groans of disappointment, met with reviews that were at best mixed and met with ticket counts that bordered on the disastrous. As noted, *The Celebration* and *Mifune* had each sold about 350,000 tickets in Denmark, yet their follow-ups were pronounced disappointments. By mid-May (2003) both were finishing up second-run engagements and the public's verdict was in: *It's All About Love* had sold just over 50,000 tickets while *Skagerrak* had sold just over 37,000. Levring's *The Intended*, which opened in Denmark on July 18, 2003, earned mixed reviews, but boded to be only marginally more popular than *The King is Alive*, which wasn't saying much.

Finally, there was von Trier's *Dogville*, received with standing ovations by the press at Cannes 2003 only to be ignored at the awards ceremony. In any case, the blessings of Cannes, where the will to experiment is so highly valued, rarely translated into success for von Trier with his home public. No matter—he travels in his own bubble, under his own power, more or less immune to the changing stylistic and critical tides that have left some of his colleagues stranded on the rocks. And as far as Dogme goes, he invented it, but owes it the least.

Lone Scherfig had better luck than Vinterberg or Kragh-Jacobsen with her next film, *Wilbur Wants to Kill Himself*, which sold 170,000 tickets, but that paled in comparison with the 800,000-plus tickets *Italian for Beginners* sold.

Different from Dogme all these films were to varying degrees, but rather than banish the ghosts of Dogme and send Danish cinema off in promising new directions, they prompted in many a strong dose of Dogme nostalgia. None of these new films had been able to recapture the simplicity and spunk which had made the Dogme films such critical and public successes. And although the "Danish New Wave" of the '90s already seems like an ancient occurrence, a closed chapter, Dogme itself continues to cast a long and stubborn shadow.

Maybe they all should have just made more Dogme films!

Lack of home-grown Danish stars in these English-language productions was commonly cited as a reason for the cool audience reception, but then again the very popular Iben Hjejle had played her heart out as the lead in *Skagerrak* and that hadn't given the film any bounce at all.

Graduating along with the Dogme brothers and sisters to bigger-budget English-language productions were, as noted earlier, Nicolas Winding Refn and Ole Bornedal, with, respectively, *Fear X* and *I Am Dina*. They too failed to meet expectations.

These are a radically mixed bunch of films that almost defy collective categorization, but their collective failure points to a clear and disturbing pattern that has led to no small amount of soul-searching in the Danish film world.

And out of that uncertainty, something good may come.

X

Appendix

Plot Synopses of All 33 Dogme Films

Note: The last two Dogme films, both Danish, specified here as films 32 (*Old, New, Borrowed and Blue*) and 33 (*In Your Hands*), were not included on the "final" list of 31 Dogme films issued by the Dogme secretariat in June of 2002 when they closed shop. This brings the total number of official Dogme films which are either completed or in production up to 33. On January 30, 2003, it was announced that two more Dogme films were in pre-production with releases slated for sometime in 2004 (see end of list for what few details are known about these two films). Additionally, the numbering system used in this index is the international count, which takes into consideration all Dogme films (as opposed to the purely domestic count, which includes only films made in Denmark).

Missing in action: It was impossible to view or find any substantive information on the Swedish Dogme film, *Babylon* (#9), by Vladan Zdravkovic, or on the American film entitled *Come Now* (#27), which was the only Dogme film put up on the final list without any information or contact numbers attached. It was not necessary for a film to be finished to receive a Dogme certificate, and possibly this film was never completed or, being one of the last, is still in some stage of production.

No contact numbers are supplied here since so many of the contact links listed on the Secretariat's final list are no longer valid, and it would be unfair to list only some. The fact is that, strictly from a business perspective, foreign Dogme was a fragile proposition and a lot of the companies that produced these films have gone out of business. This happens all the time in the film world in general, but for our purposes it renders the printing of contact information somewhat irrelevant, and thus only title, nationality, year, and director are listed below. Native title is listed first, followed by the English title (in bold) when two titles exist.

#1—*Festen/ **The Celebration***, Danish, 1998, Directed by Thomas Vinterberg: A family gathers along with friends in an old hotel to celebrate the patriarch's 60th birthday, but things go horribly wrong when the oldest son gives his father an acidly ironic toast, congratulating the old man on the sexual abuse he subjected he and his twin sister to as children. The sister has recently committed suicide. One by one family members come to grips with the truth about the old man as the facade of respect crumbles and one of the most mortifying family celebrations in film history winds to a close.

#2—*Idioterne/ **The Idiots***, Danish, 1998, Directed by Lars von Trier: A group of young Danish adults have formed a kind of collective in an old villa outside Copenhagen. They spend their time goofing on the uptight and proper townsfolk, pretending to be retarded. In so doing, they are ridiculing the conformist conventions of Danish society and challenging their own preconditioned behavior in the bargain. Eventually, things go sour and they disband their social experiment.

#3—*Mifunes Sidste Sang/ **Mifune***, Danish, 1998, Directed by Søren Kragh-Jacobsen: Upon the death of his father, a Copenhagen yuppie is obliged to travel back to the ramshackle family farm to settle affairs, and here he is reunited with his mentally retarded brother. He plans to put him in a home, but in the meantime hires a housekeeper to bring some order to the place. She turns out to be a big city call-girl on the run from a mysterious stalker. The three-some, later joined by the call-girl's troubled teenage brother, form a kind of alternative family based on mutual support.

#4—*The King is Alive*, Danish, 1999, Directed by Kristian Levring: An international group of tourists are stranded in an old abandoned mining town out in the Namibian desert after their bus driver gets lost and runs out of gas. Moving into several of the remaining tumble-down shacks, they struggle against boredom and panic in various ways, and even stage an impromptu production of Shakespeare's *King Lear* to pass the time. They battle against their own inner demons as well as each other, and when help finally arrives they have reached a state of collective spiritual transformation.

#5—*Lovers*, French, 1999, Directed by Jean-Marc Barr: A Yugoslavian painter falls in love with a French girl and their romance blossoms amid the background of classic Parisian locales and atmosphere. When police discover that he is residing illegally in France and order him to leave the country, their relationship is put to the test and his girlfriend decides to do everything in her power to protect him and to keep their love alive.

#6—*Julien Donkey-Boy*, American, 1999, Directed by Harmony Korine: A deeply schizophrenic young man named Julien spends time working in a home for blind children and wandering the streets, doing his best to survive in a bleak world. This task is made all the more difficult by his beyond-dysfunctional home life, and a tyrannical and brutal father who gives play to some of his own bizarre obsessions. Julien's pregnant sister has a miscarriage and he gets his hands on the aborted fetus and takes it home (on the bus) to hide under his bed cover.

#7—*Interview*, South Korean, 2000, Directed by Daniel H. Byun: In the process of interviewing a women for his documentary movie, the filmmaker falls in love with her. She resists his gestures of interest for reasons hidden in her past and also because she has been lying to him in these interviews and does not want that fact revealed. Finally, through her conversations with the filmmaker, she comes to terms with herself and tells the truth.

#8—*Fuckland*, Argentinean, 2000, Directed by Jose Luis Marques: A fellow from Buenos Aires who makes his living as a magician hatches a patriotic plot to win back the Falkland Islands from the British: he will travel to the islands to have sex with as many British women as possible and thereby ensure, presumably with the help of other patriotic countrymen, that the Island's next generation is of mixed race. He settles upon his "target," a women named Camilla. They go out for drinks, dinner, and sightseeing, but the final result of their meeting is ever in doubt as fact and fiction merge.

#9—*Babylon*, Swedish, 2001, Directed by Vladan Zdravkovic— no information available

#10—*Chetzemoka's Curse*, American, 2000, Directed by Rick Schmid and cast: A woman who works as a maid in a small-town hotel is haunted by the memory of her first lover and his subsequent betrayal. It seems she can't help but pass the bad karma along to others and ends up encouraging an older married man to run off with her and betray *his* wife and kids. Billed as "an acrimonious comedy."

#11—*Diapason*, Italian, 2001, Directed by Antonio Domenici: Two stories merge together over the course of one night in Rome. In his attempts to get an American actress to accept a role in his movie, the 60-year-old director, Marcello, tries to dazzle her with stories about his professional experiences with Fellini and Mastroianni and shows her locales such as Fontana di Trevi and Via Veneto, etc., where *La Dolce Vita* was filmed. The other story revolves around the actions of a desperate group of foreigners who lack moral scruples.

#12—*Italiensk for Begyndere/**Italian for Beginners***, Danish, 2000, Directed by Lone Scherfig: A group of lonely people which includes a waiter, a hair-dresser, a priest, and a baker's assistant, etc., coincidentally connect with each other in an Italian language class that they are taking for the fun of it, and romance blossoms as they form pairs. When one woman receives an unexpected inheritance, she treats her classmates to a trip to Venice where they all come together at a sumptuous feast.

#13—***Amerikana***, American, 2001, Directed by James Merendino: Two friends in their late twenties travel from South Dakota to Los Angeles on a Vespa motor scooter. They experience the journey very differently: one has romantic notions of the country while the other sees it as an empty wasteland inhabited by people without ideals or purpose. And while they have not discovered any definitive answers about America by the end of their trip, they have learned much more about themselves.

#14—***Joy Ride***, Swiss, 2001, Directed by Martin Rengel: A teenage girl starts hanging out with a group of four guys. Soon, she starts to fall in love with one of them and the two spend more and more time together away from the gang. The other three become resentful and put pressure on their pal to get rid of her, but he can't decide what to do until the fateful joy ride that brings everything to a climax.

#15—***Camera***, American, 2000, Directed by Rich Martini: A video camera is stolen from a shop and, now freed, starts doing what cameras instinctively do: filming. It films weddings, spies on people, stalks old wives and girlfriends, etc. Then the director gets his hands on the camera and attempts to make a no-budget film, but his would-be actors beg off the project since they have already appeared in the camera's own movie. In the end, someone suggests he make a film about a camera and the last shot of the film is the first shot of the film—setting up the shot in the video shop.

#16—*Bad Actors*, American, 2000, Directed by Shaun Monson: Ten actors find themselves together in a Hollywood acting class and attempt to polish their craft, but they are as pretentious and self-absorbed as humanly possible and their overblown performances give new meaning to the term "bad acting." In turn they all manage, with great effort, to become great bad actors.

#17—*Reunion*, American, 2002, Directed by Leif Tilden: Six friends come together to celebrate their 20th high school reunion, having graduated in 1981. The six characters have experienced so much since then, but are now forced to confront the old preconceptions and wisdoms about each other—and themselves. They relive old emotions and discover new truths, but their true natures inevitably surface via a series of dramatic interactions, for the passing of time has not effected who they really are.

#18—*Et Rigtigt Menneske*/*Truly Human*, Danish, 2001, Directed by Åke Sandgren: A neglected little girl dreams that the big brother she never had lives inside the walls of her house and she wills him into existence, into the real world where he must now transform himself from a fantasy figure into a real person. In the body of an adult, but with the simple nature and naiveté of a ten year old, he tries to navigate his way in the world of grown-ups. It is a world of fear, suspicion, and paranoia, and it wears him down, but he manages to help a couple of despairing adults who still have a spark of goodness left in them. In the end, having helped those who still had the capacity to be helped, he melts back into the world from which he came, the world inside walls.

#19—*Når Nettene Bli'r Lange*/*Cabin Fever*, Norwegian, 2000, Directed by Mona J. Hoel: A large family gathering takes places at Christmas in a cabin up in the mountains, but when the intense cold forces all the grown-ups, kids, Polish in-laws, and dogs to crowd inside, things get strange. The noisy and claustrophobic atmosphere brings various dormant emotional dynamics into play and dark secrets are revealed. A family that at first seemed so happy and normal is revealed to be anything but.

#20—*Strass*, Belgian, 2002, Directed by Vincent Lannoo: A teacher at a drama school demonstrates his highly controversial teaching technique to a documentary film crew. He uses what he calls the "open door" method, which consists of tormenting and humiliating his students, both physically and mentally. This has left his pupils virtual basket-cases. He insists that auditions be held for a new female student and practically rapes her in the midst of a heated "acting exercise," which the crew finally attempts to stop.

#21—*En Kærlighedshistorie/Kira's Reason—A Love Story*, 2002, Directed by Ole Christian Madsen: A married couple's happiness is shattered by the death of their infant baby. The mother suffers a mental breakdown and is admitted to a mental hospital. When she comes home she discovers that nothing is the same anymore. She must fight to regain everything she had; her ability to love, to be a mother and a wife. To be her own person. But her husband also has a lot of soul-searching to do, and their marriage is put under tremendous strain as they struggle with a raft of painful emotions. In the end they finally come together again, but there is no certainty it will last.

#22—*Era Outra Vez/Once Upon Another Time*, Spanish, 2001, Directed by Juan Pinzás: A group of friends who attended the same university meet up again ten years later to relive old times. It appears they have all done well for themselves since graduation, and they should be happy, but they aren't and this reunion triggers a range of unexpected emotions among them. Conflicts develop and humorous situations occur over the course of the weekend, bringing out the best and worst in the characters in a film that is described as a "psycho-social sexual comedy."

#23—*Resin*, American, 2001, Directed by Vladimir Gyorski: A drug dealing no-hoper spends his days on the beaches of Santa Barbara selling pot to rich college kids, but ends up in a brawl with a gang of drunk frat boys and is arrested. Back on the street again, he vows to make one last "score" that will permit him to start life afresh, but things go wrong and he ends up back in jail, caught in the clutches of California's notorious "three strikes" law which stipulates that anyone convicted of a third felony must serve a mandatory life-in-prison sentence.

#24—*Security, Colorado*, American, 2001, Directed by Andrew Gillis: Karen and her boyfriend have engaged in a long-distance relationship for some time and she now moves to his town to be with him. But it's tough going in these new and unfamiliar surroundings. Increasingly dissatisfied and frustrated, she seeks solutions in the wrong places, but eventually gains an inner strength and finally comes to realize that she herself is the only thing she can control in this life.

#25—*Converging with Angels*, American, 2001, Directed by Michael Sorenson: Against his better judgment, a high-priced male prostitute attempts to save a woman he finds in dire circumstances on the street. He takes her home. He and the girl end up falling for each other, but are soon forced to confront the bitter realities of who they are and how they have lived their lives before this chance encounter brought them together.

#26—*The Sparkle Room*, American, 2001, Directed by Alex McAulay: A woman living in rural North Carolina suffers a nervous breakdown and is eventually evicted from her apartment. Wandering in a nearby forest, she comes across an encampment constructed of cardboard boxes and garbage. It is inhabited by two brothers and a women who have rejected society. She joins them. Her parents hire a private investigator to find her, but the investigator also ends up joining them until police come to dismantle their settlement and they all commit suicide together.

#27—*Come Now*, no information available.

#28—*Elsker Dig For Evigt*/**Open Hearts,** Danish, 2002, Directed by Susanne Bier: A loving couple's relationship is destroyed when the man is hit by a car and paralyzed. Confined to a hospital bed, he becomes embittered. His girlfriend is emotionally devastated. His doctor, a married man, tries to comfort her, but by degrees their relationship turns into a physical and very passionate romance, leaving both of them consumed with guilt.

#29—***The Bread Basket***, American, 2002, Directed by Matthew Biancaniello: An aspiring Los Angeles actor sees his relationship with his girlfriend destroyed and his career short-circuited by an uncontrollable obsession with his weight that apparently has roots in his childhood. This leads to eating binges and outbursts of rage. He ends up trapped in a cycle of over-indulgence and self-loathing and ends up committing an act of self-destruction.

#30—*Dias de Boda*/**Wedding Days**, Spanish, 2002 Directed by Juan Pinzás: Two beautiful people are about to marry, but the husband, a writer with homosexual tendencies, is more interested in what his wife-to-be's connections can do for his career, her father being the administrator of a new literary prize. The wedding celebration proves to be an utter fiasco. Surprises are in store for all concerned, including the guests who reveal their dark sides and make the bride wish she had never said "I do."

#31—*El Desenlace*/**The Ending**, Spanish, 2003 Directed by Juan Pinzás: Rosendo, a successful writer, decides to accept his homosexuality and leaves his loveless marriage to start a relationship with a young gay man who works in a nightclub. But his life takes an unexpectedly complicated turn when a female journalist comes to do a story on him and gets to know his gay lover.

#32—*Se Til Venstre, Der er en Svensker/**Old, New, Borrowed and Blue/ The Dog's Called Fiat 128,*** Danish, 2003, Directed by Natasha Arthy: A young bride-to-be has everything to look forward to, but her life is complicated by the fact that she is a bit of a pathological liar. When a former male friend turns up just before the wedding, things get strange. He launches whole-heartedly into his mission of helping her find something "old, new, borrowed and blue," taking it all to extremes, and she ends up questioning her basic decisions and values.

#33—*Forbrydelser/**In Your Hands***, Danish, 2003, Directed by Annette K. Olesen: In the women's wing of a prison, inmates, guards, and other personnel interact. Here a newly ordained female priest meets a woman imprisoned for causing the death of her baby. The main tragedy in the priest's life is that she could never have a child, and their acquaintanceship has fateful repercussions.

#34 and #35—(Both Danish, as yet untitled) To be helmed by the Icelandic director, Dagur Kári and the Danish director, Charlotte Sachs Bostrup. Kári, who graduated from the Danish Film School (class of 1999), is one of Iceland's leading "art-house" filmmakers. Better known to the Danish movie-going public is Bostrup, who stands behind several commercial features that have been successful as family entertainment.

Previous Manifestos and Statements Issued by Lars von Trier

First manifesto, issued in conjunction with the release of Lars von Trier's first feature film, *The Element of Crime* on May 3, 1984. (All manifestos have been translated when necessary by the author, and all italics and capitalizations—and, as much as possible, phrasing and punctuation—are von Trier's.)

"Seemingly all is well: The filmmakers live in immaculate romantic relationships with their products, possibly love affairs which could have the taste of the routine about them, and yet they are good and solid relationships where the small problems of the day-to-day fill the time so well that these problems alone become the content! In a nutshell, an ideal marriage, the fall-out of which cannot even manage to offend the neighbors: no noisy fights at midnight . . . no compromising half-naked episodes on the stairway. A union between two partners: the filmmaker and his "film wife," which meets with everyone's approval . . . in peace with themselves . . . and yet! We can all feel that The great fatigue has taken hold!

How could such tempestuous love affairs of film history wither away to become sensible marriages? What has happened with these old men? What has corrupted the old masters of sexuality? The answer is simple. The misunderstood willingness to please, the great fear of self-disclosure (what does it matter that the potency is gone when the wife has long since learned to live without it?) . . . has gotten them to jettison that which once gave even their relationship budding life: *The Fascination!*

The fault for this situation, this state of routine, lies alone with the filmmakers. Out of despotism they have never allowed their loved one the possibility to grow and develop with love . . . In their arrogance they have refused to look the miracle in her eyes . . . and thereby crushed her . . . and themselves.

The hardened old men with hearts of stone must die! We will no longer be satisfied with 'well-meaning films with humanistic messages,' we want more—the real goods, the fascination, the experience—childish and pure as true art. We will search back to that time when the love between filmmaker and film was young, when the joy in creating was there to be read in every frame!

Surrogates cannot satisfy us any longer. We will see religion on the screen. We will see 'film mistresses' strutting with life: unjust, stupid, stubborn, ecstatic, abominable, wonderful, but not tamed and made sexless by a cranky moralistic filmmaker, a mean puritan propagating the dummed-down values of niceness.

In short, we want to see heterosexual films for, by and about men. *We seek the sensuality!"*

Second manifesto, published in English, French, and German translations in a small, 47-page booklet issued to coincide with the Cannes film festival premiere of von Trier's second feature film, *Epidemic*, on May 17, 1987. The booklet opened with von Trier's famous earlier phrase, "A film ought to be like a stone in one's shoe," and contained cast, crew, and production credits, as well as lines from the film inserted without explanation, in addition to biographical information on von Trier, writing partner Niels Vørsel, and cameraman Henning Bendtsen.

"Seemingly all is well. The young men are engaged in their steady relationship with a new generation of film. The anti-conception which is supposed to contain the epidemic only makes the birth control more effective: No unexpected creations, no bastards—the genes are intact. There exist those young men whose relationships resemble the endless stream of Grand Balls of an earlier era. There are also those who live together in rooms devoid of furniture. But their love becomes expansion without soul, reduction without bite. Their 'wildness' lacks discipline and their 'discipline' lacks wildness.

LONG LIVE THE BAGATELLE! (Ed: English translation: LONG LIVE THE INSIGNIFICANT DETAIL!)

The Bagatelle is humble and all-embracing. It exposes a corner without making a secret of eternity. Its setting is limited but magnanimous and therefore gives space to life. EPIDEMIC manifests itself in the legitimate/serious relationships of the young men as a bagatelle—for among bagatelles the masterpieces are numbered."

Third manifesto, issued in Danish by Lars von Trier on December 29, 1990 to mark the release of his film *Europa*, which premiered at Cannes on May 12, 1991, and opened in Denmark on August 16th.

"I CONFESS!

Seemingly all is well: the film director, Lars von Trier, is a scientist, an artist and a human being. And yet I say that I am a human being BUT an artist, BUT a film director.

I cry while I write these lines. How affected my attitude has been. Who am I to engage in didacticism and to chastise? Who am I to scornfully dismiss the lives and works of others? My shame becomes only that much greater as my excuse, that I was seduced by the arrogance of science, falls to the ground as a lie! For it is true that I have attempted to lose myself in a cloud of sophistry about the goal of art and the artist's obligations, that I had thought out ingenious theories on the anatomy and essence of film, but—and I now confess it quite openly—I have never remotely succeeded with this pathetic smokescreen to repress my deepest passion: MY CARNAL DESIRE.

Our relationship to film can be described and explained in so many ways: We must make film to serve pedagogic ends, our desire to exploit film can serve as a ship that can lead us on a voyage of discovery to unknown lands, or we can claim that we, through film, want to make our audience laugh or cry, or pay. It all sounds probable and yet I don't believe it.

There is only one excuse that justifies going through, or forcing others to go through, the hell that is the process of creating a film: the carnal satisfaction which arises in that fraction of a second when the cinema's speaker and projector in unison inexplicably let the illusion of motion and sound rise up—like the electron which leaves its orbit and thereby produces light—to create THE ONE THING: A Miraculous gasp of LIFE! It is only THAT which is the filmmaker's reward and hope and just due. That physical sensation, when the film magic really works, that shoots its way through the body like a shivering ejaculation . . . it is my hunt for THAT experience which always will be and always has been behind all my work and effort . . . NOTHING ELSE! So, now it is written, that did me good. And forget explaining it away with phrases like: "the childlike fascination" and the "universal humility," for here is my confession in black and white: LARS VON TRIER, THE SIMPLE MASTURBATOR OF THE FILM SCREEN.

And yet, in *Europa*, the third part of the trilogy, I have not allowed a flicker of any attempted diversionary maneuver to remain. Finally the purity and clarity is obtained! Here there is nothing to hide the reality under a suffocating layer of "art" . . . no trick is too unfair, no mode of conveyance to cheap, no effect too tasteless.

GIVE ME JUST A SINGLE TEAR OR A SINGLE DROP OF SWEAT, AND I'LL WILLINGLY TRADE ALL THE "ART" IN THE WORLD FOR THAT.

In conclusion: Let only God judge me for my alchemic experiments with life made of celluloid. One thing is certain, life outside the movie theater can never be matched, for that is His creation and thereby divine."

Manifestos and Vow of Chastity Issued by the Dogumentary Brothers

Note: On May 6, 2000, the "Dogumentary" movement—a transplantation of Dogme-like discipline to the documentary genre—was founded by Lars von Trier and three new "brothers": his uncle, Børge Høst, director of numerous documentaries; Tøger Seidenfaden, the editor of the Danish daily, *Politiken*; and Jørgen Leth (see "Jørgen Leth—The Obstructed Man"). On that day, four manifestos were published in the Danish daily, *Berlingske Tidende.* Here are reproduced the manifestos by von Trier, Høst, and Seidenfaden (*Defocus, Respect for the Public* and *Dokumentarisme*, respectively), while Leth's manifesto, *The Moment is Found,* is reprinted in the above-mentioned chapter dealing specifically with Leth.

Later, a more formal and unified manifesto was issued (in English) on Zentropa letterhead in October of 2001, and a proper new Vow of Chastity, so to speak, called *The Dogumentary Manifesto* was also included. Infused with the same kind of revolutionary ardor that characterized Dogme, it conveyed via a mixture of lofty theoretics and aggressive self-righteousness a more specific set of aims than the May 6 declarations. And then it spelled out nine hard and fast rules for the making of documentary films. This document is also reprinted here in its entirety.

Defocus

"We are searching for something that is neither fiction nor fact . . . that which cannot be contained by a 'story' or grasped by an angle.

. . . The material we are searching for is to be found in reality, the same reality where creators of fiction find their inspiration, the same reality which journalists believe they are describing but in fact cannot see because they are blinded by their techniques—techniques which have become the goal in and of itself.

To seek a story . . . is to suppress it. By emphasizing a single pattern, genuine or artificial, by presenting the world as a puzzle picture with solutions chosen in advance (is to suppress it).

In their search for The Story, The Point, The Disclosure and The Sensation, they have taken this subject matter from us—this; the rest of the world which is not nearly as easy to relate to or depict as that, but which we cannot live without!

The story is the villain . . . That which one calls the wealth of real life has vanished under our feet, squandered by journalists who worship clarity and focus above all else, draining the life out of it in the process.

How do we find it again? And how do we communicate it or describe it? That is the challenge of the future—to search without searching, to defocus! The defocusers will be the communicators of the day, no more, no less!"

March 22, 2000
Lars von Trier

Respect for the Public

Suppose, for the moment, that literature only consisted of novels and novellas to the exclusion of all else, that there were no essays, biographies or books on the thousands of topics that libraries stack together under headings such as Sociology, Folklore, Religion, Travel, Art, Natural History, Handicrafts, Industry, Agriculture, History, etc. etc.

But such a situation does almost exist today inside the film world. This is insane. In an earlier period when a bit more—and maybe also better—documentaries were produced, lack of distribution possibilities was cited as the reason why these films weren't more readily available. Today we have a plethora of television channels (to produce more), so why aren't the library shelves a mixture of books and cassettes, CD-Roms and DVDs?

What does that have to do with defocusing? Everything. As it happens, a huge amount of consumer goods are produced for television.

That most of them are not worth remembering owes to the fact that they are made without respect for their audience. They are all too often made on the presumption of what the producers believe the audience would like to have. Or even worse: what they think the viewers can understand. To produce a film of value, it is necessary that one gives one's utmost. And that means of course that one must take one's topic seriously. That one dives as deeply into it as possible. Not just in the manuscript phase but during the entire process. So that the film remains open to change right to the end. So that the end result is not just a (prearranged) meeting with a theory but with a reality.

Otherwise we are all theorists, propagandists, craftsmen. And we cannot be content with just that.

Børge Høst

Dokumentarisme

"Over the course of the 20th Century the feature film has become an art-form which in many ways equals the novel. For millions of people great film experiences play the same role as novels once did—and still do. "Read the book and see the movie," and "See the movie and read the book" are mechanisms that benefit both genres.

As far as the preserve of fiction is concerned. Here there exists both a balance and a healthy competition between the two different modes of expressive conveyance—words and pictures.

The situation is completely different when we consider how knowledge is conveyed in the real world. Here, when one talks about works of real quality which are both serious and authoritative, books come out ahead. Of course documentaries are (primarily) made for broadcast on television, and infrequently—extremely infrequently— an art documentary is shown in the movie theater. But here in the realm of reality, as opposed to fiction, there is no balance or equality between film and literature.

When one takes into account that the recording of reality gives us direct access to the object of the topic in question (the kind of access that is denied to us in the realm of fiction, since our inner spiritual lives cannot yet be recorded) and that that access can to a large extent reach back 100 years into the past, the peculiar situation we find ourselves in becomes evident. Why are the images of reality not recorded, used and conveyed with the same creativity and effectiveness as the images and completed works that we know from the world of the feature (fiction) film?

One is prone to suspect that the conventions and narrative techniques of journalism—transferred from the written to the visual medium (by journalists) with lack of creativity and imagination—are responsible for inhibiting the development (of the documentary). But just as film is not filmed theater (even though excellent films are made in that way), neither can television documentaries made with a journalistic approach be the last word in documentary filmmaking (even though excellent documentary programs are made in that way).

And these films don't need to be only for connoisseurs, either. The high ratings obtained by these strange television dramas about real life (Like how it happened that uncle Harry drowned, or how we managed to save little Sonny from cooking in the oven) testify to the irrefutable power of our fascination over the fact that something has actually taken place.

It was within the 20th century that both (broadcast) media and film became dominant, one of the most dramatic historical events that can be imagined. (But) countless are the personal tragedies, decisive turning points and high and low water marks of an existential nature which have only as yet been conveyed by small black letters on a white background.

To give Dokumentarisme real force as a social art-form is a project worthy of the 21st century."

Copenhagen, May 1, 2000
Tøger Seidenfaden

The Dogumentary Manifesto (emphasis as in original, which was published in English)

Dogumentarism relives the pure, the objective and the credible. It brings us back to the core, back to the essence of our existence.

The documentary and television reality which has become more and more manipulated and filtered by camera people, editors and directors, must now be buried.

This takes place with the following documentarist content guarantee:

The goal and content of all Dogme documentary projects must be supported and recommended in writing by at least seven people, companies or organizations who are relevant and vital.

The Documentarist Code for Dogumentarism

1. All the locations in the film must be revealed. (This is to be done by text being inserted in the image. This constitutes an exception to rule number 5. All the text must be legible.)

2. The beginning of the film must outline the goals and ideas of the director. (This must be shown to the film's actors and technicians before filming begins.)

3. The end of the film must consist of two minutes of free speaking time by the film's 'victim.' This 'victim' alone shall advise regarding the content and must approve this part of the finished film. If there is no opposition by any of the collaborators, there will be no 'victim' or 'victims.' To explain this, there will be text inserted at the end of the film.

4. All clips must be marked with 6-12 frames black. (Unless it is a clip in real time, that is a direct clip in a multi-camera filming situation.)

5. Manipulation of the sound and/or images must not take place. Filtering, creative lighting and/or optical effects are strictly forbidden.

6. The sound must never be produced exclusive of the original filming or vice versa. That is, extra soundtracks like music or dialogue
   must not be mixed in later.

7. Reconstruction of the concept or the directing of the actors is not
   acceptable. Adding elements, as with scenography, are forbidden.

8. All use of hidden cameras is forbidden.

9. Archived images or footage that has been taken for other programs must never be used.

The Closure of Dogme — Press Release from the Dogme Secretariat, June 2002

The Dogme Secretariat is Closing June 2002

Back to basic anarchism

In 1995 the Dogme brothers launched the ground-breaking manifesto, "The Vow of Chastity," and made four films that were both critically and commercially acknowledged world-wide. They encouraged filmmakers all over the world to reconsider the conventions of movie making. The challenge was taken up and to this point 31 different Dogme films have been made in Korea, Argentina, Spain, USA, France, Switzerland, Norway, Italy and of course Denmark. These films show the very diverse interpretations of the ten Dogme rules, and perhaps the need of them.

The manifesto of Dogme 95 has almost grown into a genre formula, which was never the intention. As a consequence, for our part we will stop mediating and interpreting how to make Dogme films, and are therefore closing the Dogme secretariat. The original founders have moved on with new experimental film projects, as we have moved on. In addition to that we do not have any economic foundation upon which to continue our work, which has indeed been a broadening journey.

Everyone can make a Dogme film

In case you desire to make a Dogme film, you are free to do so; you do not need to apply for a certificate anymore. "The Vow of Chastity" is an artistic way of expressing a certain cinematic point of view, it is meant to inspire filmmakers all over the world. It is an idea and not a brand, and therefore it does not imply copyrights of any kind.

For the purpose of film history

However if you do make a new Dogme film, please help us save it in the cause of film history.

Since the Dogme secretariat does not exist anymore to register the new Dogme films, we therefore advise you to send a copy of your film to:

Professor Peter Schepelern
University of Copenhagen
Department of Film and Media Science
Njalsgade 80
2300 Copenhagen S
Denmark

The University of Copenhagen will preserve the films of Dogme 95 in their film archives, as well as the individual correspondence the Dogme secretariat has held with the directors of Dogme 95, for further academic research.

Further public service

On this website you will find links to a bibliography on the essayistic and academic writings on the films of Dogme 95. As well as one solid academic article by acknowledged professor, Peter Schepelern. (Ed: the Dogme website is www.dogme95.dk. The curious should also take a look at www.zentropa.dk or www.trust-film.dk.

For academic purposes ONLY

If you are still in doubt or in need of further academic clarification, please contact Schepelern at above address.

For technical questions

If you don't know how to adjust the camera settings or have other technical questions, please check texts on this website, especially the interviews regarding *The Celebration*. Apart from that, Dogme 95 is now a well researched phenomenon, and there should be articles in all major languages concerning Dogme 95.

David Nielsen Ouro & Ann-Sofie Rørsgaard

Endnotes

1. *Politiken,* April 12, 2002

2. The January 10, 2003 issues of *Berlingske Tidende* and *Jyllands-Posten* respectively.

3. *Politiken,* September 15, 2002

4. *Weekendavisen,* May 11–14, 1998

5. Sitney, Adams P., *Film Culture Reader,* Martin Secker & Warburg, Ltd, London 1970, p.80

6. Katz, Ephraim, *The Film Encyclopedia,* HarperCollins, 1994 p. 256

7. *Weekendavisen,* August 9–15, 2002

8. One example is *Shred of Sex,* a study of erotic expression made by a collective in San Francisco in 1990, while filmmaking collectives like Groupe MTK in Grenoble, France still routinely shoot and process their own film.

9. *Politiken,* March 30, 2001

10. Armes, Roy, *French Cinema,* Oxford University Press, USA, 1985, p. 193.

11. *The Teacher's Room,* 1994, was a kind of experimental talk show conceived by von Trier, and *Big Klaus and Little Lars,* 2001, a marathon talk session between the two.

12. Armes, Roy, *French Cinema,* Oxford University Press, USA, 1985, p. 193

13. *Morgen Posten Fyn,* May 13, 1984

14. *The Element of Crime,* which was in English, had largely been funded by The Danish Film Institute whose remit was to advance the production of *Danish* film. This had caused problems and it was unlikely he would get more funding from them for another English-language film.

15. The Danish Film Institute was established in 1972 and that same year the first modern Danish Film Law went into effect. (See Danish Film Institute chapter)

16. Peter Schepelern, *Lars von Trier's Film: Tvang og Befrielse,* Rosinante Forlag A/S, 2000, pp. 118–119

17. Søren Frank, "Lars von Trier: I Lynch Stemning," *Euroman,* 1994, p. 77.

18. *B.T.,* 25 March 25, 2002

19. Von Trier was a master of post-production manipulation. In a TV series he shot in 1988 entitled *Medea,* he had filmed on 3/4-inch video tape, re-adjusted color and light, transferred it to 35mm film and then transferred it back to one-inch video tape, obtaining an image quality on the brink of dissolution. And as noted, with *The Element of Crime* and *Europa* he had also employed a wealth of lab processes. This sinner knew the meaning of temptation, and in his new found purity could be just as zealous and tiresome as a reformed alcoholic.

20. Kim Foss, Gitte Merrild, *Copenhagen Culture — A Cultural Manual,* Copenhagen Cultural Capital 96 foundation, 1996, p. 148.

21. *Politiken,* February 8, 2002

22. *The Purified* was the third installment of Jargil's documentary trilogy that he called *The Kingdom of Credibility*. All three films, including the *Exhibited*, about the World Clock art installation, and *The Humiliated*, about the making of *The Idiots*, focused on von Trier's working processes.

23. *Ekstra Bladet*, September 8, 1999

24. In his biography, *Without Cigar: the Father, the Son and the Film Merchant* (pub. 2001 by Høst & Søn, p. 31), Aalbæk Jensen describes the conception of Dogme to a group of businessmen: "It all started with a lie. We talked ourselves and others into believing that there was a new wave on the way in Danish film. We did it so effectively that we ourselves and later the press began to believe it. That here was something special. It was a lie but it worked...Then we asked ourselves, what is it that Danes would like to have the rest of the world think about them? The answer came back: 'that the whole world thinks that our little crap country is something fantastic.' Therefore we had to create a myth that would reach out beyond Denmark's borders. Without any money to market this myth. A myth that we wouldn't have to borrow 2 million DM to launch . . . . We didn't have money to carpet-bomb people like the American companies did, so we had to find something else. Hence we stole some concepts from the religious world, made a bunch of Danish films around that and turned the fact that we had no money to make them into a value. We made a virtue out of necessity and called it art. We disallowed everything that we in any case didn't have the money to buy. We said 'It's not because we don't want to use the big heavy equipment but due to religious grounds we are forced to do without it.' The Dogme concept was thus invented and launched as a kind of purification, a purity. As if we had any choice. Choices we had none of, not a lick."

25. *Politiken*, August 31, 2002

26. *Jyllands-Posten,* February 19, 1999

27. *Politiken,* August 31, 2002

28. *Berlingske Tidende,* August 12, 2002

29. *Film,* issue #15, published by the Danish Film Institute

30. *Film According to Dogme: Restrictions, Obstructions and liberation,* by Peter Schepelern as posted on Zentropa's Dogme Website

31. *Politiken,* May 11, 2002

32. Ibid

33. *Berlingske Tidende,* December 23, 2002

34. *Berlingske Tidende,* December 23, 2000

35. *Berlingske Tidende,* December 23, 2000

36. *Politiken,* January 5, 2001

37. *Berlingske Tidende,* October 27, 2002

38. *Jyllands-Posten,* August 14, 2002

39. *Weekendavisen,* November 1–7, 2002

40. *Weekendavisen,* May 3, 2001

41. *Jyllands-Posten,* October 31, 2002

42. *Berlingske Tidende,* September 6, 2002

43. *Politiken,* September 10, 2002

44. Despite all the knocks Hollywood receives in Danish film circles, you could almost hear the jealously in Steen's voice, for there is a rich bio-diversity in American film. American film is Hollywood, sure, but it's also Woody Allen, the Coen Brothers, David Lynch, and Jim Jarmusch, just to name a few independents. With its tiny film industry and tiny market, Danish film was clearly more susceptible of slipping into the kind of rut that critics were now complaining about.

45. *Politiken,* September 15, 2002

46. *Jyllands-Posten,* April 18, 2002

47. *Politiken,* August 10, 2002

48. *Berlingske Tidende,* August 9, 2002

49. Christian Braad Thomsen, being a filmmaker himself who frequently sought funding for what could be termed films with a non-commercial slant, clearly had an ax to grind, but the dominant role that grant-giving bodies like the DFI and the TV stations play in the current situation is indisputable.

50. *Politiken,* December 15, 2002

51. *Ibid*

52. Kirsten Jacobsen, *Without Cigar: The Father, The Son and The Film Merchant* (Høst & Søn publishers, Copenhagen, 2001), p. 213

53. Ibid

54. While Henning Camre had never been popular with the students (*Politiken,* January 7, 2001), he had earned a reputation as an

excellent administrator and in 1992 was head-hunted to reorganize the National Film and Television School in London. In 1997, he was brought back to Denmark to head the new Film House in central Copenhagen which included the DFI, The Film Museum, and Statens Film Central under one roof and a new unified administrative structure. Ironically, his new position would bring him into conflict with some of his old students, most notably Peter Aalbæk Jensen who savaged his decisions and leadership style almost daily in the press.

55. There was a ceiling of 3.5 million kroner which meant, in effect, that the DFI normally supplied well below half of the budget since very few theatrically-released films cost under 7 million kroner. In 1997, the state support percentage was raised to 60% and it was re-dubbed the 60/40 arrangement. Since then the ceiling was raised to 5 million kroner and plans are pending to abolish the ceiling completely in an effort to give more impetus to this system of funding.

56. *Politiken*, October 27, 2001. This finding was made by writer Per Dabelsteen.

57. *Berlingske Tidende,* November 17, 2002

58. *Jyllands-Posten*, June 13, 2002

59. Ibid

60. Peter Schepelern, Lars von Triers Film: Tvang og Befrielse (Copenhagen: Rosinante Forlag A/S, 1997, 2000), p. 113

61. *Jyllands-Posten*, June 13, 2002

62. Kirsten Jacobsen, *Without Cigar: The Father, The Son and The Film Merchant* (Copenhagen: Høst & Søn, 2001) p. 129

63. *Jyllands-Posten,* June 13, 2002

64. *Politiken,* August 1, 2002

65. Kirsten Jacobsen, *Without Cigar: The Father, The Son and The Film Merchant* (Copenhagen: Høst & Søn, 2001) p. 128

66. *Berlingske Tidende,* November 10, 2002

67. *Politiken,* November 11, 2002

68. *Berlingske Tidende,* November 13, 2002

69. *Berlingske Tidende,* November 10, 2002

70. *Politiken,* May 12, 2003

71. The "Jante Law" consists of ten rules of behavior popularized in the 1933 novel, *A Refugee Crosses His Tracks,* by the Norwegian writer, Alex Sandemose, who lived in Denmark for a period of time. These rules, such as "Do not think you are special, do not think you are good at anything, do not think you are better than us," governed life in the imaginary Danish town of Jante, and can basically be encapsulated into "don't think you are somebody." The Jante Law is constantly brought up today in egalitarian Denmark whenever somebody attempts something new and different or is considered too brash and must be "knocked back into place." Aalbæk Jensen seems in fact bound by these rules—or rather bound by an inexhaustible need to break them—every waking minute of the day.

72. Kirsten Jacobsen, *Without Cigar: The Father, The Son and The Film Merchant,* (Høst & Søn, Copenhagen, 2001) p. 117

73. Ibid, p. 110

74. Ibid, p. 111

75. Meaning prolonged and apparently not sincere on Kidman's behalf. There was a feeling that Kidman publicly spoke very positively about being in *Dogville* and working with von Trier, while at the same time her lawyer (or she herself) was purposely drawing out the negotiations.

76. *Politiken,* July 24, 2001

77. *Jyllands-Posten,* August 28, 2001

78. *Politiken,* February 17, 2002

79. *Jyllands-Posten,* October 10, 2002

80. *Politiken,* November 26, 2000

81. Ibid

82. Ibid

83. *Berlingske Tidende,* August 12, 2002

84. Ibid

85. *Jyllands-Posten,* November 19, 2002

86. *Weekendavisen,* September 13–19, 2002

87. *Dogville,* shot in early 2002 and premiered at Cannes 2003, was von Trier's very different follow up to *Dancer in the Dark*. The story took place in a Rocky Mountain village in 1930's America, and was filmed entirely in a studio with white chalk marks on a

black floor to indicate locations in the town. Atmosphere was largely provided by the interplay of light and shadow and was considered fiercely experimental. (See "*The Idiots*—Postscript")

88. *Weekendavisen,* January 18–24, 2002

89. This involved the fixed placement of 100 small digital video cameras to record the film's musical scenes so they would be recorded from a vast variety of angles, this video footage then being manipulated to produce unique variations of color and texture.

90. *Weekendavisen,* July 20–26, 2001

91. *Weekendavisen,* July 20–26, 2001

92. *Politiken,* August 3, 2002

93. *Film,* issue 22, Summer 2002, p. 25

94. *Politiken,* August 3, 2002

95. *Film,* issue #9, p. 27

96. *Jyllands-Posten,* April 18, 2002

97. Richard Kelly, *The Name of this Book is Dogma 95,* (London, Faber and Faber, 2000) p. 99

98. Ibid, p. 104

99. *Film,* issue #9, p. 27

100. *Jyllands-Posten,* April 18, 2002

101. *Politiken,* January 10, 2003

Photo Credits

Photos courtesy of:

Knud Romer Jørgensen: pp. 99, 100, 102, 187

Rick Schmidt: p. 233

Matthew Biancaniello: p. 236

SMP Archives: p. 242

Isabella Vosmikova: p. 248

Jay Archibald: p. 252

Andrew Gillis: p. 254

Alex McAulay: p. 258

Jan Willem Steenmeijer: back cover

Photos from Author's collection: pp. 26, 27, 34, 44, 160, 164, 166, 178, 182, 189

Danish Film Institute (DFI): pp. 48, 52, 54, 56, 61, 62, 69, 82, 90, 96, 109, 115, 122, 130, 135, 137, 142, 146, 152, 154, 202, 208, front cover

Index

Books Available
from Santa Monica Press

Blues for Bird
by Martin Gray
288 pages $16.95

The Book of Good Habits
*Simple and Creative Ways
to Enrich Your Life*
by Dirk Mathison
224 pages $9.95

The Butt Hello
*and other ways my cats
drive me crazy*
by Ted Meyer
96 pages $9.95

Café Nation
*Coffee Folklore, Magick,
and Divination*
by Sandra Mizumoto Posey
224 pages $9.95

Cats Around the World
by Ted Meyer
96 pages $9.95

**Discovering the History
of Your House**
and Your Neighborhood
by Betsy J. Green
288 pages $14.95

Dogme Uncut
*Lars von Trier, Thomas Vinterberg
and the Gang That Took on
Hollywood*
by Jack Stevenson
312 pages $16.95

Exploring Our Lives
*A Writing Handbook for
Senior Adults*
by Francis E. Kazemek
288 pages $14.95

Footsteps in the Fog
Alfred Hitchcock's San Francisco
by Jeff Kraft and
Aaron Leventhal
240 pages $24.95

**Free Stuff & Good Deals for Folks
over 50, 2nd Ed.**
by Linda Bowman
240 pages $12.95

**How to Find Your Family Roots and
Write Your Family History**
by William Latham and
Cindy Higgins
288 pages $14.95

How to Speak Shakespeare
by Cal Pritner and
Louis Colaianni
144 pages $16.95

**How to Win Lotteries, Sweepstakes,
and Contests in the 21st Century**
by Steve "America's Sweepstakes
King" Ledoux
224 pages $14.95

**Jackson Pollock: Memories Arrested
in Space**
by Martin Gray
224 pages $14.95

James Dean Died Here
*The Locations of America's Pop
Culture Landmarks*
by Chris Epting
312 pages $16.95

The Keystone Kid
Tales of Early Hollywood
by Coy Watson, Jr.
312 pages $24.95

Letter Writing Made Easy!
*Featuring Sample Letters for
Hundreds of Common Occasions*
by Margaret McCarthy
224 pages $12.95

Letter Writing Made Easy! Volume 2
*Featuring More Sample Letters for
Hundreds of Common Occasions*
by Margaret McCarthy
224 pages $12.95

Nancy Shavick's Tarot Universe
by Nancy Shavick
336 pages $15.95

Offbeat Food
*Adventures in an
Omnivorous World*
by Alan Ridenour
240 pages $19.95

Offbeat Marijuana
*The Life and Times of the
World's Grooviest Plant*
by Saul Rubin
240 pages $19.95

Offbeat Museums
*The Collections and Curators of
America's Most Unusual Museums*
by Saul Rubin
240 pages $19.95

Past Imperfect
*How Tracing Your Family Medical
History Can Save Your Life*
by Carol Daus
240 pages $12.95

A Prayer for Burma
by Kenneth Wong
216 pages $14.95

Quack!
*Tales of Medical Fraud from
the Museum of Questionable
Medical Devices*
by Bob McCoy
240 pages $19.95

Redneck Haiku
by Mary K. Witte
112 pages $9.95

**The Seven Sacred Rites
of Menarche**
*The Spiritual Journey of the
Adolescent Girl*
by Kristi Meisenbach Boylan
160 pages $11.95

**The Seven Sacred Rites
of Menopause**
*The Spiritual Journey to
the Wise-Woman Years*
by Kristi Meisenbach Boylan
144 pages $11.95

Silent Echoes
*Discovering Early Hollywood
Through the Films of Buster
Keaton*
by John Bengtson
240 pages $24.95

Tiki Road Trip
*A Guide to Tiki Culture in
North America*
by James Teitelbaum
288 pages $16.95

What's Buggin' You?
*Michael Bohdan's Guide to
Home Pest Control*
by Michael Bohdan
256 pages $12.95

Order Form 1-800-784-9553

	Quantity	Amount
Blues for Bird (epic poem about Charlie Parker) ($16.95)	_____	_____
The Book of Good Habits ($9.95)	_____	_____
The Butt Hello . . . and Other Ways My Cats Drive Me Crazy ($9.95)	_____	_____
Café Nation: Coffee Folklore, Magick and Divination ($9.95)	_____	_____
Cats Around the World ($9.95)	_____	_____
Discovering the History of Your House. . . ($14.95)	_____	_____
Dogme Uncut ($16.95)	_____	_____
Exploring Our Lives: A Writing Handbook for Senior Adults ($14.95)	_____	_____
Footsteps in the Fog: Alfred Hitchcock's San Francisco ($24.95)	_____	_____
Free Stuff & Good Deals for Folks over 50, 2nd Ed. ($12.95)	_____	_____
How to Find Your Family Roots . . . ($14.95)	_____	_____
How to Speak Shakespeare ($16.95)	_____	_____
How to Win Lotteries, Sweepstakes, and Contests . . . ($14.95)	_____	_____
Jackson Pollock: Memories Arrested in Space ($14.95)	_____	_____
James Dean Died Here: America's Pop Culture Landmarks ($16.95)	_____	_____
The Keystone Kid: Tales of Early Hollywood ($24.95)	_____	_____
Letter Writing Made Easy! ($12.95)	_____	_____
Letter Writing Made Easy! Volume 2 ($12.95)	_____	_____
Nancy Shavick's Tarot Universe ($15.95)	_____	_____
Offbeat Food ($19.95)	_____	_____
Offbeat Marijuana ($19.95)	_____	_____
Offbeat Museums ($19.95)	_____	_____
Past Imperfect: Tracing Your Family Medical History ($12.95)	_____	_____
A Prayer for Burma ($14.95)	_____	_____
Quack! Tales of Medical Fraud ($19.95)	_____	_____
Redneck Haiku ($9.95)	_____	_____
The Seven Sacred Rites of Menarche ($11.95)	_____	_____
The Seven Sacred Rites of Menopause ($11.95)	_____	_____
Silent Echoes: Early Hollywood Through Buster Keaton ($24.95)	_____	_____
Tiki Road Trip ($16.95)	_____	_____
What's Buggin' You?: A Guide to Home Pest Control ($12.95)	_____	_____

	Subtotal	_____
CA residents add 8.25% sales tax		_____
Shipping and Handling (see left)		_____
	TOTAL	_____

Shipping & Handling:
1 book	$3.00
Each additional book is	$ .50

Name _____

Address _____

City _____ State _____ Zip _____

☐ Visa ☐ MasterCard   Card No.: _____

Exp. Date _____ Signature _____

☐ Enclosed is my check or money order payable to:

Santa Monica Press LLC
P.O. Box 1076
Santa Monica, CA 90406

www.santamonicapress.com 1-800-784-9553